s and conflict
ineteenth-century England
5-1850

s and Conflict in
eteenth-Century England

Birth of Modern Britain series

General editors:

A. E. Dyson
Senior Lecturer in English Literature,
University of East Anglia

and

R. T. Shannon
Reader in English History,
University of East Anglia

Titles in the series:

Nonconformity in the nineteenth century
edited by David M. Thompson

Class and conflict in nineteenth-century England 1815–1850
edited by Patricia Hollis

The idea of the city in nineteenth-century Britain
edited by B. C. Coleman

Class and conflict in nineteenth-century England 1815-1850

Edited by

Patricia Hollis

School of English and American Studies,
University of East Anglia

Routledge & Kegan Paul

London and Boston

First published in 1973
by Routledge & Kegan Paul Ltd
Broadway House, 68–74 Carter Lane,
London EC4V 5EL and
9 Park Street,
Boston, Mass. 02108, U.S.A.
Printed in Great Britain by
Unwin Brothers Limited
The Gresham Press, Old Woking, Surrey, England
A member of the Staples Printing Group

ISBN 0 7100 7419 0 (c)
ISBN 0 7100 7420 4 (p)

General editors' preface

The series is concerned to make the central issues and topics of the recent past 'live', in both senses of that word. We hope to appeal to students of history and literature equally, since each has much to offer, and learn from, the other. The volume editors are encouraged to select documents from the widest range of sources, and to convey the 'feel' of particular controversies when passion ran high. One problem for the modern student is hindsight: often, we fall back on over-simplified versions of history—Whig or Marxist, progressive or conservative—because we fail to imagine events as they were. We hope here to re-create situations through the passions and commitments of participants and contemporary commentators, before the outcome was known. In this way, students are encouraged to avoid both over-simplified judgments and that dull sense that whatever happened was inevitable which can so devitalize our understanding of any period's history, or its art.

We believe that this treatment of the recent past, bringing out the sense of immediacy and conflict, is also the soundest basis for understanding the modern world. Increasingly, we realize that continuity is more striking than discontinuity: nothing could be more naive than a claim for 'modernity' which assumes that the past is 'irrelevant' or dead. It was during the age of Arnold and Gladstone, Disraeli and Tennyson, Darwin and Chamberlain that our most distinctive modern problems defined themselves—the growth of great cities and technology; the battle between individualism and collectivism; the coming of democracy, with all its implications for education, class, vocation and the ordinary expectations of living; the revolutions in travel and communication; the shifting relationships between individuals and the state. Many of the major ideas that shape our world were also born: and in the ferment of day-to-day crises and perplexities, prophetic and widely-ranging hopes and fears, we see the birth of modern Britain, the emergence of our world of today. Volume editors have been encouraged in their selection of material from contemporary sources to illuminate that density and complexity of things which is the essence of 'reality'.

In this volume Dr Patricia Hollis explores the crucially important area of the origins of modern ideas in Britain of the nature of class and the conflicts between classes. What is particularly to be welcomed in her approach to these themes is the way in which for the first time three distinct streams of contributory analysis and activity are brought into an integrated relationship: firstly, the theoretical shift in the movement of secular dissent from an analysis of an illegitimate aristocratic political dispensation to one of capitalist economic exploitation; secondly, the way in which the new movements among the working people set about finding methods to put their wrongs to right; and thirdly, just as important but in general so neglected, the way in which the upper classes responded to these dissenting movements by a counter-attack to reassert traditional values. In so doing Dr Hollis contributes a very persuasive voice to the vigorous historiographical debate now in progress on the origins and nature of the British working class as a social and political force.

For suggestions for further reading, see the introductions to each group of documents.

Contents

Chronological table

1812	Founding of the Hampden clubs; Major Cartwright's tours
1813–14	Repeal of the statute of artificers (and control over apprentices)
1816	Cobbett's *Political Register* became a working-class 2*d* paper
	Spa Fields riots of the Spenceans
1817	March of the Blanketeers
	Suspension of habeas corpus
	Cobbett's flight to America
1818	Formation of societies of Political Protestants; Philanthropic Society
1819	Peterloo
	Six Acts
1820	Cato Street conspiracy
1821	Mudie's Co-operative and Economical Society
1824	Select Committee on working of the Combination Acts
1825	Repeal of the Combination Acts
	Founding of First London Co-operative Society
	Founding of *Trades Newspaper*
1826	T. Hodgskin, *Labour Defended*
1828	Brighton Co-operative Society
1829	Catholic emancipation
	British Association for Promoting Co-operative Knowledge
1830	Birmingham Political Union
	Launching of Short Time movement
	National Association for the Protection of Labour
	Launching of unstamped penny papers
	Swing agricultural riots
1831	National Union of the Working Classes and National Political Union; *Poor Man's Guardian*
1832	Reform Act
	Labour exchanges under impact of Owen
1833	Factory Act limiting child labour
	Cold Bath Fields riot
	National Regeneration Society for eight-hour day
	Derby lock-out by masters

1834	Grand National Consolidated Trades Union
	Tolpuddle martyrs
	New Poor Law
1836	Stamp duty reduced to 1*d*
	London Working Men's Association; Short Time Movement on to the attack
1837	Revival of Birmingham Political Union
	East London Democratic Association formed
	Launching of *Northern Star* and rise of O'Connor
	Poor Law commissioners moved north and anti-Poor Law agitation under Stephens
1838	London Working Men's Society publicize Charter which was nationally adopted
	Great Northern Union founded at Leeds
	Select Committee on Combinations investigated Glasgow cotton spinners' strike of 1837
1839	The National Convention in London, moved to Birmingham where Bull Ring riots, and arrest of Lovett
	Emergence of Anti-Corn Law League
	House of Commons rejected first petition
	Newport rising; trial of John Frost
1840	Mass Chartist arrests
	Chartism organized into National Charter Association at Manchester
	Publication of Lovett's *Chartism*, recommending a New Move
1841	Growth of knowledge Chartism, temperance Chartism, Christian Chartism
1842	Complete Suffrage Union conferences
	Plug Plots; miners' strikes
	House of Commons rejected second petition
1843	Chartist trials
	Midland mining commission
1844	Rochdale Pioneers Co-operative Society
1845	Land plan
	National Association of United Trades
1846	Repeal of the Corn Laws
1847	Ten Hours Factory Act
1848	House of Commons rejected third petition
	Conspiracy and arrests
	Hume's Little Charter for household suffrage
1850	Harney and Jones reorganized Chartism

Introduction

Marx wrote of the French peasantry in *Eighteenth Brumaire*:

> In so far as millions of families live under economic conditions of existence that separate their mode of life, their interests and their culture from those of other classes, and put them in hostile opposition to the latter, they form a class. In so far as there is merely a local identification among these smallholding peasants, and the identity of their interests begets no community, no national bond and no political organization among them, they do not form a class.

Marx makes it clear that a common economic mode of existence is a necessary but not sufficient ingredient of class; what is crucial is a consciousness of class, an attitude or stance to other groups in the community. Class on this account is essentially a relationship, an experience and not just an economic location.

It is with this in mind that I have drawn these documents together. They do not provide a history of working-class movements in this period; they are certainly not an account of what 'really happened' to the impoverished and vulnerable in society during the first half of the nineteenth century. What I believe they illustrate are the attitudes and relationships of working men towards each other and against other groups in society. I have therefore brought the material under three headings: what I have called the analysis of class in terms of economic and political theory; class relations in the years between the end of the French wars and the move into mid-Victorianism; and finally, the response to the more disturbing aspects of class by the appropriate vehicles of social control, religion, education and philanthropy, mechanisms, among other things, for inculcating values more conducive to social stability and class harmony. The proportion of material devoted to the first of these parts, and the juxtaposition of the material in the third part, represent the claims of the book perhaps to its novelty and hopefully to its utility.

Several things follow from this. 'Events' are covered only in so far as they were the occasion for statements of class attitude. To take an example, I have not tried to illustrate the new Poor Law by offering an assessment of its losses and gains, its dietary sheets or its educational provisions; nor even have I discussed whether the working-class response to it was well-founded. Instead, I have drawn heavily on J. R. Stephens's speeches, and the comments of Richard Pilling and the *Northern Star* on the interdependence of wage rates and poor relief. Likewise, the Newport Rising and '1848' are documented only very briefly. There is little on the occupational and regional roots of Chartism. But by contrast I have included a possibly disproportionate amount of material on the relations of Chartism with trades unions and with the middle class.

It means also that this material is very far from being 'objective' or balanced in its totality. The documents are deliberately partisan and polemical. Inevitably they are drawn from a less than comprehensive range of sources. They include statements made at State Trials suggesting the views of judge and judged, but little from the Home Office papers. They include comments by Robert Lowery or Thomas Cooper on the effect of poverty on political judgment, but little on the depth of working-class poverty as revealed, say, in the select committees on the handloom weavers. Above all, these documents are drawn from working-class journalism, speeches made to shivering colliers, editorials for pondering in Lovett's reading room. Some of the papers of the 1830s, the *Poor Man's Guardian* and the *Pioneer*, have recently been reprinted; but those of the 1820s, the *Republican* and the *Trades Newspaper*, and for the 1840s, the *Northern Star*, are accessible only on microfilm for most readers. The *Northern Star* in particular has remained remarkably unquarried outside of Ph.D. theses.

Finally, this approach to the material means that the book is in no way self-sufficient. It assumes the basic background information, about Robert Owen for example, that is to be found in secondary textbooks; and the introduction to each cluster of documents is meant to point up a coherent argument or a common theme, rather than to provide a chronological narrative. The book does not seek to replace G. D. H. Cole and A. W. Filson's *British Working Class Movements, selected documents 1789–1875*, even if it could. The suggestions for further reading at the end of the introduction to each cluster of documents are indeed meant to be taken seriously.

The first of the three parts is devoted to the analysis of class, to descriptions of the geography of social cleavage, and to depictions of privilege dependent on oppression, of power on injustice, of wealth on exploitation.

Paine reshaped the old rallying cry of 'No taxation without representation' by embedding it in a critique of Old Corruption. The political system, he argued, was dominated by an aristocratic clique, together with their sycophants, sinecurists, placemen and priests, who fed off the people by virtue of their political power to levy taxes. If taxes were lowered, then the well-being of the people would grow and the aristocratic grip on resources would be undermined. Francis Place and the philosophic radicals on the one side, and Cobbett and the men of 1819 on the other, were equally heirs to this tradition. Both saw politics as a struggle of aristocracy against the people. It was an analysis common to middle- and working-class radicals alike.

But from the 1820s this account of social cleavage was increasingly displaced, though never fully replaced, by a more obviously socialist account, that of Robert Owen, and that of Thomas Hodgskin through to O'Brien, both of which were developed to challenge the new political economy of Malthus, Ricardo and McCulloch. The enemy here was capitalist economics rather than aristocratic privilege, property rather than taxes, a profiteering middle class rather than a parasitic upper class. Working men were exploited in their very labour, because they did not receive back as wages the true value of the goods their labour produced. Within this socialist analysis, the Owenite strand bypassed political radicalism and developed the economic self-help of co-operation and syndicalism, whereas O'Brien's writing accommodated itself to traditional political radicalism. Only universal suffrage, he argued, would remedy economic exploitation. But the effect of both socialist strands, with their assertion that property and profits were theft, was to alienate those middle-class radicals who affirmed orthodox political economy, and to open up a cleavage within the radical camp between working men and all others which in intellectual terms was at least as significant as the traditional political division between aristocracy and people.

To a considerable extent, as these documents show, this debate on the nature of class was self-sustaining, with O'Brien, for one, challenging simultaneously middle-class political economy, old-style radical concern with taxes, and the newer syndicalist concern with trades unionism. In some cases one can trace the diffusion of certain ideas, from the theoretician, Hodgskin or Ricardo, through their popularizers such as O'Brien or Francis Place, and see them reflected back by their readers, the Know-Nothings who wrote in to the *Poor Man's Guardian*. But these debates also received dynamic and occasionally direction from the material grouped in Part Two—most obviously in the discussion of syndicalism which was prompted by the moves towards the Grand National Consolidated Union in the winter of 1833–4.

Documents in Part Two have been chosen to illustrate the methods adopted by working men to secure their rights: political radicalism which centred on the demand for the vote; co-operation, trades unionism and the factory movement as ways of economic betterment; and finally moral self-help as an assertion of working-class dignity and self-discipline.

Political radicalism proved most attractive in the years around Peterloo, the 1832 Reform Act, and the opening years of Chartism. Throughout the period, radicals steadily argued that politics was about the distribution of power and therefore of wealth and wellbeing; and that only if working men had the vote with which to purify and to control the House of Commons, could they ensure that their economic interests were protected; though whether this entailed a straightforward reduction in taxation on the model of Old Corruption or a more elaborate recasting of the laws preserving landed and financial property, was up for debate. If politics was ignored, they feared, any working-class scheme which challenged established institutions could be smashed whenever those in political power saw fit.

Frequently attached to the demand for the vote were other traditional radical planks, reform of local government and the legal system, repeal of the taxes on knowledge and all monopolies, the end of tithes and the state church's grip on education, the suspicion of any growth in central government or its standing army, all concerns shared by radicals of the National Union of the Working Classes with more middle-class radicals of the National Political Union.

The usual technique was to develop a network of political clubs, strongest often in the provinces, especially in Lancashire, Yorkshire and the Midlands, such as the Hampden clubs at the end of the French wars, the political unions of the early 1830s, and the Chartist branches a few years later. These were held together by itinerant lecturers, a radical press, and in later years by the organization of petitions, conventions, and subscriptions.

But the radicalism of 1819 was smashed by the counter-revolution of the Six Acts; and that of 1832 was quickly overcast by the Irish Coercion Act of 1833, overshadowed by the rise of trades unionism, and more subtly undermined by the reassertion of social discipline in the forms of the new Poor Law and political economy.

Chartism lasted much longer, partly because the loss of craft controls during a deepening depression forced artisans, no less than handloom weavers or factory workers, to sell their labour power and to join the ranks of the proletarianized. Remedies for sweating in the tailoring or carpentering trades, or for wage-cutting in the textile trades, hinged on the control of hours and wages; and because this in turn touched on such questions as child labour, the level of poor relief, or on projected local boards of trade, parliament seemed to many working men in these years a more suitable source of help and appropriate point of pressure than the traditional trades union. The Charter was in this way conceived as a legislative means for the correction of economic ills; and this meant that even when class relations were at their most antagonistic, class co-operation was always theoretically available and often, as in 1839, 1842 and from 1847 on, actually available to those middle-class reformers willing to soft-pedal political economy and pursue an enlarged franchise. The other source of Chartism's staying-power was its catholicity, drawing on the campaigns and campaigners of the 1830s, touching local government, land and currency reform, and enrolling Irish nationalists, feminists, secularists and Methodists, republicans, internationalists, teetotallers, vegetarians and a few socialists into its ranks.

Co-operation and trades unionism offered other ways of restructuring society which did not involve the apparently futile quest for the franchise. Co-operative theory developed two forms, the wholesale store of the late 1820s, and the community, such as Manea Fen and Queenswood, of the late 1830s. The wholesale stores were a device to accumulate funds for community building; some several hundred at their peak, they sustained a series of co-operative congresses and several co-operative journals; and the strongest of them developed into labour exchanges offering a just wage and self-employment before they were absorbed into the general unionism of the winter of 1833. When they were re-founded in the 1840s, however, profits were retained by individual members and the wider community ideal phased out.

Trades unionism was legitimized with the repeal of the Combination Acts in 1825. At each of its three peaks it moved out into a general unionism which drew quite specifically on socialist theory—in 1829, when the Lancashire cotton spinners made common cause with Yorkshire textile workers in the National Association for the Protection of Labour, before their adherents moved on into the factory movement; in 1833–4 when London tailors joined with other London and provincial trades to smash the growing gulf between honourable and dishonourable trades in the Grand National Consolidated Trades Union; and again in the mid-1840s with the formation of the National Association of United Trades.

The third style of working-class activity was moral self-help; the educational activity of the radical press and the pamphleteering of the working men's associations; the anticlerical drive which took radicals into Chartist churches; the exhortations to temperance and the distaste for *ad hominem* vitriol and demagogy; the restraint of exclusive dealing and the engagement in local politics; all were ways to encourage working men to acquire the self-control and moral weight that preceded social control and political weight. In Bamford's words, 'Canst thou not control thyself, and wouldst thou govern a household? Canst thou not govern a household, and yet wouldst thou direct a nation?' The vote would have meaning just in so far as men were morally fit to exercise it. But the difficulty with this position, as Lovett himself saw, was that it offered too many hostages to class enemies, to those who argued that politics was an élitist activity and required appropriate training, or to those who believed that politics was a limited activity and that most things that mattered were beyond the power of government to affect.

Though these documents are grouped to suggest that these were alternative methods of action, they were of course intellectually complementary and practically related. The London political unions of the 1830s stemmed from trade clubs and co-operative societies; the trade and co-operative societies came together around the labour exchange; outside London, the short time movement was an extension of trades unionism and in turn provided much of the organized opposition to the new Poor Law; early Chartism drew on all of these sources, and was itself greatly strengthened in the 1840s when the trades began to adhere to it in their corporate capacity. Hetherington, for example, was a founding father of the NUWC, of the first printing union in London and one of the first co-operative groups; he used the Unstamped press to hold all these threads together, as well as to recommend temperance and useful knowledge; and he went on to become one of the most influential of London Chartists as well as a guardian of the St Pancras poor. A Richard Pilling, to take a provincial example, moved between the trades union, factory and Poor Law movements and carried them into Northern Chartism. In O'Brien's words (*Poor Man's Guardian*, 2 November 1833):

> Let us deal with no middleman who refuses to vote or petition for Universal Suffrage—let us deal with no villain who is opposed to Trades Unions, or in any other way hostile to our rights and privileges. Let us resist every attempt of the shopocrats to cut down the workman's wages, and uphold every effort of the men to obtain equitable advances. Let us support one another in all struggles against the mercenary combinations of slave-drivers, and encourage exclusive dealing with the people's friends in all lines of business . . . Let us as far as possible promote mutual exchanges of labour for labour, on the cooperative principle, so as to intercept the profits of trade in addition to the wages of labour . . . But, meanwhile, neglect no opportunity of seeking Universal Suffrage, which is the grand panacea for all our evils.

Part Three suggests some of the ways in which members of the upper classes sought to reassert traditional values and exact conciliatory behaviour.

The government's hold on law and order, particularly up until the 1840s, was never as firm as it would have liked. Until the introduction of a professional police force in 1829 in London and from the late 1830s in the provinces, government had only the army and its variants, yeomanry and militia, with which to keep order. It therefore had to control popular unrest and seditious radicalism through the law courts where possible. The counter-revolution of the 1790s, the Six Acts of 1819, were legislative alternatives to the much hated standing army or a new police.

Far more effective than this official response, however, was the private non-governmental response to problems of political order and social discipline. One strand in this was political economy which, as is clear from Part One, allowed industrialists from the 1820s to argue the harmony of interests between masters and men, the social utility of high profits and wage restraint, the futility of unionism, the inescapable rigidity of the laws of competition, the necessity of a free market. One consequence of political economy was to develop the distinction between poverty and pauperism, between the independent poor who quite properly laboured each and every day for their daily bread, and the dependent poor, paupers, parasites on the labour of others. The older, less critical attitude to the poor, entailed by a belief that God had ordained each man to his lot in life, and often softened by casual almsgiving and soup kitchens, was now toughened by political economy. The function of philanthropy became to inhibit the independent poor from descending into the ranks of the pauper; indigence was to be stigmatized, and philanthropy must strengthen the moral will which encouraged men to remain self-supporting against all economic odds. To aid the undeserving was simply to destroy the incentive of the struggling; to support social parasites and their offspring without requiring any labour in return was to destroy the equilibrium of the market created by political economy.

Similarly, many who advocated extending religious instruction to the poor and to the turbulent, shared the views of Archdeacon Sinclair: 'Nothing will ever improve the character of the lower orders, or give the upper security and peace, but a multiplication of schools and churches'. Every church that Bishop Blomfield built in London in the 1830s was supposed to become a spiritual lighthouse to penetrate rookeries, gin palaces and infidel reading rooms; and to be the centre of a network of philanthropic agencies which would reconstruct the pastoral image and restore social sympathies.

Where philanthropy and religion sought to reform the adult, education sought to form the child. Educationalists from Robert Owen to Shaftesbury to HM Inspectors, all harp on the 'impressionableness' of the child. He was a plant to be pruned, where his father was metal, from which the dross must be refined out, and which must be hammered into shape. But popular education only inadequately produced a literate and disciplined adult, so reformers moved into the field of adult education, there both to remedy faulty juvenile training and to neutralize the propaganda circulated by socialists hostile to political economy. 'Useful knowledge', it was hoped, would empty prisons, workhouses and Chartist lecture halls simultaneously; and would enhance the quality of life for working men and stabilize the society in which they were an unreliable element. But just as many working men scorned the social contract entailed in philanthropy's 'chain of sympathy', and practised mutual aid of their own; and just as they despised the passivity which seemed to be an integral part of otherworldliness, and instead channelled their religious aspirations into a Christianity 'purified' of its church structure and Tory clergy; so too they rejected the manipulative functions of useful knowledge, while happy to enjoy its fiction.

None the less it remains true that the moral self-help wing of working-class movements shared the dominant and puritan values of Victorian society, its emphasis on thrift, sobriety and self-discipline; and as the economic depression lifted, which had done much to brutalize the relations of the enfranchised and the propertied with the excluded and exploited, so articulate working men were increasingly absorbed into popular politics, into the demand for a wider franchise, if not always for universal suffrage; the quest for land reform, common to Owen, O'Connor and the League; the diminution of taxes and monopolies and patronage; the extension of state education and the end of an over-privileged state church. Working men and middle-class men might and did remain suspicious of each other's intentions and aspirations; but by the year of the Great Exhibition, leading radicals of both classes had come to appreciate that they needed each other for leverage—both within parliament and without. And this meant abandoning the old relations of deference and protection built into conservative politics. The poor were to enter into moral and political adulthood—at the price of abandoning their stance of class hostility on the one hand and their claim to paternalist protection on the other. 1867 was a concession to consensus politics, and not to class politics.

Part One

Class and conflict—the analysis

1 Old Corruption and the attack on privilege

The attack on privilege became the classical radical case for parliamentary reform. Paine (1737–1809), writing to rebut Burke's attack on the French Revolution, analysed the nature of government and asked what made it legitimate (1a). Where earlier writers, in social contract theories for example, had explored the origins of government, Paine argued that government was legitimate only in so far as its actions promoted the general happiness, and this was best secured by universal suffrage and republicanism. He asserted the right of men to self-government, free both from the dead hand of the past and of the self-interest of an existing aristocratic minority. Twenty years later, Colquhoun (1745–1820), a London police magistrate, whose professional interest in pauperism (see p. 321) led him to analyse the production and distribution of wealth, provided the statistics of appropriation (1b). He showed that the producers (those who added to the national wealth—they included employers) maintained a class of non-producers, only some of whom were useful members of society. His calculations were frequently re-published, sometimes, as in Owen's *Crisis* (1c) with a distinctly radical gloss. William Cobbett (1762–1835), the first great working-class journalist (see p. 94), and John Wade (1788–1875) editor of the *Gorgon* and later a proponent of middle-class political economy (see p. 44) together turned Colquhoun's neutral economic analysis into a scathing political attack on Old Corruption, the parasitic ruling class of aristocrats, priests, pensioners, placemen, boroughmongers and fundholders, who lived off taxes levied on working men (1d and 1e). Only a radically reformed parliament would reduce taxation, allow working men to keep the fruits of their labour and thus end their poverty. A later statistician, R. M. Martin (1803–68), in his evidence to the *Select Committee on Handloom Weavers* in 1834, documented the regressive nature of taxation, which was levied mainly on food and drink (1f); and showed that as half of these taxes (some £27 millions in a budget of £50 millions) went to service the National Debt, they also redistributed wealth upwards.

Subsequent analyses of capitalism by the Ricardian socialists and Bronterre O'Brien (see p. 25) deflected the attack from taxation to profits (1g). But Feargus O'Connor (1796–1855) was still describing Old Corruption as the source of the people's sorrows in the *Northern Star* of 1847 (1h); and it remained the traditional radical critique of Aristocratic Privilege *versus* the People which was common to working-class and to middle-class radicals alike, to a William Lovett as well as to a Rev. Miall.

Suggestions for further reading

For Paine and Cobbett, see E. Thompson, *The Making of the English Working Class* (1964); for Paine, see E. Hobsbawm, *Labouring Men* (1965); for Cobbett, see G. D. H. Cole, *William Cobbett* (1924).

1a Hereditary government

T. Paine, *The Rights of Man*, Part I (1790), pp. 3–4; Part II (1791), p. 174 in the 1937 edn.

There never did exist, nor never can exist a parliament, or any description of men, or any generation of men, in any country, possessed of the right or the power of binding or controlling posterity to the 'end of time', or of commanding for ever how the world shall be governed, or who shall govern it . . . Every age and generation must be as free to act for itself, *in all cases*, as the ages and generations which preceded it. The vanity and presumption of governing beyond the grave is the most ridiculous and insolent of tyrannies. Man has no property in man; neither had any generation a property in the generations which are to follow . . . That which a whole nation chooses to do, it has a right to do. Mr. Burke denies it. Where then does the right exist? I am contending for the right of the *living*, and against their being willed away, and controlled and contracted for, by the manuscript-assumed authority of the dead . . . Every generation is equal in rights to the generation which preceded it, by the same rule that every individual is born equal in rights with his contemporary.

Government is nothing more than a national association; and the object of this association is the good of all, as well individually as collectively. Every man wishes to pursue his occupation, and to enjoy the fruits of his labours and the produce of his property in peace and safety, and with the least possible expense. When these things are accomplished, all the objects for which government ought to be established are answered.

1b Producers and parasites

Patrick Colquhoun, *A Treatise on the Wealth, Power and Resources of the British Empire* (1814).

Contemplating, therefore, the gradations of society . . . it becomes a matter of interesting enquiry, *by what proportion* of the community at large those different classes are maintained. Assuming . . . that it is by the annual labour of the people employed in agriculture, mines, minerals, manufactures, shipping, commerce, fisheries, and inland trade, assisted by capital, machinery, and skill, that the means of subsistence are obtained; it can be demonstrated that all other classes of the community, although many of them partake largely in the new property annually produced, have no share whatever in its production, and, whatever they may do to diminish, do nothing to increase the national wealth. Many of them indeed labour with great zeal and ability in the affairs of the state and in its judicial and revenue departments, while others are laboriously occupied in offensive and defensive war. . . . But like menial servants their labour adds to the value of nothing, since not like the agriculturist, the manufacturer, and the trader, they work upon no material that possesses a reproductive quality, and yet their consumption of the labour of others generally exceeds that allotted to many of the labourers themselves . . . [None the less] all who labour in any useful pursuit contribute to the general comfort and happiness of every well governed community. It is only those who pass their lives in vice and idleness . . . who are real nuisances in society—who live upon the land and labour of the people, without fulfilling any useful station in the body politic, or making the smallest return or compensation to society for what they consume . . .

More than 1/5 part of the whole community are unproductive labourers, and these labourers receive from the aggregate labour of the productive class about 1/3 part of the new property created annually. But it does not follow . . . that a very great proportion of these unproductive labourers are not highly useful in their different stations in society.

1c Producers and parasites illustrated

Crisis, 17 *May* 1834.

FIRST CLASS THE LABOURING POPULATION *The Producers of all Wealth*	Individual Income	Aggregate Population	Aggregate Amount
	£	NUMBERS	£
Agricultural and mining labourers	11	3,154,142	33,396,795
Aquatic labourers and seamen	11	400,000	8,100,000
Mechanical and manufacturing labourers	11	4,343,389	49,054,752
Umbrella, parasol makers, embroiderers, chair coverers, lace workers, etc.	12	150,000	3,800,000
Artists, sculptors, etc.	56	25,000	1,400,000
Pauper labourers	5	774,200	3,871,000
Pensioners receiving for labour	2	46,000	420,000
		8,892,731	99,742,547
SECOND CLASS DISTRIBUTORS, SUPERINTENDENTS, AND MANUFACTURERS *Necessary, but too numerous*			
Farmers	22	1,540,000	33,600,000
Capitalists in manufacturing and mechanical operations	134	264,000	35,376,000
Ditto in clothing, etc.	36	218,750	7,875,000
Ditto in building and engineering	60	43,500	2,610,000
Ship builders and ship owners	124	46,750	5,652,000
Merchants, wholesale dealers, brokers, and bankers	140	200,000	28,177,600

SECOND CLASS DISTRIBUTORS, SUPERINTENDENTS, AND MANUFACTURERS *Necessary, but too numerous*	Individual Income	Aggregate Population	Aggregate Amount
	£	NUMBERS	£
Shopkeepers and retail dealers	40	700,000	28,000,000
Innkeepers and publicans	14	437,500	8,750,000
Clerks and Shopmen	14	262,500	6,750,000
Hawkers and pedlars	11	5,600	63,000
Physicians, surgeons, etc.	60	96,000	5,400,000
	—	3,814,600	162,253,600
THIRD CLASS GOVERNMENT *Much too numerous and expensive*			
The Royal Family	1670	300	501,000
Persons in higher and lesser civil offices	77	114,500	8,830,000
Judges, barristers, attorneys' clerks, etc.	80	95,000	7,600,000
Army and navy officers	96	65,000	6,295,000
Common soldiers, militia, seamen and marines	9½	770,000	17,004,680
Lunatics, and keepers of lunatic asylums	48	4,700	195,000
Half-pay and pensions	24½	60,500	1,486,600
Persons included in the above, receiving incomes from funds and church	—	—	5,211,063
Prisoners for debt	6	17,500	105,000
Paupers	7¾	774,200	6,000,000
Vagrants, prostitutes, rogues, gipsies, vagabonds, in and out of prison	12	308,741	3,704,892
		2,210,441	56,933,235
FOURTH CLASS INSTRUCTION AND AMUSEMENT *Indispensable and eminently useful*			
Clergymen, working	40	87,500	3,500,000
Dissenting ministers	25	20,000	500,000
Universities and chief schools	150	3,496	524,400
Lesser schools	34	210,000	7,140,000
Theatres, concerts, and musicians	50	3,500	175,000
		324,496	11,839,400

FIFTH CLASS *The most wealthy and least useful*	Individual Income	Aggregate Population	Aggregate Amount
	£	NUMBERS	£
Nobility and Bishops	396	13,620	5,400,480
Dignified clergymen	120	9,000	1,080,000
Baronets, knights, and esquires	205	122,915	25,022,110
Greater and lesser landholders and freeholders	28	1,435,000	40,250,000
Gentlemen and ladies living on incomes in the funds, etc.	100	280,000	28,000,000
		1,860,535	99,752,590

	£
Total amount of wealth created annually in Great Britain and Ireland	430,521,372
Amount received by the productive classes	99,742,547
Amount received by the non-producers	330,778,825
	No.
Total number of the productive classes	8,892,731
Total number of the non-producers	8,210,072
The whole population in 1812	17,102,803

1d Taxation and working men

Cobbett's *Political Register*, 2 November 1816.

Friends and Fellow Countrymen,

Whatever the Pride of rank, of riches or of scholarship may have induced some men to believe, or to affect to believe, the real strength and all the resources of a country, ever have sprung and ever must spring, from the *labour* of its people . . . Elegant dresses, superb furniture, stately buildings, fine roads and canals, fleet horses and carriages, numerous and stout ships, warehouses teeming with goods; all these, and many other objects that fall under our view, are so many marks of national wealth and resources. But all these spring from *labour*. Without the Journeyman and the labourer none of them could exist; without the assistance of their hands, the country would be a wilderness, hardly worth the notice of an invader.

As it is the labour of those who toil which makes a country abound in resources, so it is the same class of men, who must, by their arms, secure its safety and uphold its fame . . .

With this correct idea of your own worth in your minds, with what indignation must you hear yourselves called the Populace, the Rabble, the Mob, the Swinish Multitude; and, with what greater indignation, if possible, must you hear the projects of those cool and cruel and insolent men, who, now that you have been, without any fault of your own, brought into a state of misery, propose to narrow the limits of parish relief, to prevent you from marrying in the days of your youth, or to thrust you out to seek your bread in foreign lands, never more to behold your parents or friends? But suppress your indignation, until we return to this, after we have considered the *cause* of your present misery and the measures which have produced that cause.

. . . It is the *enormous amount of the taxes*, which the government compels us to pay for the support of its army, its placemen, its pensioners etc. and for the payment of the interest of its debt. That this is the *real* cause has been a thousand times proved; and it is now so acknowledged by the creatures of the government themselves . . . The tax gatherers do not, indeed, come to *you* and demand money of you: but, there are few articles which you use, in the purchase of which you do not pay *a tax* . . .

The *remedy* is what we have now to look to, and that remedy consists wholly and solely of such a reform in the Commons', or People's, House of Parliament, as shall give to every payer of *direct taxes* a vote at elections, and as shall cause the Members to be *elected annually* . . .

But, this and *all other things*, must be done by a *reformed parliament*.—We must have *that first*, or we shall have nothing good; and, any man, who would, *before hand*, take up your time with the detail of what a reformed parliament ought to do in this respect, or with respect to any changes in the form of government, can have no other object than that of defeating the cause of reform, and, indeed, the very act must show, that *to raise obstacles* is his wish . . .

I know of no enemy of reform and of the happiness of the country so great as that man, who would persuade you that we possess *nothing good*, and that *all* must be torn to pieces. There is no principle, no precedent, no regulation (except as to mere matter of detail), favourable to freedom, which is not to be found in the Laws of England or in the example of our Ancestors. Therefore, I say we may ask for, and we want *nothing new*. We have great constitutional laws and principles, to which we are immoveably attached. We want *great alteration*, but we want *nothing new*. Alteration, modification to suit the times and circumstances; but the great principles ought to be, and must be, the same, or else confusion will follow.

1e The structure of Old Corruption

Gorgon, 8 August 1818.

. . . It will be proper to say a word or two on the various classes into which society is divided. And first of the upper classes in which are included the first dignitaries in the Church and Law, the Aristocracy, the last of which, according to Burke, forming the *capital* of the Corinthian Pillar, and is considered by many as the grace, polish, and ornament of the whole community; and by others as the disgrace, disease etc. engendered from the old age and corruptions of the body politic. In this class reside the master-springs of the system, and for sake of which the whole machine may be said to live and move. After the upper come the middling classes; among which are included the *loyal parsons*, Commissioners of Taxes, and in general all those employed in the highest departments of the Revenue, which together with the magistracy of the country, form the active, working *journeymen* of Corruption; and of which the upper classes may be considered the employers. These form the system *in toto* . . . The different classes . . . are identified with Corruption, and from a Principle of self-preservation will resolutely oppose every attempt at Reform. Opposed to this phalanx, with interests quite distinct and even incompatible, are arrayed, the PRODUCTIVE CLASSES of society . . . Productive classes are those who, by their labours increase the funds of the community, as husbandmen, mechanics, labourers, etc.; and are thus termed to distinguish them from the *unproductive* classes, as lawyers, parsons, and aristocrats; which are termed idle consumers, because they waste the produce of the country without giving anything in return. To render our enumeration complete, we ought to notice the class of paupers and public creditors, and we shall then have mentioned all the elements, which form that strange compound, English society.

. . . From this statement our readers may form some idea of the fraud, robbery, and spoliations that are practised upon the productive classes, and the very small proportion which every man enjoys of his own toil and industry . . .

The whole borough-mongering fabric depends upon our financial system, on the ability of Ministers to levy the taxes; when the latter fail, from whatever cause, the whole system will dry up and instantly vanish. This is the *spring* that supports it, and the people are masters of this *spring*, and whenever they choose to interrupt the current the machine will stop for want of the principle that maintained it in motion. The more taxes the people of any country pay, the greater is the power they possess over their Rulers . . .

Such being the basis and strength of the system, it would be the easiest thing in the world for the People to resist it. Let us suppose that the classes of society we have mentioned have agreed to some Plan of Reform, and this plan the borough proprietors think proper to reject, what ought to be done in such a case? *We ought to resist the payment of taxes.* There is nothing either unjust, impracticable, or dangerous in such a mode of procedure. A majority of the people being opposed to the system it establishes both the right and power of resistance . . . What folly then to think of violence, of plots, and conspiracies, when there remains a measure so effectual, and which has never been tried . . . There is no need of pikes, gunpowder or blunderbuss, nor anything else of a dangerous nature. . .

1f The burden of taxation

R. M. Martin's evidence to the *Select Committee on the Handloom Weavers' Petition* (1834), qus 3875–7.

I have prepared an analysis of a few of the articles bearing more particularly on the labouring classes.

Malt liquor . . . on 365 pots of stout, the working man pays an annual tax of £4.11.3*d*. . . . Sugar; if a labouring man consumes 1 lb. of sugar weekly . . . he pays an annual tax of 17*s*. 4*d*. . . . If a labouring man consumes 4 oz. of tea per week . . . valued at 4*s*. a pound . . . therefore 12 lbs. of tea per annum consumed imposes on him a direct tax of £1.4*s*. annually . . . Soap; if a labouring man uses 1 lb. of soap weekly . . . he pays . . . 13*s*. per annum . . . On housing . . . the annual tax is not less than 12*s*. per annum . . . We will estimate the cost of bread and meat to a labouring man or artizan at 10*d*. per diem, or £15.4.2*d*. per annum, the minimum of supply to a hard working man, who is thus directly mulcted, at the very least, £3 per annum. On clothing; the poorest clad man will require in shoes, stockings, shirts, smock-frock, trowsers, hat and hankerchief, at least 60*s*. worth in the year . . . a tax of 10*s*. per annum . . . Total taxes on the labourer per annum, £11.7.7*d*. Taking a labourer's earnings at 1/6*d*. per diem . . . his income will be £22.10*s*.; thus it will be admitted that, at the very least, 100% or half of his income is abstracted from him by taxation.

1g Old Corruption or capitalism?

Bronterre O'Brien, *Operative*, 18 November 1838.

Mr. Cobbett, like his predecessor Paine, was everlastingly referring the evils of the country to taxation. Now this is all delusion. Enormous taxation is no doubt an evil; but it is only one of a number of evils, many of them equally oppressive as taxation, and all growing out of, and equally inseparable from, the present constitution of society . . . RENTS, and TITHES, and INTEREST of money, and tolls, and above all, of the *profits realized on Capital*, which is greater than all the other burdens put together.

1h Times to try men's souls

Chartist Circular, 7 March 1840.

Deprived of the first and distinguishing privilege of freemen; the productive classes of this country have fallen unresisting victims to exclusive privilege, partiality and injustice . . . Were these masses not slaves, would they permit fifty millions of pounds to be extracted from the hard-earned fruits of their industry, per annum? Were they freemen, would they allow ten hundred thousand pounds of their money to be lavished upon one family—a family, too, from whom these masses never received tenpence worth of benefit? Were they not the most degraded of human beings, as far as political status is concerned, would they continue to pay thirty millions of interest for debts . . . ? Were they freemen, would the present horde of state paupers, pensioners, and placemen, be permitted to wallow in luxury at the expense of the industrious poor? Were they freemen, would the present corn-laws be allowed to exist, at an expense of fifteen to fifty million per annum? Would the present currency laws remain unchanged—laws which palpably enrich one class by openly robbing another? and last though not least, had the unenfranchised been freemen, would State Churches have been so richly endowed, or dissenting clergy received such enormous stipends? We fearlessly answer—No . . . The evils resulting from kingcraft and priestcraft, could never have reached the fearful magnitude which they have now obtained.

O'Connor, *Northern Star*, 23 January 1847.

I tell you, that, sooner or later, thin gaunt men, dying of famine, pestilence, and hunger, must have been the result of the usurpations of a bloated aristocracy—an overpaid staff of Ministerial menials—a well-fed standing army—a gorged church, over-paid officials, and pensioned paupers; of the absorption of the honey of the factory bee, by the drone who owns the key; of a useless police, only rendered necessary to reconcile men to their degradation, of over grown bankers, merchants, and traders, speculating upon the blood, the misfortunes, and the distresses of their country; and above all, that such must be the result so long as the rich oppressor monopolizes all power over the poor oppressed.

2 Old Corruption—the attack on priestcraft

Richard Carlile (1790–1843), a journalist repeatedly imprisoned for seditious libel and blasphemy during the 1820s (see p. 143) seized on priestcraft as the core of corruption, for it preached slavery in the name of Christianity and lived off the revenues of the poor (2a and 2b). This was a theme echoed by later secularists, such as Henry Hetherington (1793–1849), printer and Chartist who died of cholera (2c), G. J. Holyoake and subsequently Charles Bradlaugh.

Suggestions for further reading

For Carlile, see W. Wickwar, *The Struggle for the freedom of the Press, 1819–1832* (1928); and on the wider theme, E. Royle, *Radical Politics 1790–1900: Religion and Unbelief* (1971).

2a The tyranny of the mind

R. Carlile, *Republican*, 22 February 1822.

No effectual reform will ever take place in this country whilst an established Priesthood draws an immense revenue from the industry of the country, and exercises in return a despotic power over the minds as well as the bodies of the people . . . The Priests are as much a political body as a standing army, the former are kept up to keep your mind in awe, the latter your body . . .

J. B. Smith of Stamford, *Republican*, 1 October 1819.

To Richard Carlile.

While I was under the influence of the Christian religion . . . instead of being thankful for my creation, I had ample reason to execrate the day of my birth and so far from the worship of a real Christian being the service of a true God and perfect freedom, it is in my opinion, nothing less than complete slavery; this I know from terrific experience . . . [it is] through your instrumentality that I have arrived at such a degree of happiness as I now enjoy.

2b Kingcraft, priestcraft, lordcraft

R. Carlile, *Prompter*, 18 June 1831.

I charge upon the existence of kings, and priests, and lords, those useless classes, the common poverty of the labouring classes of mankind. I charge upon them the common warfare and slaughter of mankind. I charge upon their wicked usurpations, their false pretensions, and their general and tyrannical dishonesty, all the social evils that afflict mankind . . . The man is a social villain, a thief, a pickpocket, a cheat, a liar, who preaches to another man in the name of God . . . *Down with the priests.* There can be no general human welfare, where they are allowed to hold influence. The lords of the two islands are like the aristocrats of every other country, pursuing their family aggrandisement at the risk of the peace, the lives and the health of the labouring people. They have monopolized, hitherto, the legislative power, and have made laws pursuant to their own desires, and not pursuant to the general welfare . . . *We must put down those lords.* Neither kings, nor priests, nor lords, are useful to a people. We can work without them, eat without them, be skilful without them, be happy without them, make good laws without them, administer well those good laws without them, govern the country without them, communicate with other countries without them, and protect ourselves as a nation without them. They are the profligate consumers of a nation's wealth, a prey upon her strength, a chain to her neck, so many mill stones tied to her heels, clogs to her ankles, gyves to her limbs, vultures to her liver, and bad examples to her manners . . . Either in war or in peace, kingcraft, priestcraft, and lordcraft, is a system of plunder, murder and spoliation. THEN DOWN WITH KINGS, PRIESTS AND LORDS . . .

2c The testament of a secularist

Henry Hetherington, 21 August 1849, reprinted in G. J. Holyoake, *Life and Character of Henry Hetherington* (1849).

As life is uncertain, it behoves everyone to make preparations for death; I deem it therefore a duty incumbent on me, ere I quit this life, to express in writing, for the satisfaction and guidance of esteemed friends, my feelings and opinions in references to our common principles . . .

In the first place, then—I calmly and deliberately declare that I do not believe in the popular notion of an Almighty, All-wise and Benevolent GOD—possessing intelligence, and conscious of His own operations; because these attributes involve such a mass of absurdities, and contradictions, so much cruelty and injustice on His part to the poor and destitute portion of His creatures—that, in my opinion, no rational reflecting mind can, after disinterested investigation, give credence to the existence of such a Being.

Second, I believe death to be an eternal sleep—that I shall never live again in this world, or another, with a consciousness that I am the same identical person that once lived, performed the duties, and exercised the functions of a human being.

Third, I consider priestcraft and superstition the greatest obstacle to human improvement and happiness. During my life I have, to the best of my ability, sincerely and strenuously exposed and opposed them, and die with a firm conviction that Truth, Justice, and Liberty will never be permanently established on earth till every vestige of priestcraft and superstition be utterly destroyed.

Fourth, I have ever considered that the only religion useful to man consists exclusively of the practice of morality, and in the mutual interchange of kind actions. In such a religion there is no room for priests and when I see them interfering at our births, marriages and deaths pretending to conduct us safely through this state of being to another and happier world, any disinterested person of the least shrewdness and discernment must perceive that their sole aim is to stultify the minds of the people by their incomprehensible doctrines that they may the more effectually fleece the poor deluded sheep who listen to their empty babblings and mystifications.

Fifth, as I have lived so I die, a determined opponent to their nefarious and plundering system. I wish my friends, therefore, to deposit my remains in unconsecrated ground, and trust they will allow no priest, or clergyman of any denomination, to interfere in any way whatsoever at my funeral . . .

These are my views and principles in quitting an existence that has been chequered with the plagues and pleasures of a competitive, scrambling, selfish system; a system by which the moral and social aspirations of the noblest human being are nullified by incessant toil and physical deprivations; by which, indeed, all men are trained to be either slaves, hypocrites or criminals. Hence my ardent attachment to the principles of that great and good man—ROBERT OWEN. I quit this world with a firm conviction that his system is the only true road to human emancipation . . .

3 The theft of land—the attack on property

The theorists of Old Corruption argued that the poor were poor because their taxes supported a profligate government. The Spenceans, attuned to the distress caused by enclosure, stated that the poor were poor because they were dependent on a profiteering landlord class. Thomas Spence (1750–1814), a London bookseller, claimed that all land was originally held in common, but that the poor had been dispossessed by the powerful and become landless and exploited labourers (3a). Only if land were again communally owned would poverty and exploitation end. Allen Davenport ([?]–1847), a radical London shoemaker, showed how such a parish commonwealth might function (3b), and set it against the current monopoly of land (3c). Working-class writers in the early 1830s associated agrarian reform with political reform (3d), Bronterre O'Brien (1805–64), the leading working-class journalist of the 1830s and 1840s associated it with a reform of the currency and credit systems which developed the labour exchange schemes of 1833 (3e) (see p. 24). From the 1830s on, land reform developed three main styles, the community-building schemes of Robert Owen (1771–1858) (see p. 154); the labour-intensive farming of O'Connor's land-plan (see p. 306) and home colonization, both methods of absorbing surplus labour; and finally the radical attack on aristocratic primogeniture and entail made by Cobden, the Anti-Corn Law League (see p. 279) and the Freehold Land Society (see p. 357).

Suggestions for further reading

For Spenceanism, see O. D. Rudkin, *Thomas Spence and his Connections* (1969); for O'Brien's views on land, A. Plummer, *Bronterre* (1971).

3a The land, the people's farm

T. Spence, *The Real Rights of Man* (1775).

That property in land and liberty among men in a state of nature ought to be equal, few, one would be fain to hope, would be foolish enough to deny . . . To deny them that right is in effect denying them a right to live . . .

[But] if we look back to the origin of the present nations, we shall see that the land, with all its appurtenances, was claimed by a few, and divided among themselves, in as assured a manner as if they had manufactured it and it had been the work of their own hands . . . Accordingly . . . no man, more than any other creature, could claim a right to so much as a blade of grass, or a nut or an acorn, a fish or a fowl . . . without the permission of the pretended proprietor; and not a foot of land, water, rock or heath but was claimed by one or other of those lords; so that all things, men as well as other creatures who lived, were obliged to owe their lives to someone or other's property . . . Whether they lived, multiplied, worked or fought, it was all for their respective lords; and they, God bless them, most graciously accepted of all as their due. For by granting the means of life, they granted the life itself; and of course, they thought they had a right to all the services and advantages that the life or death of the creatures they gave life to could yield. . . . Thus were the first land-holders usurpers and tyrants; and all who have since possessed their lands, have done so by right of inheritance, purchase etc. from them . . .

Let it be supposed, then, that the whole people in some country, after much reasoning and deliberation, should conclude that every man has an equal property in the land in the neighbourhood where he resides. They therefore resolve that if they live in society together, it shall only be with a view that everyone may reap all the benefits from their natural rights and privileges possible.

Therefore a day is appointed on which the inhabitants of each parish meet, in their respective parishes, to take their long-lost rights into possession, and to form themselves into corporations. So then each parish becomes a corporation, and all men who are inhabitants become members or burghers. The land, with all that appertains to it, is in every parish made the property of the corporation or parish, with as ample power to let, repair or alter all or any part thereof . . . but the power of alienating the least morsel . . . is denied . . .

Then you may behold the rent which the people have paid into the parish treasures, employed by each parish in paying the Government its share of the sum which the Parliament or National Congress at any time grants; in maintaining and relieving its own poor, and people out of work; in paying the necessary officers their salaries; in building, repairing and adorning its houses, bridges and other structures . . . in a word, in doing whatever the people think proper . . . all affairs to be determined by voting, either in a full meeting of the parish . . . or in the house of representatives . . .

3b The parish commonwealth

Allen Davenport, *Republican*, 18 October 1822.

If the land of the whole empire was divided amongst her population, it would run to nearly seven acres each, but I will say six. Now, the miniature commonwealth I am going to describe, shall contain a population of one thousand souls: the land, therefore, will be six thousand acres . . . This commonwealth shall hold their land as joint stock. The land, and the houses may be let on leases, and lease-holders may let it to tenants at will: mechanics, and labourers, would follow their usual occupations, and be paid their wages according to their agreement. But all the rents of this commonwealth, must be paid into the hands of a committee, or board, who shall be appointed for that purpose, and who shall quarterly, after deducting all the expenses this little government may incur, in building, repairing, etc. divide it in equal shares, to every man, woman, and child in the community. In such a commonwealth, all would be happy, because all would be free; all would be brothers and sisters, because all would be equal; all would be contented, because all would be just; all would be generous, because all would be exempt from present, and the dread of future want! If a whole country were divided into districts, or communities on this plan, each district would send its deputy, or deputies to the National Convention to enact such laws as would best suit such a state of society.

To see mankind restored to this happy state is my sole ambition, and whether the road to it be through Radical, Republican, or Revolutionary principles, it matters not to me.

3c Monopoly in land

Allen Davenport, *Republican*, 1 October 1824.

What liberty can you enjoy without possessing land? If you traverse a field, do you not commit a trespass? If you pluck a berry, do you not violate a law? If you carry off one single grain of sand, do you not commit a larceny? . . . The dust is *my lord's*, the sand is *my lord's*, the berry is *my lord's*, for the field is *my lord's*, into which you cannot intrude though under the most pressing necessity, without the risk of a prosecution . . . *My Lord* in possessing the land as private property, possesses all the other elements, fire, water, and air, as far as his domains extend . . . I should not be surprised, if I were to hear of an action brought against some of the balloon gentlemen, for trespass in passing the atmosphere over some great Lord's fields.

I feel as certain as I do of my own existence, that equal liberties will never be obtained, that equal rights will never be enjoyed, and that a fair and impartial administration of justice will never be established, till the system of private property in land is abolished . . .

The monopoly in land by individuals, who transfer, by the laws of primogeniture their entire estates to one sole heir, and the holding the same in perpetuity, are the greatest of all political evils. Does not the landholders of England, at the present moment, hold the Power not only to enslave, but even to starve the landless part of the population?

3d Pledges for reform

'Agrarius' (George Petrie), *Man*, 21 July 1833.

Let no man obtain your suffrages, who will not give the following pledges:

1. To resign, when recalled by a majority of his constituents.
2. That he will strenuously and unceasingly exert himself to procure the total repeal of the following laws: the odious law of Primogeniture, Mortmain, and Entail; the law of freehold, copyhold and leasehold; the legislative powers of the House of Lords, and the abolition of all titles; the dismemberment of the Church from the State, that her priests may be placed on a footing with dissenters; and the substitution of a national guard (by annual ballot) in lieu of the present military and demi-military police force.
3. That he shall exert himself to establish a land office, the ministers of which shall be the stewards of the State, and who shall be empowered to let the land at a rent, the average of which shall be sufficient to cover the expenses of the State; they will also have the power to grant reasonable indemnity to the possessor of freehold by purchase (not exceeding a given amount), provided such purchase shall have been made within the last 20 years; the said land to revert to the State on the payment of the indemnity. All other lands to be considered the property of the State; and as there is no punishment awarded to the previous holders of that kind of stolen property, neither will they receive any reward for delivering up the same, other than the gratification of an approving conscience, for having performed an act of justice and equity.

3e Land and currency reform

Bronterre O'Brien, *National Reformer*, 16 January 1847.

1st. The Land of the United Kingdom must be made the public property of the whole people of the United Kingdom.

2nd. That the only rational way of doing that is, to abolish the private ownership of land altogether, make all rents payable to and for the state, make the tenant right, or right of occupancy, equal to all, and secure to every leaseholder full value for all *bona fide* improvements made by him on the soil during his occupancy.

3rd. That the only safe, peaceable and humane way of effecting such settlement is, to restore the land gradually to the public, as the landlords die off, so as not to disturb any proprietor existing at the time of passing the law, during his or her life; and on the lapse of their estates to the nation, at their death, to secure to their heirs, assigns, or representatives, the full money value of each estate, payable, by annual instalments, out of the future rents, so that even the remotest appearance of confiscation or spoilation may be avoided, and the aristocracy left without a shadow of pretext for rebelling against the law.

4th. That the National Debt, and all other public debts, be legislated for on the same principle as the land, namely, the capitals to be recognized, and payment of them guaranteed by annual instalments. But no more plundering of the tax-payers and debtor interests, by ever-lasting usury and law expenses, kept up merely to feed one portion of the community in idleness at the expense of the rest.

5th. Gold and silver to be forever abolished as currency and standards of value, and to be treated as mere mercantile commodities, which they are. The quarter or bushel of wheat to be henceforward the recognized standard of value—its average price (measured by labour) to be the unit of account—the Bank of England, and all other privileged corporations for the issue of money, to be abolished—the Government itself to be sole issuer of the legal tender money of the country. . . .

6th. Public marts or bazaars to be established for the deposit and sale of all manner of goods and commodities, on the principle of equitable exchanges. No manufacturer or depositor to appraise or sell his own goods, but all sales and exchanges to be effected by salaried officers, selected by the depositors. Such officers to appraise all goods upon delivery, and to give the depositors the money price of them in a paper currency that shall fairly represent them, by expressing their value in labour or corn—such notes to be of the same denomination as the Government notes, and convertible into the same when required for payment of taxes, etc., into gold and silver, at the market price, when required for exportation. All depositors to be able, on presenting the notes of the bazaar, to extract from it other goods, to the amount of their notes. . . .

7th. In order to enable industrious men to stock farms, and to manufacture goods on their own account, District Banks should be established, into which should be paid the rents of each district; and, from those rents, loans should be made to every deserving man who could bring competent testimony as to character and fitness to be trusted with an advance. . . . Next to the nationalization of landed property, and the establishment of an efficient currency, this system of credit would be the most effectual instrument conceivable for emancipating the industrious classes. For, who would be a hired bondsman of another, if he could till the soil, or manufacture goods, on his own account? And what properly constituted Democratic Government could refuse to establish banks, the object of which was to make freemen of its citizens? Remember, my friends, that if we owe the Government allegiance, it owes us, in return, protection. But what protection has a man from a Government which suffers rapacious profit-mongers to take advantage of his poverty to make him a slave for life? As society is now constituted, the productive classes are mere slaves to capitalists and usurious profitmongers. The wealth they produce is not their own. It is scized by the profit-monger, the moment it comes into existence. And out of this slavery the wretched producer can never hope to emerge; for, the more wealth he produces, the greater is the power he gives his employer of oppressing him, and the more and more unfit he becomes, every day, for resistance.

To escape from that soul and body crushing slavery, there is but one door open to him. It lies in the direction of the above propositions.

4 Competition—the attack on poverty

Critics of Old Corruption and the Spenceans had both focused on poverty as the key social evil, although they disagreed as to its cause and its remedy. The Rev. T. Malthus (1766–1834) voiced one of the great fears of the propertied—that the growth in pauperism, born by the rates, might eventually swallow up all property (4a). Hence Harriet Martineau's Warning Tales against indiscriminate charity which merely encouraged the poor to breed and worsen their situation (see p. 326); hence the severity of the new Poor Law of 1834 (see p. 206) and the bitterness of its opponents. Robert Owen (1771–1858), the philanthropic manager of the New Lanark cotton mills, disagreed with this pessimism (4b). Working men produced more in a week than they needed to live on; so any industrious man was entitled to a living wage, and the present profits of capitalists were stolen at his expense, because working men competed with and undercut each other. Equitable Labour Exchanges and co-operative communities (see p. 154) were ways for working men to work for themselves. George Mudie, printer and founder of *The Economist*, showed that poverty could be eradicated in this way without robbing the rich (4c). But Wooler (1786–1853) in the *Black Dwarf* criticized Owen's paternalism (4d), and the *Poor Man's Guardian* (4e) his disdain for politics.

Suggestions for further reading

For Owen, see V. Gatrell (ed.), *A New View of Society* (1970); A. Bestor, *Backwoods Utopias* (1952); and J. F. Harrison, *Robert Owen and the Owenites* (1969); for Malthus, D. Glass, *Introduction to Malthus* (1953).

4a Population and poverty

T. Malthus, *A Summary View* (1830) (a revised and condensed version of his *Essay on Population*, 1798).

If the natural increase of population, when unchecked by the difficulty of procuring the means of subsistence or other peculiar causes, be such as to continue doubling its numbers in twenty-five years, and if the greatest increase of food which, for a continuance, could possibly take place on a limited territory like our earth in its present state, be at the most only such as would add every twenty-five years an amount equal to its present produce, then it is quite clear that a powerful check on the increase of population must be almost constantly in action . . . These checks . . . have been classed under the general heads of preventive and positive. It will be found that they are all resolvable into *moral restraint*, *vice* and *misery* . . .

The existence of a tendency in mankind to increase, if unchecked, beyond the possibility of an adequate supply of food in a limited territory, must at once determine the question as to the natural right of the poor to full support in a state of society where the law of property is recognized . . . The concession of such a right, and a right of property, are absolutely incompatible and cannot exist together.

4b Unemployment and the world of plenty

R. Owen, *A Report to the County of Lanark* (1820).

The Evil for which your Reporter has been required to provide a remedy, is the general want of employment, at wages sufficient to support the family of a working man beneficially for the community . . . [Owen lists his propositions].

1st—That manual labour, properly directed, is the source of all wealth and of national prosperity.
2nd—That, when properly directed, labour is of far more value to the community than the expense necessary to maintain the labourer in considerable comfort.
3rd—That manual labour, properly directed, may be made to continue of this value in all parts of the world, under any supposable increase of its population, for many centuries to come.
4th—That, under a proper direction of manual labour, Great Britain and its dependencies may be made to support an incalculable increase of population, most advantageously for all its inhabitants.
5th—That when manual labour shall be so directed, it will be found that population cannot, for many years, be stimulated to advance as rapidly as society might be benefited by its increase . . .

It is well known that, during the last half century in particular, Great Britain, beyond any other nation, has progressively increased its powers of production, by a rapid advancement in scientific improvements and arrangements . . .

It appeared to your Reporter that the natural effect of the aid thus obtained from knowledge and science should be to add to the wealth and happiness of society in proportion as the new power increased and was judiciously directed; and that, in consequence, all parties would thereby be substantially benefited. All know, however, that these beneficial effects do not exist. On the contrary, it must be acknowledged that the working classes, which form so large a proportion of the population, cannot obtain even the comforts which their labour formerly procured for them, and that no party appears to gain, but all to suffer by their distress.

Having taken this view of the subject, your Reporter was induced to conclude that the want of beneficial employment for the working classes, and the consequent public distress, were owing to the rapid increase of the new productive power, for the advantageous application of which, society had neglected to make the proper arrangements. Could these arrangements be formed, he entertained the most confident expectation that productive employment might again be found for all who required it; and that the national distress, of which all now so loudly complain, might be gradually converted into a much higher degree of prosperity than was attainable prior to the extraordinary accession lately made to the productive powers of society . . .

His opinion on this important subject is founded on the following considerations:

First—It must be admitted that scientific or artificial aid to man increases his productive powers, his natural wants remaining the same; and in proportion as his productive powers increase he becomes less dependent on his physical strength and on the many contingencies connected with it.

Second—That the direct effect of every addition to scientific, or mechanical and chemical power is to increase wealth; and it is found, accordingly, that the immediate cause of the present want of employment for the working classes is an excess of production of all kinds of wealth, by which, under the existing arrangements of commerce, all the markets of the world are overstocked.

Third—That, could markets be found, an incalculable addition might yet be made to the wealth of society, as is most evident from the number of persons who seek employment, and the far greater number who, from ignorance, are insufficiently employed, but still more from the means we possess of increasing, to an unlimited extent, our scientific powers of production.

Fourth—That the deficiency of employment for the working classes cannot proceed from a want of wealth or capital, or of the means of greatly adding to that which now exists, but from some defect in the mode of distributing this extraordinary addition of new capital throughout society, or, to speak commercially, from the want of a market, or means of exchange, co-extensive with the means of production.

Were effective measures devised to facilitate the distribution of wealth after it was created, your Reporter could have no difficulty in suggesting the means of beneficial occupation for all who are unemployed, and for a considerable increase to their number . . .

One of the measures which he thus ventures to propose, *to let prosperity loose on the country* (if he may be allowed the expression), *is a change in the standard of value* . . .

THAT THE NATURAL STANDARD OF VALUE IS, IN PRINCIPLE, HUMAN LABOUR, OR THE COMBINED MANUAL AND MENTAL POWERS OF MEN CALLED INTO ACTION.

And that it would be highly beneficial, and has now become absolutely necessary, to reduce this principle into immediate practice; . . . as it forms the essence of all wealth, its value in every article of produce may also be ascertained, and its exchangeable value with all other values fixed accordingly; the whole to be permanent for a given period.

Human labour would thus acquire its natural or intrinsic value, which would increase as science advanced; and this is, in fact, the only really useful object of science.

The demand for human labour would be no longer subject to caprice, nor would the support of human life be made, as at present, a perpetually varying article of commerce, and the working classes made the slaves of an artificial system of wages, more cruel in its effects than any slavery ever practised by society, either barbarous or civilized.

4c The virtues of Owenism

G. Mudie, *The Economist*, 7 July 1821; 19 May 1821.

The *opposition* of the *interests* of all individuals, then, being the true source and only cause of *poverty* . . . it became specially *necessary*, in framing such a scheme of society, to provide arrangements which should RECONCILE the now *conflicting interests of individuals*;—should substitute the greatest possible *facilities* and *inducements*, for the *unlimited production and distribution of wealth* . . . and to render it *impossible* that any *individuals* should *ever* be destitute of *abundance of the necessaries and comforts of life*.

That Mr. Owen's scheme does effect this reconcilation of interests . . . is irrefragably proved . . .

One of the inherent features and intrinsic properties of the plan we are considering, is, that it overthrows nothing. The only enemies it has to combat and which it must inevitably destroy, are poverty, wretchedness, ignorance and vice. It leaves everyone in possession of all he has now; and so far from diminishing, it will greatly add to the present private wealth, even of the most wealthy individuals. It proposes to enrich all—not by dispossessing the present wealthy classes of their riches, and distributing them amongst the poor,—but by placing all in a condition to create new wealth, for themselves, and for society at large . . .

4d The morality of Owenism

Black Dwarf, 20 August 1817.

The plan itself seems to be, in plain terms, the establishment of a nursery for men (if their situation would leave them deserving of the name) so completely under the control of the 'existing authorities', as to be only in one respect distinguished from *a military force*. Soldiers are generally maintained in idleness, by the nation; but the soldiers of the pauper-barracks, are to *maintain themselves*, by working in the agricultural department principally. Imagine a state of things, in which the ministry of a country shall have so completely reversed the natural order of society, that those who can work, and earnestly seek employment, are in great numbers unable to find it, and are compelled to subsist upon *the charity* as it is called, not of the men who have reduced them in the scale of society, but of those who are not yet quite sunk to the lowest gradation in the scale. Imagine then a speculative enquirer to propose to take these individuals, and to enclose them in establishments, consisting of 1,200 each, men, women, and children; that a sort of Spencean community shall be established amongst them, in which they shall be reduced to mere automata, and all their feelings, passions, and opinions are to be subjected to certain rules, which Mr. Owen, the tutelary deity of these novel elysiums will lay down. They are to work in common, live in common, and have all things in common, except their wives. The children, at the age of three years are to be separated from their parents, and classed together for the duties which are to be required from them. And in these places, Mr. Owen presumes that all the bad passions will be eradicated; that secure of *subsistence* and *clothing*, the poor will wish for nothing further: that 'malice, envy, hatred, and all uncharitableness', will cease, and a new golden age return to bless the world . . .

All the mischievous effects resulting from the operation of the common laws of nature are to be superseded, and Mr. Owen like a new Creator is to stand forward with a rod of power, more powerful than that of Moses, and more beneficent than that of deity.

The principal justification of Mr. Owen's pretensions are that he has succeeded in *changing*, as he calls it the moral habits of the persons under his employment in a manufactory at Lanark, in Scotland. For all the good he has done in that respect, he deserves the highest thanks. It is much to be wished, that all who live by the labour of the poor would pay as much attention to their wants, and to their interests as Mr. Owen did to those under his care at Lanark. A little kindness, or rather a little *justice* to the labourer, would be the best means of destroying those bad habits which are generally acquired by ill treatment; but the case is materially different to improve the appearance and external manners of men *entirely dependent* upon an employer for support, and holding all their comforts in his fiat. In such cases, men will be easily induced to adopt anything that may be recommended to them, provided it do not too much shock these prejudices which are interests in the bosoms of all men at the manufactory; the persons are only obliged to obey while they remain; and they are *rewarded* for their obedience . . .

It is very amusing to hear Mr. Owen talk of *re-moralizing* the *poor*. Does he not think that the RICH are a little more in want of re-moralizing; and particularly that class of them, which has contributed to *de-moralize* the poor, if they are de-moralized, by supporting measures which have made them poor, and which now continue them poor and wretched? . . . Talk of the poor being de-moralized! It is their would-be-masters that create all the evils that afflict the poor, and all the depravity that pretended philanthropists pretend to regret.

In one point of view Mr. Owen's scheme might be productive of some good. Let him abandon the labourer to his own protection;

cease to oppress him, and the poor man would scorn to hold any fictitious dependence upon the rich. Give him a fair price for his labour, and do not take two thirds of a depreciated remuneration back from him again in the shape of taxes. Lower the extravagance of the great. Tax those *real luxuries*, enormous fortunes obtained without merit. Reduce the herd of locusts that prey upon the honey of the hive, and think they do the bees a most essential service by robbing them. LET THE POOR ALONE. The working bee can always find a hive; LET THE POOR ALONE. Do not take from them what they can earn, to supply the wants of those who will earn nothing. Do this; and the poor will not want your splendid erections for the cultivation of misery, and the subjugation of the mind.

4e Owenism and politics

Poor Man's Guardian, 1 September 1832; 22 September 1832.

Let all the Co-operators join the working classes in demanding their POLITICAL RIGHTS; for despite the contempt in which Mr. Owen and his friends may hold the right of voting for those who make the laws, the working classes know full well that without it they must ever continue the victims of unjust legislation. Without this important RIGHT, they seek in vain for political protection against the incessant exactions of *land-stealers*, *monopolists*, and *capitalists*, well knowing that it is the want of this right which has made them the abject slaves they are . . .

The Owenite thinks that without property the working classes can never get represented in Parliament, and therefore he sets to work with his 'Equitable Labour Exchange' to get property; while the Radical thinks that without representation they will never be able to acquire property at all, and accordingly he begins to work at the other end, and goes to work for Universal Suffrage . . . No one can admire Mr. Owen more than we do, nor entertain a higher opinion of his enlightened views; but, at the same time, we are of opinion that if he supposes that the wealth-producers of England will ever reap the fruits of his benevolence, until they shall have first obtained their political rights, he greatly deceives himself, and will find it so, when it is too late.

5 Capitalism—the attack on political economy

Until the late 1820s, working-class writers had located poverty as the gap between the value of a working man's labour, and the value of his wage; and taxes, parasites, the theft of land, and competition were held to account for it. The enemy was primarily aristocratic government buttressed by land and by church. The result was a radical analysis of wrongs, a view of society that Chartists could and did share with the Anti-Corn Law League. Middle- and working-class radicals saw themselves confronting a common enemy in the aristocracy. But the articulation of political economy in the 1820s, justifying the new industrial capitalist system, encouraged working men to compare their wage with that of the capitalist. The discrepancy was held to be exploitation, the enemy was the capitalist and the middle man, profits rather than taxes were the other side of poverty, and the result was a socialist analysis of working-class wrongs. Former middle-class allies in the radical attack on aristocracy were now class enemies. (See Place's comments, p. 132.)

J. R. McCulloch (1789–1864) stated the classical case for political economy (5a). The rate of wages depended on the ratio of capital to population. Wages could rise only if either population fell, or capital increased and with it the amount available for investment and employment. Profits, therefore, which created capital, were socially desirable; trades unionism, which sought to raise wages higher than the wage fund could support, was harmful; and the interests of master and man were identical. The function of government was simply to promote free trade so that the market could determine the natural level of wages, prices and profits. Harriet Martineau (1802–76), a writer of moral tales, put these tenets into popular form for working-class consumption (5b).

Thomas Hodgskin (1787–1869) and William Thompson (1785?–1833) offered an alternative analysis of profits and wages (5c and 5d). The labourer, and not the capitalist, produced the goods and he should rightfully retain them; but as he was dependent on the capitalist for a wage, he was dispossessed. Capitalists were thieves and profits were theft.

The middle-class economists returned to expose the fallacies of socialism. Poulett Scrope (1797–1876) argued that profits were not stolen from wages (3e); they were the fund from which wages were paid. Only as profits increased could wages increase, and thus the bond of harmony between capitalist and labourer was made clear. John Wade, now a proponent of political economy, stated boldly that labour was an object for sale in the open market (5f) and could claim no privileges and no protection. *The Trades Newspaper*, a working-class paper founded in 1825 to prevent the re-imposition of the Combination laws, bitterly attacked (5g) the notion that labour was a commodity whose price was determined by supply and demand. John Scott, a Manchester silk-weaver, soberly pointed out to a House of Commons committee (5h) that to strip labour of its defences in the name of free trade was to starve the labourer out of existence.

Suggestions for further reading

For middle-class political economy, see M. Blaug, *Ricardian Economics* (1958); L. Robbins, *The theory of economic policy in English classical political economy* (1952); for Harriet Martineau, the biography by R. K. Webb, *Harriet Martineau* (1960); for Thompson and Hodgskin, H. L. Beales, *The early English socialists* (1933); R. Pankhurst, *William Thompson* (1954); E. Halevy, *Thomas Hodgskin* (1903).

5a Classical political economy

J. R. McCulloch, *Principles of Political Economy* (1825), pp. 316–19, 337 of the 1864 edn.

The capacity of a country to support and employ labourers is not measured by advantageousness of situation, richness of soil, or extent of territory . . . but on the amount of its capital applicable to the employment of labour, and on the disposition of the owners of capital to apply it. . . .

The quantity of produce apportioned to each labourer, or his wages rated in commodities, is determined by the ratio which the capital of the country bears to its labouring population. When, on the one hand, capital is increased without an equivalent increase of population, the portions of it that go to individuals, or their wages, are necessarily augmented; and when, on the other hand, population happens to increase more rapidly than capital, the latter having to be distributed among a greater number of persons, their wages or shares are proportionally reduced . . . The well-being of the labouring classes is, therefore, especially dependent on the relation which they bear to capital. If they increase faster than it, their condition is deteriorated; and if they increase more slowly, it is improved. This oscillation determines 'their weal and their woe' . . . We may be assured that every scheme for improving their condition which is not bottomed on this principle, or which has not an increase of the ratio of capital to population for its object, must be nugatory and ineffectual.

And yet it has been said, that an increase of capital may be hostile to the working classes, and that their interests and those of the capitalists may be, and in fact are, frequently opposed. But there is no real room or ground for any such statement. Labour and capital are alike dependent upon, and necessary to each other; without the former the latter cannot exist, and without the latter the former would be valueless. The notion that an increase of machinery, food, and clothing (for of such articles does capital consist), can be injurious to the labourer, is too plainly contradictory and absurd to be entitled to any notice. The truth is, that whatever tends to promote accumulation, to increase the desire for and the means of amassing additional wealth, and to give confidence and security to its possessors, contributes in the most effectual manner to advance the interests of the labourers. A capitalist cannot increase his own stock without at the same time, and to the same extent, increasing the wealth or the means of subsistence, of the working classes. Hoarding is no longer practised in any country in which property is protected. Wherever this is the case, all savings go to swell, directly or indirectly, the amount of the fund for the employment of labour . . . An increase of capital is but another name for an increased demand for labour; and it is the only way in which it can be really and permanently increased.

But, supposing this to be admitted, it will perhaps be alleged that capitalists endeavour to reduce wages to the lowest possible limits; that, being able to stop their works for a time, they have a great advantage in the deadly struggle which they are always carrying on against the labourers, who can rarely afford to be idle—at least for any considerable period—and that, consequently, the latter are too often reduced to a state bordering on helotism and wretchedness . . . A capitalist has a certain sum of money to expend on wages; and it is, of course his object to get the largest possible amount of labour in exchange. But thousands of other capitalists are in the same situation; all of them are employers of labour, and have certain sums to expend upon it. Inasmuch, however, as the supply of labour in the market is limited, wages cannot be artificially reduced. All the capital is sure, through the higgling of the market, to be equitably divided among all the labourers; and with every increase of the former, as compared with the latter, wages will necessarily rise . . . It is idle, therefore, to suppose that the efforts of capitalists to cheapen labour can have the smallest influence over its medium price . . .

[This shows] the paramount importance, with a view to the well-being of the community, of the increase of population being subordinate to that of capital. But how desirable soever, legislation can do but little to bring about this result. When government has secured the property and the rights of individuals, and has given that freedom to industry which is so essential, it has done nearly all it can to promote the increase of capital. If it interfere in industrial undertakings, its proceedings will be productive of injury. The reliance of individuals on their own efforts, and their desire to advance themselves, are the only principles on which any dependence can be safely placed.

5b Political economy popularized

Harriet Martineau, 'The Manchester Strike', *Illustrations of Political Economy* (1832 edn), pp. 57–60.

[*The Manchester Strike:* the argument between Allen, leader of the moderates within the Union, Clack, the demagogue, and Mr Wentworth, one of the masters.]

'You do not deny, sir', said Allen, 'that our real wages are less than they were?'

'I am afraid it is as true as that our profits are less. There is less surplus remaining over from our manufacture for us to divide . . . We cannot afford higher wages. . . . Your wages consist of the proportion you receive of the return brought by the article you manufacture. You know how the value of this return varies; how, when an article is scarce, it brings in a large return, and how, when it is plentiful, our customers give less for it; and you must therefore see how your wages vary independently of our will.'

'But whose doing is it, sir, that the return varies so much?' . . .

'If', observed one of the masters, 'you brought only half the present quantity of labour to us, we must, whether we liked it or not, pay double for it. If you choose to bring up large families who will in turn rear large families to the same occupation, it is a necessary consequence that wages will fall to the very lowest point.'

'What do you call the lowest point?'

'That at which the labourer can barely subsist. If he cannot subsist, he cannot labour, of course. If he can do more than merely subsist, his wages are not at the lowest point . . . Upon the proportion of your labour to our capital depends the rise and fall of wages through the whole scale of payment.'

'What would you call the highest payment?' inquired Allen.

'The greatest possible proportion of the return that the capitalist can spare, so as to leave it worth his while to manufacture; and this highest rate is, of course, paid only when labour is difficult to be had.'

'We cannot wait till that time,' said Clack. 'If we waited till a war or a fever carried off part of our numbers, it would do little good; for there are plenty of young ones growing up. We must bestir ourselves and see if a strike will not do as well. The plague would no doubt be more acceptable to gentlemen, as long as it did not stop their manufacture, like a strike; but the poor must raise themselves by such means as are in their own hands, and not wait for a judgement of Providence.'

'I quite agree with you,' said Mr. Wentworth. 'Providence would have men guide themselves by its usual course, and not by uncommon accidents. But I doubt whether a strike is one of the means which will gain your point. It will leave your case worse than in the beginning, depend upon it. A strike works in the wrong way for your interest. It does not decrease your numbers, and it does decrease the capital which is to maintain you.'

5c The capitalists' monopoly of the produce of labour

T. Hodgskin, *Labour Defended Against the Claims of Capital* (1825) (1922 reprint).

Throughout this country at present there exists a serious contest between capital and labour . . . To suggest some arguments in favour of labour, and against capital, is my chief motive for publishing the present pamphlet. . . .

. . . I shall proceed to EXAMINE THE EFFECTS OF CAPITAL; AND I SHALL BEGIN WITH CIRCULATING CAPITAL . . . To enable either the master manufacturer or the labourer to devote himself to any particular occupation, it is only necessary that he should possess—not, as political economists say, a stock of commodities, or circulating capital, but a conviction that while he is labouring at his particular occupation the things which he does not produce himself will be provided for him, and that he will be able to procure them and pay for them by the produce of his own labour . . . The effects usually attributed to a stock of commodities are caused by co-existing labour, and that it is by the command the capitalist possesses over the *labour of some men*, not by his possessing a stock of commodities that HE is enabled to *support* and consequently employ other labourers.

I come now to examine, secondly, the NATURE and EFFECTS of FIXED CAPITAL. Fixed capital consists of the tools and instruments the labourer works with . . . Are they, or are they not, the produce of labour? . . . Are, or are they not, so much inert decaying and dead matter, of no utility whatever, possessing no skilful hands? . . . Fixed capital does not derive its utility from previous, but present labour; and does not bring its owner a profit because it has been stored-up, but because it is a means of obtaining a command over labour . . .

The labourer subsists on what is called circulating capital; he works with fixed capital . . . and profit is derived in both cases from the power which the capitalists have over the labourer who consumes the circulating and who uses the fixed capital . . .

Betwixt him who produces food and him who produces clothing, betwixt him who makes instruments and him who uses them, in steps the capitalist, who neither makes them nor uses them, and appropriates to himself the produce of both. With as niggard a hand as possible he transfers to each part of the produce of the other, keeping to himself the larger share . . . While he despoils both, so completely does he exclude one from the view of the other that both believe they are indebted to him for subsistence. He is the *middleman* of all labourers . . .

Masters, it is evident, are *labourers* as well as their journeymen. In this character their interest is precisely the same as that of their men. But they are also either capitalists, or the agents of the capitalist, and in this respect their interest is decidedly opposed to the interest of their workmen . . .

I have shown that it [capital] has no just claim to any share of the labourer's produce, and that what it actually receives is the cause of the poverty of the labourer . . .

Should it be said, then, as perhaps it may, that unless there be profit, and unless there be interest, there will be no motives for accumulation and improvement, I answer that this is a false view, and arises from attributing to capital and saving those effects which result from labour; and that the best means of securing the progressive improvement, both of individuals and of nations, is to do justice and allow labour to possess and enjoy the whole of its produce.

5d Equality of distribution

W. Thompson, *An inquiry into the Principles of the Distribution of Wealth* (1824).

It is not the mere possession of wealth, but the *right distribution* of it, that is important to a community . . . The tendency of the existing arrangements of things as to wealth, is to enrich a few at the expense of the mass of the producers; to make the poverty of the poor more hopeless, to throw back the middling classes upon the poor, that a few may be enabled, not only to accumulate in perniciously large masses the real national, which is only the aggregate of individual, capital, but also, by means of such accumulations, to command the products of the yearly labour of the community. Who is not alarmed at the every day increasing tendency to poverty on the part of the many, to the ostentation of excessive wealth on the part of the few?

. . . Every producer of wealth should have the entire use of the products of his labour or exertion. But as long as the labourer stands in society divested of everything but the mere power of producing, as long as he possesses neither the tools nor the machinery to work with, the land or materials to work upon, the house and clothes that shelter him, or even the food which he is consuming while in the act of producing; as long as any institutions or expedients exist, by the open or unseen operations of which he stands dependent, day by day, for his very life on those who have accumulated these necessary means of his exertions; so long will he remain deprived of almost all the products of his labour, instead of having the use of all of them . . . As long as a class of mere capitalists exists, society must remain in a diseased state. Whatever plunder is saved from the hand of political power, will be levied in another way under the name of profits, by capitalists, who, while capitalists, must be always the law-makers . . .

Representative institutions . . . tend to the dissolution of the league between capitalists and the holders of political power; because the great and paramount interest of those not possessed of capital would be as fully represented as that of those possessing it.

5e The fallacies of socialism

G. Poulett Scrope, *Political Economy* (1833), pp. 98, 100, 103–9 of the 1873 edn.

If the entire capital a labourer works with belongs to himself, whether by right of purchase or by production, the whole produce of his labour will likewise properly belong to him. But if he works with the capital of another, it is evident that a part of the produce which results from the joint employment of his labour and the other's capital, belongs of right to the owner of the capital . . . It is to be viewed in the light of a compensation to him for abstaining for a time from the consumption of that portion of his property on his personal gratification . . .

[Yet some still] declaim against capital as the poison of society, and the taking of interest on capital by its owners as an abuse, an injustice, a robbery of the class of labourers! . . . Such blindness is to me truly unaccountable . . . That any sane person should attribute the evil [of general misery] to the *existence of capital*—that is, to the employment of wealth, instead of being unproductively consumed . . . —is indeed wonderful . . .

But perhaps it is in the imagination of these schemers, that there should not be a general destruction but only a general division, of the capital at present existing, among the present race of labourers; so that each, it is thought, would, for some time at least, be provided with a stock of food, clothes and tools with which to continue the business of production . . . But, in a very short time, a large part of the population, all the idle—and in such a crisis there will be little industry—will have consumed their share of the plunder in riot and excess . . . Either they will, if sufficiently strong and numerous, call for another division of property, that is, once more plunder of the barns, granaries, homesteads, and warehouses of the industrious, or if they are not strong enough to attempt this, they will humble themselves to the owners of these same barns and warehouses, and petition for food and clothing in return for all they have to offer, their labour; that is to say, they will apply to them for employment and wages . . . If their request is acceded to, the old system of masters and men, capitalists and labourers, will recommence . . .

There is an unhappy impression prevalent among the labouring classes, that because it is for the interest of the employer to pay no larger wages than they can get their work done for, while it is of course their (the labourers' interest) to get as much as they can, therefore the two classes have permanently hostile interests and none in common . . . Wages are . . . determined [by the capitalist] on a calculation made by him that the produce of their joint industry will reach an amount sufficient at least to cover his expenditure in wages, etc., and leave such a surplus, or profit, as will repay him in the ordinary sense on his capital, and a full remuneration for his skill and attention to the business. If when the returns come in from his sales they amount to more than this, his profits are by so much increased. But this increase has been in no degree taken out of the wages of his labourers. On the contrary, should the increase in the amount of returns prove to be permanent, the higher profits obtained in the particular business would soon attract fresh capital to it, occasioning an increased demand for labour and before long an increase in wages. So far then from its being true that increased profits are necessarily taken out of wages and improved wages out of profits, the very reverse is the case. Profits and wages may, and generally do, rise and fall together . . . Of course when profits, on the other hand, fall off, the labourers must, under the stern influence of the law of supply and demand, submit to a reduction of wages—or they will find their employers reducing their establishments, or perhaps withdrawing their capital from the business altogether.

It is clear then that the true interests of both employers and labourers are in the long run identical . . . All attempts to obtain an artificial rise in wages, such as the profits of the trade cannot bear, can only drive it away to other localities, perhaps to foreign countries, and leave the local labouring population with lessened occupation and means of maintenance.

5f Labour for sale

John Wade, *The history of the middle and working classes* (1834 edn) pp. 236–7.

Labour is a commodity for sale, differing from other commodities chiefly in its more perishable nature, in the greater difficulty and expense of storing up a surplus quantity of it beyond the current demand, and in the circumstances that the supply of it cannot be augmented or diminished with the same facility as the supply of a merely physical product. All the principles of trade, therefore, which are applicable to buyers and sellers, are alike applicable to workmen and their employers. Wages, like prices, must be determined by the free competition of the market; there must be no arbitrary interferences either on the part of the state or of individuals; any compulsory attempt to fix the market price of labour would be as indefensible as an attempt to fix the market price of bread or butcher's meat. Labour is the property of the working man, and merits the same protection as other property; but no more. The trade in it ought to be free, neither protected by immunities, nor restricted by penalties.

5g Masters and men

T. Single, *Trades Newspaper*, 13 November 1825.

Men are told not to *demand* of their masters an advance of wages, to enter into combinations for that purpose is criminal, and to submit to their dictation is justice. What! is that justice, that they who purchase labour shall fix the price they are to pay for it? Are men to have no *power* to defend and protect their own interests? If they have any, it must have some weight: if it has none, it is of no use. Wages, in most cases, are regulated in a great degree *by the power* the men have to oppose their masters. This is one reason why in some trades they are well paid, in others badly . . . For instance, the agricultural labourers have *no power*, either by combinations or otherwise; they are therefore *badly off*. The various classes who are employed in other pursuits are more voiced and have more means to defend their rights, consequently are better paid. . .

Among masters there exists one general feeling to get work done as cheap as they can. Not one among them but what has a stronger desire to oppose any rise of price than to promote it. I appeal to every employer if this is not a positive fact. Examine your own feelings, and I am sure you must admit it. Then is it not absurd to suppose that they will ever, of their own accord, advance the value of Labour? . . .

The interests of masters and men are as much opposed to each other as light is to darkness. The object of the one is to get as much labour for as little money as possible, and the other just the contrary: hence arises that unanimous feeling on each side to oppose the other. The whole of the working classes are as naturally disposed to promote an advance of wages whenever an opportunity occurs, as masters are to lower them . . . Any *act* which tends to lessen the *power* of the men, is, in fact, an act for the lowering of wages, and increasing the wealth of employers.

Some are continually talking about leaving the rate of wages to regulate itself, like every other commodity. The Scotch economists say, that wages are and must be always regulated by the demand for labour. When there is plenty of work and short of hands the price will rise; and when there are more hands than there is labour to do, it, as a matter of course, will fall.—This is an excellent idea for a theory; but, like most others, it is nothing in reality, and no use in practice.

Every body that knows anything of men must know, that at all times there are, and always have been, a great number of hands out of work. Now ask any man out of employment, who is almost in a state of starvation, to go to work in his calling, for *much* less than the regular prices which are paid, and you will find that in nine hundred and ninety-nine cases out of a thousand he would sooner beg, steal, or starve, than do it. Every person who knows anything about the employment of men knows this to be the fact. What nonsense, then, to talk about wages being regulated by the demand.

The wages are now, ever were, and ever will be, regulated by a variety of circumstances; it is impossible that they can be by one general rule. To call labour a commodity that is to be brought to the market like wheat or any other article, is sheer nonsense—the one is a shadow, and the other a substance. Before you can order Englishmen to be worked like cattle, you must first deprive them of all the natural passions and feelings which are implanted by God. When you have succeeded in this, then you may compare them to cattle, or any other commodity, and not before.

Men are not those manageable beings who are to be regulated by their masters with as much ease as a horse or an ass. They possess pride, envy, hatred, and all the passions which those do who style themselves their betters. The love of independence and uprightness of conduct, too, operates as strongly on the minds of the poor as the rich. There must be some very powerful cause or other on the mind of a poor man, else he could never hear his children cry for bread, suffer the tortures of hunger, commit acts wherein his life is in danger, suffer almost every privation and disgrace imaginable, rather than *undersell his labour*, or work for much less than his fellow workmates. . . .

An economist in the Paper called the *Scotsman* says 'they', the men, 'can only raise wages by providence of conduct—by taking care that capital shall accumulate in a higher ratio than they increase in numbers. This is the only method', says he, 'by which they can diminish their working hours and improve their condition'. Here you see is the same error; he seems to think that men's minds are to be regulated like a machine. . . Is he such a fool as to imagine that men can *aggregately* add to or diminish their number in as easy a manner as we can the number of dogs or cats?

To tell men that their bad pay and poverty arises from there being too many people will never be believed, while there is in the country more than a sufficiency of food for the whole. When there is a scarcity and every one in a certain degree feels it, then is the time such a doctrine may be believed, and not before.

5h Labour and capital contrasted

Evidence of John Scott, silk weaver, to the *Select Committee on the Handloom Weavers' Petition* (1835), qus 2685–91.

You have heard it asserted that labour, like every other marketable commodity should find its own level; do you think that the wages of the weavers have found their level?—I do not think that the wages of labour have found their own level; yet neither do I think there is a similarity between what is called capital and labour . . . Capital, I can make out to be nothing else but an accumulation of the products of labour; and the very supposition that a man has capital, includes in it that he has the power of refusing to part with his articles if an insufficient price be offered for them. In the dealings of capitalists with each other, they are generally the one as much in need of buying as the other is of selling, and they can either of them abstain from buying or selling if they consider improper terms are demanded of them. But how stands the case with the labourer? Labour is always carried to the market by those who have nothing else to keep or sell, and now, therefore, must part with it immediately, whether the price pleases them or not, or suffer privations, most likely severe want: labour is always purchased by capitalists, who can abstain from purchasing until they can have it on their own terms, without suffering either privation or want. That, Sir, I presume to call one great distinction essential to the very existence of labour and capital. Another is, that all kinds of commodities (capital or accumulations of the products of labour) having assumed a tangible, visible, substantial form, can be retained if an inadequate price be offered for them, and the fortune of another day, week, month, year be tried for them, as they will generally keep for some time without suffering much damage; many of them will keep any length of time without any damage at all. But how fares labour in this respect? The labour which I ought to perform or might perform this week, if I, in imitation of the capitalist, refuse to part with it, that is, refuse to perform it, because an inadequate prices is offered me for it, can I bottle it? Can I lay it up in salt? In what way can I store it, that, in imitation of the capitalist, I may either get the same price for it, or a higher or lower price, as the case may be, at some future period? That I presume to call another essential distinction inseparable from the very nature of labour and capital. These two distinctions between the nature of labour and capital (viz. that labour is always sold by the poor, and always bought by the rich, and that labour cannot by any possibility be stored, but must be every instant sold or every instant lost) are sufficient to convince me that labour and capital can never with justice be subjected to the same laws; and I must continue to be of that opinion, until somebody convinces me these distinctions do not exist, or that their existence forms no real difference.

Do you think that on that account the weaver is more entitled to protection in his wages than the capitalist is?—I do not wish to withdraw what protection capital has, but I do say that labour ought not to be left unprotected. We see the shopkeeper protected by the license of the hawker, and we see the land protected by the corn law, that both the land and the shopkeeper may pay their taxes; but the labourer, while he pays his taxes, is altogether unprotected . . .

Do you think that the capital which has been already accumulated would ever have been accumulated, unless with a view to this command over the immediate wants and necessities of the day?—I think that has been the chief view that capitalists have had in accumulating it.

Then do you not conceive it to be part of the design of Providence, that that should be one of the main stimulants to effect an accumulation of capital?—I think that Providence has deigned that labour, which is the capital of the working man, should be protected, and not to be taken from him by those who have the power, that is, the capital.

6 Capitalism—the attack on exploitation

Central to the attack on capitalism was the sense of exploitation. Working men were robbed of the produce of their labour in the name of profits, robbed of the power to protect their labour in the name of free trade, robbed of the price of their labour, because competition, machinery and sweating together made it cheap.

A verse sent into the *Poor Man's Guardian*, the leading working-class paper of the 1830s (6a) showed how this theft occurred. It was accumulated robbery. The *Co-operator*, edited for the co-operative movement by Dr King of Brighton, described working men as mere counters in the capitalists' power game (6b). *Blackwood's*, a Tory Review deeply hostile to *laisser faire*, said that free trade and competition turned men into mere labour power (6c), without rights, without defences, and excluded from the economic public. The middle-class Society for the Diffusion of Useful Knowledge challenged such anti-social views, and their *Penny Magazine* (6d) carried a poem by Barry Cornwall praising the virtue and value of toil; the working-class reply, not by Barry Cornwall, suggested the hatred working men felt towards an economy that destroyed their dignity as well as their livelihood. James Morrison's *Pioneer*, the organ of the Builders' Union (see p. 169), grimly forecast (6e) that if exploitation continued, capitalism would end in revolution. Ernest Jones, one of the leaders of later Chartism, developed (6f) the concept of surplus value, that gap between the value of what the labourer produced for the capitalist and what he received back as wages, which was the core of exploitation. In his *Song of the Low* (6g) he explored the bitter irony borne by the exploited towards the exploiters.

Suggestions for further reading

For the notion of exploitation, P. Hollis, *The Pauper Press* (1970); W. Oliver, 'The Grand National Consolidated Trades Union', *Economic History Review* (1964).

6a On wages

Poor Man's Guardian, 7 January 1832.

Wages should form the price of goods;
Yes, wages should be all,
Then we who work to make the goods,
Should *justly have them all*;
But if their price be made of rent,
Tithes, taxes, profits all,
Then we who work to make the goods,
Shall have—*just none at all.*

One of the Know-Nothings.

6b Exploitation

Cooperator, 17 September 1829; 18 October 1829.

The capitalists produce nothing themselves; they are fed, clothed and lodged by the working classes . . . In the present form of society, the workmen are entirely in the power of the capitalists, who are incessantly playing at what is called *profit and loss*—and the workmen are the counters, which are pitched backwards and forwards with this unfortunate difference—that the counters do not eat and drink as workmen do, and therefore don't mind being thrown aside at the end of the game. The game could not be played without the counters; and capitalists could not play at profit and loss without the workmen. But the workmen are as much in the power of the capitalists, as the counters are in that of the players; and if the capitalists do not want them, they must go to the wall . . . We claim for the workman the rights of a rational and moral agent . . . the being whose exertions produce all the wealth of the world—we claim for him the rights of a man, and deprecate the philosophy which would make him an article of merchandize, to be bought and sold, multiplied or diminished, by no other rules than those which serve to decide the manufacture of a hat.

'Senex', *Pioneer*, 14 June 1834.

I would banish the word *wages* from the language, and consign it, with the word slavery, to histories and dictionaries. *Wages* is a term of purchase; it means the piecemeal purchase of your blood, and bones, and brains, at weekly payments; it is the present name for the *Saturday's market price of man, woman, and child*!

6c Free trade and the public good

'The Influence of free trade upon the Condition of the Labouring Classes', *Blackwood's*, April 1830.

The advocates of Free Trade contend that if this branch [silk] of our manufactures cannot sustain itself against foreign rivalry, it is proof that it is not of a profitable nature with respect to the community at large; and that therefore it ought to be left to its fate. The silk-weavers reply, that this may be true as far as the non-productive classes are concerned; and add, that with the declension and fall of the silk trade, their means of subsistence must be greatly diminished, or perhaps entirely fail, when no alternative would be left them except starvation or the work-house . . . The foreign competition which has been let in on him, forces the British manufacturer to put up with half the remuneration which he had been accustomed to receive from his labour. If he has succeeded in keeping the field against foreign rivalry, it has been done by the application of a double portion of industry; and the fall which has taken place in British silks, to the level of continental prices, is therefore a benefit reaped by the non-productive classes—by those who live on incomes derived from profit, or capital lent out at interest, at the expense of the producing classes—of those classes who subsist solely upon the earnings of manual industry . . . The changes projected by the Economists benefit the affluent and non-productive classes, by diminishing the cost of the commodities which they consume; but this advantage is purchased solely at the expense of the productive classes, by diminishing their wages and adding to their toil. This system is admirably calculated to minister to the luxury and enjoyments of the idle and opulent portion of the community; to foster the dissipation, and augment the splendour of the palace and the hall; but the virtuous and hard-working inmate of the cottage it robs of his comforts, and almost of his necessaries. What it adds to the enjoyment of bloated wealth, it takes from the scanty earnings of pining industry. . . . For our own part, we feel no hesitation in avowing that we would rather waive all the glittering advantages which are held out to us as likely to result from the practical application of the most wonderful discoveries of Political Economy, than consent to reap them at the expense of any class of our fellow subjects . . .

There is indeed nothing in the conduct of the advocates of Free Trade so deserving of reprehension, as the hypocritical pretences with which they attempt to disguise or conceal the real object of their measures. If we credit their professions, this amiable and enlightened tribe of philosophers has nothing in view except the public good, and the improvement of the condition of the industrious classes. . . . We must, however, be allowed to assure the labouring and industrious classes, that they constitute no portion of that public, of whom the Whigs and the Economists talk so loudly and so frequently. In the vocabulary of this sect, the personification called 'the public' includes only the idle capitalists, the consuming classes, the '*fruges consumere nati*'; but has no reference whatever to the working portion of the community. The Whig Economists regard this class merely as beasts of burden, as animal machinery produced by nature for the purpose of 'hewing wood and drawing water' in the service of the non-productive and consuming classes. We apprehend, however, that the moment is arriving, when the Free Traders will no longer find shelter from public scorn and indignation, under the hollow and false pretence of intending to benefit the working classes. The time is approaching when they must cease to insult the understandings of those whom they have irreparably injured. . . .

6d The weaver's song

Barry Cornwall, *Penny Magazine*, 7 July 1832.

Weave, brothers, weave!—Swiftly throw
  The shuttle athwart the loom,
And show us how brightly your flowers grow,
  That have beauty but no perfume!
Come, show us the rose, with a hundred dyes,
  The lily, that hath no spot,
The violet, deep as your true love's eyes,
  And the little forget-me-not!
    Sing,—sing, brothers! weave and sing!
      'Tis good both to sing and to weave:
    'Tis better to work than live idle:
      'Tis better to sing than grieve.

Weave, brothers, weave!—Toil is ours;
  But toil is the lot of men:
One gathers the fruit, one gathers the flowers,
  One soweth the seed again!
There is not a creature, from England's King,
  To the peasant that delves the soil,
That knows half the pleasures the seasons bring,
  If he have not his share of toil!
    So,—sing, brothers! etc.

The weaver's song, not by Barry Cornwall

Poor Man's Guardian, 3 November 1832.

Why should I toil from morn till night,
  Producing wealth I can't enjoy?
Why should base robbers thus unite
  The honest to destroy!
Why should I live deprived of all
  The countless blessings nature gave?
Oh, why not rouse at nature's call
  And cease to be a slave?
Deprived of all that blesses man,
  Why should I live in pain,
To bless a greedy tyrant clan
  Who make my labour vain?
Why should I ceaseless toil for those
  Who care not for my sad distress?
Who cruelly increase my woes
  And make each comfort less!

The idle poet's lay I scorn!—
  The coldly reasoning brute I hate!
I feel my heart, my soul forlorn—
  I cannot bear my state!
Hot indignation burns me up—
  My thoughts, my words are all in flame—
I now have drained sad sorrow's cup.
  And Justice now will claim!

6e A warning

'Concord', *Pioneer*, 12 October 1833.

The present movements of society are tending rapidly to its dissolution —anarchy and convulsion must ensue, unless the saving hand of union is stretched forth. Thousands of working men are weekly being displaced by the new inventions of machinery, which are daily coming into use. Their condition is becoming more and more degraded, and the more facilities of production are discovered, the more wretched becomes their lot. There is a point beyond which patience will not be able to endure; there is a point of oppression, which if once passed will produce a dreadful reaction. I warn every accumulating capitalist, that safety does not consist in individual abundance, but in a proper distribution of comfort amongst all. I warn the great monopolists of a truth which is of vast importance for them to know—that machinery, by which their great accumulations are made, and by which the condition of the labourer is becoming daily more and more degraded, must speedily come into the hands of the working men, to *work for them, and not against them*, or all property of every kind will be unsafe in England, and a revolution more terrific than any that has been experienced in France, will be experienced in this country.

It behoves all classes who respect their own safety, to respect the comfort and happiness of the working mass. The capitalist is continually accumulating, and the working man is continually going down; and this will continue to operate until the injured labourer, galled by intolerable oppression, shall rise with a determination which nothing can quell, and effect a dreadful revolution.

It would be folly amounting to madness for the rich capitalist to assure himself of safety. Twenty-four hours can overthrow the whole labours of his life, and involve his family in the misery and insecurity which he is now bringing upon his fellow men . . . I cannot help shuddering at the prospect before us: I know that a fire is kindled, that will burn up the whole earth; I see that continued oppression will result in violence, and no power can stop it.

6f Exploitation and surplus value

Ernest Jones, *Notes to the People* (1851), i, pp. 442–3.

. . . I assert, that you, as a *Capitalist*, as an *employer*, are a nuisance in society—that you are a stumbling block in the way of happiness—that your whole order must be done away with before labour can be emancipated, and man obtain his rights . . .

. . . You talk of your men receiving from 40*s*. to 60*s*. per fortnight for their work—there are very few workmen in England that receive quarter of this. But supposing they do, *what do you receive by their work?* That is the standard by which to measure their wages. It suits your purpose to pay them that—or you would not pay it; then what right have you to vaunt the payment as something for which they owe you gratitude? Which is the greater gainer—they or you? If you,—as you indisputably are,—it is you who owe gratitude to them, not they to you.

But, let us go a step further: do you not withhold more *from* them, than you give *to* them? If you pay them 20*s*. per week, could they not make 40*s*. or 60*s*. per week, were not you and your class in existence? Why, of course they could! and I'll show you how: you pay them something for their labour—and *make an enormous profit out of it besides*. If you were not there, they would have the labour payment just the same, and *all the profit into the bargain*. Therefore you capital employing-classes are as injurious as you are unnecessary; injurious—because you intercept between God and man, between labour and the means of work. Unnecessary—because you did not create the means of work,—and they being there without you, you are not wanted that the labourer may work and live.

6g The song of the low

Ernest Jones, *Notes to the People* (1852), ii, p. 953.

We're low—we're low—we're very very low
As low as low can be;
The rich are high—for we make them so—
And a miserable lot are we!
And a miserable lot are we! are we!
A miserable lot are we!

We plough and sow—we're so very very low,
That we delve in the dirty clay,
Till we bless the plain with the golden grain
And the vale with fragrant hay.
Our place we know—we're so very low,
'Tis down at the landlords' feet;
We're not too low—the bread to grow,
But too low the bread to eat.
We're low, we're low, etc.

Down, down we go—we're so very very low
To the hell of the deep sunk mines.
But we gather the proudest gems that glow,
When the crown of a despot shines;
And whenever he lacks—upon our backs
Fresh loads he deigns to lay.
We're far too low to vote the tax,
But not too low to pay.
We're low, we're low, etc.

We're low, we're low—mere rabble, we know,
But at our plastic power,
The mould at the lordling's feet will grow
Into palace and church and tower—

Then prostrate fall—in the rich man's hall,
And cringe at the rich man's door,
We're not too low to build the wall,
But too low to tread the floor.
  We're low, we're low, etc.

We're low, we're low—we're very very low
Yet from our fingers glide
The silken flow—and the robes that glow
Round the limbs of the sons of pride.
And what we get—and what we give,
We know—and we know our share.
We're not too low the cloth to weave—
But too low the cloth to wear.
  We're low, we're low, etc.

We're low, we're low—we're very very low
And yet when the trumpets ring,
The thrust of a poor man's arm will go
Through the heart of the proudest king!
We're low, we're low—our place we know,
We're only the rank and file,
We're not too low—to kill the foe,
But too low to touch the spoil.
We're low, we're low, etc.

7 Capitalism—the analysis of under-consumption

Wages were low because there were more men than jobs. This situation was made worse by two trends, the growth of sweating and the introduction of machinery. If they continued, working men argued, labourers would no longer be able to buy the goods produced, and capitalism itself would be destroyed. Only control of hours and wages would break the spiral of sweating, produce enough employment and turn producers into consumers, with consequent prosperity for all.

The most depressed of all trades was weaving which, even before the advent of the power loom, was being destroyed by unlimited cheap labour (7a). The artisan trades, shoemaking, carpentering and tailoring could no longer control entry to the trade after the repeal of the apprenticeship laws in 1813–15, and so they too were increasingly swamped by 'dishonourable' men who worked by the piece in sweat shops for long hours and low pay. Henry Mayhew in his survey of the London poor in 1849 showed how over-work made under-pay and under-pay made over-work (7b). Wages spiralled down.

Machinery, now being introduced into the textile and printing trades, increased unemployment, because it displaced adult labour, produced more and cheaper goods, and thus cheapened still further the price of labour. The *Advocate* (7c), speaking for the printers, would limit machinery while men were unemployed. The middle-class economists, Charles Knight of the Society for the Diffusion of Useful Knowledge (SDUK), W. Cooke Taylor of the Anti-Corn Law League, and Andrew Ure for the manufacturers, replied (7d) that machinery made more jobs and higher wages, and so bound masters and men together in common interest. William Longson, for the weavers, pointed out that the benefit of cheap goods was received by the foreigner (7e) at the expense of working men, O'Brien that increased employment would be for the machine and not for men (7f). He challenged Lord Brougham's *Companion to the Newspaper* which argued that working men were producers rather than consumers (7g); and he was supported by William Carpenter (1797–1874), his fellow radical journalist, who predicted that if men lacked the wages to buy goods, the country would collapse into general depression (7h). With this in mind, Richard Oastler, speaking for the Short Time movement (see p. 192), told the Committee on the handloom weavers that to regulate wages and hours was to control the supply of labour, increase its price, and release the extra purchasing power which alone could buy the country out of its slumps (7i). O'Connor picked up a theme of William Thompson (7j): working men should value themselves as consumers and not merely as producers. But at the trial of Ernest Jones in 1848 Chief Justice Wilde could still ask, in the language of Hannah More fifty years earlier, what would the poor do without the rich?

Suggestions for further reading

For Henry Mayhew, E. P. Thompson and E. Yeo, *The Unknown Mayhew* (1971).

7a The freedom of the weaver

The committee of the Macclesfield silk weavers, *Trades Newspaper*, 9 July 1826.

Amongst all distressed objects . . . the weaver appears the most prominent. His loom is the emblem of his poverty . . . for in proportion as he exerts himself, in the same proportion is the price of labour reduced, until unable to live by his labour . . . he is compelled to apply to that miserable and degrading substitute, the parochial fund . . . What will benefit the weaver, and restore him to that rank in society, to which, as an industrious artisan, he is entitled? We answer, a minimum price for their labour, fixed by the joint approbation of the majority of the masters and men, and made valid by legislative enactment, so as to prevent the avaricious master from preying on the very vitals of the poor . . . Will the Legislature interfere? No. Because they consider it infringing on the principle of free labour . . . Though they can legislate for the protection of rabbits and hares, yet they consider it unjust to legislate to protect the labourer's wages—his only property . . .

7b The economy of sweating

Reported to the National Association of United Trades, *Northern Star*, 21 March 1846.

Mr. Worsey of Manchester tailors.

For the past 16 or 17 years I have been connected with the respectable portion of the trade. When I first pointed out the ruin that was about to overtake us, I was told that I was a marked man; this I have been and have suffered accordingly. Prior to last August I was paid at the rate of 27*s*. per week for 13 hours labour daily, including dinner hour; now, however, owing to the spirit of unjust competition, and the blight which the system of 'sweating' has thrown over the trade, I can only earn 14*s*. 6*d*. a week, never working less than 15 hours per day for that miserable pittance.

Overwork and underpay

H. Mayhew, *London Labour and the London Poor* (1861–2 edn), pp. 301–4.

The labour of the men who depend entirely on the slaughter-houses for the purchase of their articles is usually seven days a week the year through. That is seven days—for Sunday work is all but universal—each of 13 hours, or 91 hours in all; while the established hours of labour in the 'honourable trade' are six days of the week, each of 10 hours, or 60 hours in all . . . This system, of over-work exists in the 'slop' part of almost every business—indeed, it is the principal means by which the cheap trade is maintained . . . From people being obliged to work twice the hours they once *did* work, or that in reason they *ought* to work, a glut of hands is the consequence, and the masters are led to make reductions in the wages . . .

Not only is it true that over-work makes under-pay, but the converse of the proposition is equally true, that under-pay makes over-work . . . for the workman in such cases seldom or never thinks of reducing his expenditure to his income, but rather of increasing his labour, so as still to bring his income, by extra production, up to his expenditure. Hence we find that, as the wages of a trade descend, so do the labourers extend their hours of work to the utmost possible limits—they not only toil earlier and later than before, but the Sunday becomes a work-day like the rest . . . and when the hours of work are carried to the extreme of human industry, then more is sought to be done in a given space of time, either by the employment of the members of their own family, or apprentices, upon the inferior portion of the work, or else by 'scamping it'.

7c The Moloch of machinery

Advocate, 16 February 1833.

It is a monster that devours the bread of thousands. It is an insatiable Moloch. It is callous to all feeling; it is insensible at the sight of the emaciated form, the hollow cheek, and the sunken eye; it turns like the deaf adder from the appeal of misery; it can behold unmoved the poor man's table without a meal, and his hearth uncheered by a feeble blaze . . . The labour of the working man is his only inheritance; if you take from him that, you deprive him of all. Yet this the growth of machinery has done, or what is nearly the same thing, it has rendered his labour valueless, for he is denied adequate employment for its exercise . . . Machinery has made labour too cheap, because it has made it too plentiful; there is not a sufficient demand for it.

7d A defence of machinery

Charles Knight, *The Results of Machinery* (1831), p. 179; pp. 186–7.

There are great temporary inconveniences in the introduction of a new machine . . .

[However] there is no such thing . . . as a limit to the wants of consumers . . . the cheaper an article of necessity becomes, the more of it is used; that when the most pressing wants are supplied, and supplied amply by cheapness, the consumer has money to lay out on new wants: that when these new wants are supplied cheaply, he goes on again and again to other new wants; that there are no limits, in fact, to his wants as long as he has capital to satisfy them. . . . The working man stands in a double character; he is both a producer and a consumer. But we will be bold to say that the question of cheapness of production is a much more important question to be decided in his favour as a consumer than the question of dearness of production is to be decided in his favour as a producer . . . When the price of every article that he uses should be doubled, trebled, and in nine cases out of ten, put beyond the possibility of attainment:—what we ask would be the use to him of his advance in wages? Let us never forget that it is not for the employment of labourers, but for the benefit of consumers, that labour is employed at all.

Machinery and the bond of interest

W. Cooke Taylor, *Notes of a Tour in the Manufacturing Districts* (1842), pp. 117–20 of the 1968 edn.

It is a common error to suppose that very large capitals invest the possessors with a disproportionate power over the rights of labour . . .

[On the contrary] from this condition of factory investment there results a great degree of certainty for the employment of the operative. A landlord may clear his estate with profit, but a factory capitalist cannot discharge his operatives without ruin. He must often work his mills at a positive loss, or he will not only lose the interest on the capital he has invested, but also deteriorate the capital itself, as rust destroys his machinery, and the moth consumes his materials . . .

Another result from the large amount of capital invested in factories is the creation of a perceived identity of interest between the employer and the employed . . . the proprietor feels every instant his dependence upon those whom he employs, and his workmen can never hide from themselves that the mill and the machinery must have been provided for them, or else they could not have found a market for their industry.

Machinery and high wages

A. Ure, *Philosophy of Manufactures* (1835), p. 329.

The main reason they [industrial wages] are so high is, that they form a small part of the value of the manufactured article, so that if reduced too low by a sordid master, they would render his operatives less careful, and thereby injure the quality of their work more than could be compensated by his saving in wages. The less proportion wages bear to the value of the goods, the higher, generally speaking, is the recompense of labour.

7e Foreign trade and foreign benefits

William Longson, *Trades Newspaper*, 30 October 1825.

By starving the industrious workmen, we can boast of underselling all foreign manufacturers; but of what advantage has this been to Britain, when foreigners impose heavy duties on those articles which we offer to them at lower prices than their own manufacturers? What has been thus wrung from the distressed families of Englishmen, is now paid away to foreigners in the shape of duties!!! . . . Every other class must suffer, by thus depriving the working classes of the means of consumption—diminishing the home consumption to the amount of 100 millions annually, must diminish the prosperity of every trade and occupation whose produce or manufactures are consumed by the working classes . . .

7f Machinery and consumption

Bronterre O'Brien, *Poor Man's Guardian*, 5 September 1835.

As machinery extends it necessarily displaces manual labour, and unless the parties so displaced can find other employment as profitable as *that* they left, the change is to *them* one of evil. The capitalists, we know, will say that machinery cures the evil it creates; he will tell us that by making goods cheaper, it extends consumption, and that increased consumption causes increased employment. So it does, we reply, but it is increased employment for *the machine* not for *the workman* . . . It has not merely cheapened goods for the public, which it has thereby benefited, but it has also cheapened the workman's labour, to his very great injury . . . Machinery has been made an instrument for widening the distance between rich and poor . . .

7g Under-consumption or over-production?

Companion to the Newspaper, December 1833.

Let one very simple and incontrovertible truth be kept in view, and the whole matter is clear. *No operations of the unions can increase consumption.* In other words, they cannot give more employment to the body of workmen than they had before. On the contrary, if they raise the nominal rate of wages, they will infallibly diminish consumption. They will reduce the quantity of employment. They can never therefore remedy a state of things in which the distress of the workmen is occasioned by the want of sufficient employment for their whole number.

Poor Man's Guardian, 28 December 1833.

This absurd paragraph is based on the supposition that some men are born only to *slave*, and the rest only to *consume*, and that the existence of the *many* ought to depend upon the mere appetites, or consuming powers, of the *few*. The proper answer is that the Trades' Unions will admit no such supposition. They are resolved that *consumption* and *production* shall henceforth be united in the same persons . . . Any operation that will give the workmen increased wages, will give them increased means of consuming; and this is all the consumption they trouble themselves about, for as to *that* of their oppressors, they would rather *diminish* than *increase* it . . . But what a strange doctrine that traces our distress, not to our inability to produce enough for all, but to the difficulties of finding bellies and backs to consume it . . . from having too much, not too little! . . . If all that is wanted be merely to increase consumption, what better remedy for the evil than *that* of putting all the people in a condition to consume? If the millions are distressed simply because the thousands cannot consume enough, will it not meet all the difficulties of the case to make the millions consumers too?

Companion to the Newspaper, December 1833.

The amount at which wages naturally settle down, is always that at which the greatest possible quantity of employment is given to the general body of the workmen. Any thing the effect of which is permanently to disturb this level . . . cannot benefit, but must injure the interests of the general body of workmen . . . Either these persons will have less constant employment than they otherwise would have, or the number will be greater than it otherwise would be of those who have no employment at all.

If the wages of all classes of workmen were to be thus raised above their natural level . . . everything would be only so much the dearer. The higher wages of the mason would raise the rent of houses; those of the cabinet-maker would raise the price of furniture; those of the journeyman baker would raise the price of bread; those of the cotton-spinner, wool-comber, and the other descriptions of artisans employed in the fabrication of clothing would render that in a corresponding degree more expensive; and so with every other article. The rise of wages would be merely nominal.

Poor Man's Guardian, 28 December 1833.

The fallacy of this passage . . . consists in the *implied* assumption that the producers consume *all they produce*. Were this the case, the rise of wages would indeed be 'merely nominal' . . . But Brougham forgets that the great consumers of wealth are parties who produce nothing at all. It is against *these* that high prices operate . . . It ought always to be borne in mind that so long as the present system lasts, the working classes will have a paramount interest in high prices. And this for the reason once stated by Mr. Attwood, 'because the working classes are sellers of all things, while they are *purchasers* of only a part'. The non-producers consume perhaps four-fifths of the wealth of the country; the producers hardly a fifth. Let the latter only succeed in doubling the prices of all commodities, and (supposing production to continue the same) the consequence will be THE TRANSFERENCE OF TWO-FIFTHS OF THE WEALTH OF THE COUNTRY FROM DRONES AND VAGABONDS TO THE USE OF THE CLASSES WHO PRODUCE IT, AND WHO OUGHT THEREFORE TO ENJOY IT. Do you understand *that*, Brougham? Do you *now* think the Trades' Unions insane for seeking a revolution of comforts through a revolution of prices? . . .

7h Machinery and mass misery

William Carpenter, *Political Letters*, 4 February 1831.

The whole of the community may be divided into these two classes; . . . the capitalists . . . and the labourers . . . The one, the capitalist, being familiar only with the amazing productive power of machinery, in the various branches of manufacture, contends that its results must be necessarily beneficial to society, by multiplying and increasing the several articles of food, clothing, and so forth; and that therefore it ought to be protected: while the other, the labourer, being familiar only with the amazing power of machinery, in superseding his labour, which is *the only commodity* he has to offer in exchange for the necessary articles of subsistence, contends that machinery necessarily produces poverty, and ought therefore to be suppressed or destroyed.

On which side lies the truth in these conflicting opinions? Is it with the capitalists and political economists? Or is it with the practical and impoverished labourer?

That the natural, which is the theoretical tendency of mechanical inventions, and the application of mechanical power to the production of useful articles, is to increase the number of human enjoyments while the quantum of human labour is diminished, is an obvious and indisputable truth. But there are two things never to be lost sight of, in order to render the practical results of machinery accordant with its natural tendencies. The first is, that it should not be permitted to come into *competition* with human labour, so long as human labour furnishes to any portion of society the only means of subsistence; the second is, that society should be placed in a condition to purchase and consume the articles fabricated by the aid of machinery; and that, too, at such a price as will leave to the producers an excess over the actual cost of production. If these precautions be lost sight of, or are disregarded, the whole value of machinery is destroyed, and a frightful mass of human misery, instead of an incalculable amount of human happiness, is produced, as the inevitable result. And in this result—though not so immediately, yet not the less certainly—must the capitalists, or the possessors of machinery, be involved, equally, with every other class of society.

While the present mode of employing machinery and appropriating its productions are retained, every individual whose labour is displaced by its application, and who is therefore deprived of the means of supporting himself and his family by his own exertions—or in other words, of providing for his own wants and necessities—not only ceases to be a consumer of the products of machinery, and thereby contracts the market, or diminishes the demand for such productions; —but the burden of supporting him and his family, or of, at least, supplying them with a sufficient quantity of food and clothing to preserve their existence, must inevitably fall upon those who possess and employ the power by which the condition of these men and their families has been changed. Thus, the immense numbers of labourers, who, in consequence of the introduction into manufactures of scientific power have had their wages reduced one-half or two-thirds, . . . go entirely without various articles of clothing and furniture which they formerly possessed, or to use such descriptions of them as were formerly destroyed, as worn out and useless. Then, there is the immense number of paupers, the greater part of whom are persons deprived of the means of supporting themselves by their individual labour—not in consequence of sickness or old age, but in consequence of their labour having been superseded by mechanical power . . .

What a frightful prospect does this view of the subject throw up before us! The discoveries and improvements which are daily and hourly being made in mechanical invention, must ultimately supersede, almost entirely, the demand for mere manual labour; but manual labour being that by which, alone, nine-tenths of the whole population are furnished with the means of subsistence for themselves and families, such a supersedure of their labour must reduce them to the condition of paupers, and throw the burden of supporting them in idleness upon the other tenth, who alone possess the powers of production. But the powers of production are only valuable in proportion to the demand for the articles of production; and as this is regulated by the means and not by the wants of the individuals composing society, the destitution of the nine-tenths must inevitably diminish the demand to such an extent, as to render it impossible for the tenth, who possess the means of production, to furnish the whole with the necessary articles of subsistence. They must themselves become involved in the ruin which their folly and cupidity have produced, and then lament that one of heaven's best gifts—the faculty of invention—has been so perverted and misapplied as to have become a curse and a scourge to mankind.

7i The demand for a regulated wage

Evidence of Richard Oastler to the *Select Committee on the Handloom Weavers' Petition* (1834), qus 3776–807.

You would put an end to the freedom of labour?—I would put an end to the freedom of murder, and to the freedom of employing labourers beyond their strength; I would put an end to anything which prevents the poor man getting a good living with fair and reasonable work; and I would put an end to this because it is destructive of human life . . .

Suppose you were to raise the price very considerably, and in consequence of that you could not export your goods?—We can use them at home.

You would not use so much, would you?—Three times as much, and a great deal more than that, because the labourers would be better paid, and they would consume them. The capitalists do not use the goods, and there is the great mistake . . . If the wages were higher, the labourer would be enabled to clothe himself, because his wages would be better and to feed himself, because his wages would be better; and those labourers are the persons who are after all the great consumers of agricultural and manufacturing produce, and not the capitalist, because a great capitalist, however wealthy he is, wears only one coat at once, at least, he does certainly seldom wear two coats at once; but 1,000 labourers, being enabled to buy a thousand coats, where they cannot now get one, would most certainly increase the trade . . . The English merchants send their goods to different foreign ports, and there they compete with each other, and absolutely cut one another's throats, always giving the foreigner more cloth etc. for less money.

Is not all your reasoning founded upon the supposition that if the wages to the labourer are raised very considerably, a greater quantity of employment would remain to the weaver?—A great deal more would go to the weaver; we should consume a great many more goods, because the wages would be increased, and it is the wages that form the customers to the shopkeepers and so on . . .

What is the effect of the reduction of wages upon the supply of goods?—It increases the quantity, because the manufacturer generally acts upon the foolish plan of reducing wages, and then the weaver has to make more goods in order to provide for himself and his family, and thus the quantity increases. The wisest plan, in case of a great quantity of goods being on hand, is to reduce the quantity of making (i.e. to shorten the hours of labour) and to keep wages up . . . I do not think that the Government can claim on any ground the allegiance of the operatives, when they see that capital and property are protected, and their labour is left to chance.

7j Producers and consumers

F. O'Connor at a London meeting: *Northern Star*, 9 October 1841.

There is one character you working men seem proud of giving yourselves—that of being producers of wealth. At all your meetings you reiterate this. Now, I seek to make you consumers of wealth. Production is one thing, but consumption is another. I am satisfied that machinery should be the producer so long as you can become the consumer. Machinery requires no consumption, save a few tons of linseed oil, or a few hogsheads of grease. But you require beef, bread, solid nutriment . . .

The summing up of C. J. Wilde, at the trial of Ernest Jones for sedition and unlawful assembly, 10 July 1848; *State Trials* (new series), vi, col. 814.

'There shall be no peace in the country . . . until the poor man has his rights, and until the rich man has brought his nose to the grindstone.'

That is undoubtedly an extraordinary passage. The learned counsel has pointed out a degree of insensibility on the part of the rich, which I hope and believe has no existence in this country at all; and he talked about the indulgences of the rich and the feasting of others, and so on. Why how in the world could the rich better use their wealth, than in expending it in those articles of manufacture which employ the poor? Would the poor be more benefited if the rich did not keep carriages, which leads to the consumption of iron and wood, and glass and cloth, and silk and leather . . . What is to become of the coachmakers? The rich man can eat no more than the poor man, and seldom has so good an appetitite; he can wear but one suit of clothes at a time. How much of what a rich man spends is consumed upon himself? Not one thousandth part. What the rich man spends is so much dispersed among the poor; and those who grumble at the equipages of the rich, and of the expenditure of their houses and establishments, grumble at their expending their money in the only way in which the poor can benefit.

8 Politics and economics

The attack on Old Corruption had led Cobbett to demand a political remedy—a radical reform of parliament to cut taxation and to ease the burdens on working men. But the attack on capitalism had seemed to suggest industrial remedies, co-operation, as outlined by Robert Owen, trades unionism as organized by John Doherty (see p. 166). The growth of the parliamentary reform movement from the late autumn of 1830 again encouraged political action. Parliament, said Bronterre O'Brien, was controlled by the privileged and the propertied who made laws to perpetuate their privilege and their property (8a). Profits, rents and taxes robbed the poor to benefit the rich. Day-to-day poverty, therefore, was due to the workings of capitalism; but that this exploitation could continue was because working men were denied the vote. Only if working men were enfranchised could they reshape the industrial system and retain the produce of their labour. Without the vote, their co-operative or union activity could be smashed whenever government chose. The Reform Act of 1832, on this account, worsened the position of working men, for it added the new industrial and commercial middle class to their old enemy, the aristocracy (8b). William Carpenter thought such cynicism unjustified (8c): those who were newly enfranchised would be the allies and not the enemies of working men.

8a Property

Bronterre O'Brien, *Poor Man's Guardian*, 26 July 1834.

About one-seventh of the population possess votes. The other six-sevenths are outcasts from the laws. The former, or privileged fraction, comprises all the 'property' people. The latter, all the *work* people, or those who live by labour. Now, since all the wealth is the produce of industry, and as the privileged fraction produce nothing themselves, it is plain that they must live on the labours of the rest. But how is this to be done, since everybody thinks it enough to work for himself? It is done partly by *fraud* and partly by *force*. The 'property' people having all the law-making to themselves, make and maintain fraudulent institutions, by which they contrive (under false pretences) to transfer the wealth of the producers to themselves. All our institutions relating to *land* and *money* are of this kind . . .

Bronterre O'Brien, *Operative*, 25 November 1838.

We must have laws and institutions which shall not only throw the burdens of society on the 'property' of the country, but which shall also give the productive classes a concurrent power with the other classes, over the *land* and *currency* of the kingdom. The land being the great fountain of wealth, and the currency being the measure of value, whatever parties are in possession of these have an absolute power of life and death over the rest of the community. At present our upper and middle classes hold *exclusive* dominion over the land and currency . . . Armed with this two-fold monopoly, their power is perfectly irresistible. The landlord divides the bulk of our agricultural produce between himself, the farmer and the parson. The money-monger divides the bulk of our manufactured produce between himself and the merchant. The parties then exchange their respective surpluses with each other, but as to the unfortunate labourer and artisan, they never receive more from either party than what will barely keep them alive from day to day . . .

8b A last warning on the accursed Reform Bill

One of the Oppressed, *Poor Man's Guardian*, 14 April 1832.

Fellow countrymen, Manchester 19 March 1832

I have given you my opinion in several letters, at various times, on the present measure of *Reform* . . . That measure, if carried into effect, will do you an incalculable deal of harm. I have told you that the evils under which you labour are not produced by taxation . . . the abolition of the whole government would relieve you to the amount of only one half-penny a day. I have told you that the *remote* cause of your poverty is your not having seats, *personally*, in that which ought to be your house; and that you are thereby prevented from assisting, like the land-stealers, the merchants, the manufacturers, and the tradesmen, in your own persons, to make the laws by which you are governed; and I told you that the *immediate* cause of your poverty is the exorbitant *rents, tithes, interest on money, profits on labour, and profits on trade*, which are imposed on you by laws made by the land-stealers, merchants, manufacturers, and tradesmen in that house from which you are excluded, and by which exclusion you are prevented from making laws to regulate your wages. I have told you that the government taxes are only a natural consequence arising out of the rents, interest, and other profits which are imposed on you—that those taxes are, in short, only a sum of money given to the government to beat and torture you into a submission to those rents, tithes, interest, and profits, by which you are robbed to more than twenty-times the amount of those taxes . . .

As soon as the land-stealers, merchants, manufacturers, and tradesmen acquire the privilege of law-making, they begin to legislate for their own individual interest; that is, to increase their rents and profits, by which they deprive you of the produce of your industry; and in proportion as their influence in law-making is increased, so are those rents and profits increased, and so likewise is your poverty increased accordingly . . . The influence of these men who live by these impositions is to be increased in making the laws, by this Bill more than ten-fold!! Will you believe now that you have any interest in the passing of this Bill, or that your interest does not consist in its being kicked out, as it was before? . . . I therefore conjure you to prepare your coffins if you have the means. You will be starved to death by thousands, if this Bill pass, and thrown on to the dung hill, or on to the ground, naked, like dogs . . .

Of all the Bills, or *plots* (for it is nothing else) that ever was proposed on earth, this is the most deceptive and the most mischievous. This Bill proposes to extend the number of electors to about five times the present amount. This on the face of the measure appears, at first sight, a most liberal alteration. What! extend the number of voters from one hundred and fifty thousand, to six or seven hundred thousand? *Most liberal indeed!!!* But now, when we come to see that the liberality is all on one side, and none on the other—when we come to see that those whose influence is already tenfold too great, are to have that influence tenfold increased, while you whose influence is already tenfold too little, are to have that influence (through the great increase of the other) incalculably diminished, it is the most *illiberal*, the most *tyrannical*, the most *abominable*, the most *infamous*, the most *hellish* measure that ever could, or can be proposed. Your number is four-fifths of the whole population. Your influence, therefore, at elections (in addition to your right of being elected yourselves) ought to be four times as great as all the rest of the community. Yet your influence will not be more than *one twentieth part* of that which will be exercised by those who live on the fruits of your labour. You will in reality therefore, from fear and fewness of number, have no influence at all.

This Bill proposes to disenfranchise a number of rotten boroughs, and to transfer the elective franchise to large populous towns. This is another of the *supposed liberal features* of the Bill . . . These individuals in these large towns want to get as large profits on their manufactures as the others do on corn, and thereby impoverish you three times as much as you are. Their profits, already, are three times as great, aye, *ten times* as great, in those towns as they ought to be. These profits are the main cause of your poverty in those towns now. So much for the *liberality* of disenfranchising small towns to enfranchise large ones! . . .

When I hear master manufacturers and tradesmen say—*We must get large profits to enable us to pay you high wages*, my blood curdles within me, and I wish at once that I were a dog, or anything else, rather than a man. *Those large profits are the sole cause why wages are low*. They are got by keeping wages down . . . Go and ask the land-stealers, and the agricultural labourers, whether their interests are alike. Ask old Peel and his workmen whether their interests are alike. When I hear a set of masters telling such a story, I can find an excuse for them, but when I hear a working man endeavouring to consolidate his own poverty by the same language, I wish I were any other animal rather than what I am . . . This word *capital* is a capital word for a man to get hold of, who does not know what capital in reality is, nor how it is obtained. His large capital is obtained (like all other large capitals) solely by employing a number of men, women, and children, and instead of paying them in wages little short of what they earn, or what he obtains for the produce of their industry, he sends them home with empty pockets, and keeps the money himself. Thus does he obtain his *large capital*—live in a capital state of luxury—pay capital wages to a set of *worthless household servants*, who live in luxury, like himself, on the fruits of other people's industry, and thereby keep his *useful workmen, women and children in a capital state of poverty and distress*. But I suppose the delusion must go on for six or seven hundred years more, although this fact, like the sun, stares us in the face that in exact proportion as these large capitals are obtained, so is the poverty of the working people most *capitally increased* . . .

[Four estates, land-stealers together with capitalists, the priesthood, the government, and the stamped press exploit working men.] They rob you by means of rents, tithes, interest, taxes and various other impositions, of more than two-thirds of all your productions. But being unable to devour and otherwise consume that produce, as fast as you can create it, they then tell you that *there is no trade*; and that you must starve and wait for employment *till trade revives*; that is, till they have devoured and consumed the contents of the warehouses. When the warehouses are partially emptied, you are then told that trade is *a little revived*, and you are set to work again for a time. But, as one-third of you, if fully employed, is sufficient to keep pace with the jaws and other consumptive powers of these four estates, they then tell you that *you are too numerous*—that you *must emigrate*—that you must leave the land of your birth; or otherwise, if you do not, you can only be employed *occasionally*, as you can scramble up a day's work, at *one-third of the wages which you ought to receive* . . . and so you continue, first working, then standing idle and starving, till these four estates have consumed what you last made, and so on, year after year . . .

Instead of this state of things you ought to receive as much wages as will enable you to purchase and consume the produce of your own labour yourselves, by which means your consumption would keep pace with your industry, and your industry with your consumption; you would never be too numerous, the warehouses would never be filled to excess, and you would never be idle, except when your ingenuity and consumption [*sic*] might happen to surpass your own consumption. It is a fact that ought to be inscribed in letters on the face of the sun, that it is as *practicable* to make the price of everything consist *almost entirely of wages as of profits*—that profits ought only to be as much as will enable every profit-man to live as well as yourselves, and no better—that *fortunes are all an excess of profits*, which are obtained by a reduction of, or by keeping down your wages—that if rents, tithes, interest, profits on labour and trade, and taxes were reduced to what they ought to be, every useful man of you in the kingdom might receive, at the present time, nearly three times as much wages as you do receive, without any one thing being one farthing dearer than it is now. These are facts. Do you not see then that all you want is *high wages and low profits*? You must see it. But then you will say, how are we to get these rents, tithes, interest and other profits down? Why I will tell you plainly—*you must get your own wages up, and then they must fall*, for the price of things in this country must assimilate in price to the price of things in other countries, and other countries to this; and therefore, when wages rise, every species of impost or profit must fall. They cannot be both high nor both low. Whenever those profits are high, your wages must be low; and when your wages in this, as in any other country, are high, those rents, tithes, interest and other profits must be relatively low . . .

8c The Reform Bill

William Carpenter, *Address on the Reform Bill* (1831).

If I have succeeded in convincing you, that although this plan of reform is not such a one as we should frame ourselves, nor such an one as would be framed by a statesman who took a just or statesman-like view of the subject, it is nevertheless a great improvement upon the present system; that although it leaves many evils unredressed—many rights in abeyance—many imperfections unamended, it nevertheless suppresses many abuses—gives a great accession to popular influence in the House of Commons—and, above all, recognizes the principle, that the institutions of society should be modified or altered in accordance with *public opinion* . . . then I am entitled to urge upon you . . . your duty to give it your support.

But then, it has been said, the enfranchisement of the MIDDLE CLASSES for whom the bill is intended, will greatly injure your interests, and indefinitely postpone the time of YOUR enfranchisement.

. . . Those who thus address you, insist that the middle classes, or 'middle-men' . . . have an interest *separate* and adverse from yours; and it is greatly to be regretted, that the language they employ, whenever speaking of this class, is such as is calculated to alienate from each other the *two* classes of society—if two classes they *will* have them to be . . . I most confidently state, that the middle classes of 1831 . . . are not only *not* a class of persons having interests different from your own; but that they *are not a different class* from your own. They are the *same* class; they are, generally speaking, *working* or *labouring* men—and working, too, in such a sphere as to be almost wholly overwhelmed by anxieties and difficulties, of precisely the same description, and arising from the same causes, as your own. It is quite true, that there are a few large manufacturers, and commercial men, and monopolists, who have in some sense an interest separate from yours' . . . but then they are not the men who are to be enfranchised by the Bill; they are enfranchised pretty well already . . .

In whatever light we view the attempt to set the working classes against the Bill, it appears extremely foolish and mischievous . . . The Bill lays the foundation for securing the rights of all. It is like a wedge . . . I have felt it to be my duty to do what I can to prevent the calamities that must ensue upon the working and 'middle classes' being placed in hostility to each other. If not the same class, identically, your interests are alike. You are equally interested in getting cheap government, and a due reward for your skill and labour; but if the *enemies of reform*, the men who *hate* you both . . . can but succeed in separating you, in arraying you against each other, in prevailing upon you to pull in opposite directions, they gain their point, and both of you become sacrificed to your own folly.

9 The language of class

Radicals and socialists alike operated a We–They analysis of society, pitting the idle against the industrious, the parasites against the producers, the useless against the useful. Radicals, such as Francis Place or Richard Cobden, saw this as a line between the Aristocracy and the People, and both middle and working men were among the People (9a). Socialists, however, drew the line between a middle and upper class who possessed the power to exploit and a working class that was exploited. Political allies on the first theory were class enemies on the second. But O'Brien emphasized (9b) that exploitation existed only because working men were denied the vote; if middle-class men favoured universal suffrage, then class co-operation was possible. G. J. Holyoake, a socialist and a secularist (1817–1906), denied this (9c), for reasons presented by Ernest Jones (1819–69), one of the leaders of the later Chartist movement. Class conflict would exist while the interests of classes conflicted (9d). However when Jones spelled out the cast of his exploiting class, it included sinecurists as well as capitalists, the old radical as well as the new socialist enemies. Marx's definition of class (9e) was much stricter, demanding common economic modes of existence as well as a common class-consciousness. The letter of Alexander Yates to the *Red Republican* (9f) offered three generations of radical language —Cobbett's Old Corruption, O'Brien's attack on profit-mongers, the appeal to a proletariat—layered on each other.

Suggestions for further reading

For Holyoake, his autobiographies, *Bygones Worth Remembering* (1905), *Sixty years of an agitator's Life* (1892); for E. Jones, J. Saville (ed.), *Ernest Jones* (1952).

9a The people

Place to Sir J. Hobhouse, 2 June 1832, quoted in G. Wallas, *Life of F. Place* (1951 edn), p. 192.

By the word 'people' when, as in this letter I use the word in a political sense, I mean those among them who take part in public affairs, by whom the rest *must* be governed.

Senex, *Pioneer*, 28 June 1834.

Those who call themselves the liberal statesmen of the present day, must go progressively with the people; but in the word PEOPLE (a word very much misunderstood) they must, brethren, include *us*, the productive labourers, for what are the people without us? And yet, brethren, while we work not for ourselves, but for the capitalists and profit-mongers, we can hardly rank with the PEOPLE. The people have a political position, but we have none that we can make any use of with benefit to ourselves . . .

9b Class and politics

H. Hetherington, *Poor Man's Guardian*, 3 December 1831.

At the point where the franchise is withheld injustice begins; when the demand for Universal Suffrage becomes general, and not till then, the whole country will be united;—then indeed the term *classes* will merge into some comprehensive appellation, and no bloodshed will ensue, for the claims of united millions will be irresistible.

Bronterre O'Brien, *Poor Man's Guardian*, 12 October 1833.

We have over and over again said in the *Guardian*, that no man is to be blamed for his particular trade or vocation, no matter how obnoxious it may be to the general interests of the community, providing he is willing to allow each and all of his fellow-subjects an equal voice with himself in determining how far such trade or vocation should prevail in society . . . We have blamed those of all classes who are opposed to political equality, and those of no class who are the friends of equal laws and equal rights for all the people. Point us out a merchant, or manufacturer, who is the friend of universal suffrage, and then see whether we will hold him up as the enemy of the working man. No! fellow-countrymen, our creed is this—the man who would place you on a political equality with himself is your friend. The man who would not,—is your enemy; and he is your enemy only because he wants to live on the fruits of your labour, without doing any useful work himself.

Bronterre O'Brien, *loc. cit.*, 19 October 1833.

. . . An entire change in society—a change amounting to a complete subversion of the existing 'order of the world'—is contemplated by the working classes. They aspire to be at the top instead of at the bottom of society—or rather that there should be no bottom or top at all!

9c The chimera of class conciliation

G. J. Holyoake to his father, 11 March 1842 (Holyoake Collection, Manchester).

I delivered a lecture last night at which Hetherington and other reformers were present and spoke—I took up the position that the now much-talked-of reconciliation between the middle and working classes was worse than a chimera a dangerous chimera—First I said we must do away with class distinctions—*middle men* and *working men* may unite, and cordially, but the *two classes* never can—Hetherington who came to oppose me could scarcely be said to do so, he found, and acknowledged also, so much of truth in what I advanced—I maintain that the most advanced democratical party must not serve or waver an iota any junction must take place from others to them not from them to others or they will be left in the lurch after they had gained the Reform bill for the middle classes.

9d The boundaries of class

Ernest Jones, *Notes to the People* (1851), i, pp. 312–14, 511.

That system which causes the large capitalist to destroy the lesser one—that system of competition, in the long run must make the large capitalists *destroy each other* . . . Not so with the small shopkeeper—he is suffering already. . . . he feels it in poor's rate and taxation on the one hand, and in the death of home trade upon the other.

Therefore working-man and shopkeeper may unite, and will unite, as soon as the latter ceases to be blind to his true interests. Therefore the capitalists of all kinds will be our foes as long as they exist, and carry on against us a war to the very knife. Therefore, they must BE PUT DOWN. Therefore, we MUST have class against class—that is, all the oppressed on the one side, and all the oppressors on the other. *An amalgamation of classes is impossible where an amalgamation of interests is impossible also.* Let all those whose interests are identical unite in the same phalanx—don't trouble your head about the rest—you may preach to them till doomsday . . . What, therefore, the leaders of democratic movements have to examine, is: how widely can we extend the basis of our operation?—which means in other words, how many classes will be benefited by our success? . . . All beyond that pale are our enemies by the law of nature—unconvertible, (excepting of course individual cases of generous and elevated feeling), and therefore not worth the wasting of a single thought or moment. Next, they must consider, are those, having an identity of interest on the side of democracy, the stronger, or the weaker portion of the people—are they the many or are they the few? (I don't allude here only to those who are enlightened as to their own interests, but to those whose interests are identical, whether they know it yet or not). If they are the *few*, give up agitation, for even a temporary victory could not result in a sustained triumph . . . But if they are the *many*—then go-ahead! The result is as certain as that of a mathematical problem. It is a mere calculation of powers—and, unless you make a mistake in *working out* the problem—that calculation can end in but one solution. If you make a mistake, you must begin it over again, that is all.

Now, in this country, the basis of operation is very wide—those having identical interests consists of working-men, small shopkeepers, small farmers, (many of the larger in both classes also), soldiers, and policemen. Those having interests opposed to these, are landlords, mine-owners, factory-lords, bankers, usurers, merchants, state church parsons, placemen, great pensioners, and sinecurists—all of which latter, with their families, form about six millions, as opposed to twenty-four millions. These two portions of the community must be separated, distinctly, dividedly and openly from each other. CLASS AGAINST CLASS—all other mode of proceeding is mere moonshine. Once achieve this—nay!—*once turn the balance*—and who can doubt the result.

It has been said by many that the actual proletarian class—the wage slaves and the destitute—form the minority in our country—that nobles, capitalists, professionals, middle class, small retail shopkeepers and aristocracy of labour, form a large majority . . . But all this is changing rapidly. The strength of the proletarian is growing, while that of the privileged is growing more circumscribed by the operations of the very system the latter are upholding: the aristocracy of labour is being driven fast down into the ranks of the wage slave—the small retail shop keeper and the small farmer are fast disappearing beneath the dull level of hired labour—while the class below this again is widening with fearful celerity . . . Now mark the contrast: the 'higher class' is one-twentieth of the population—the parish class (below the lowest hired labour) constitutes one-eighth! and take the bulk of the two orders—the rich and the poor, what do we find? Three to one, stands the reckoning.

9e The definition of class

Karl Marx, *The Eighteenth Brumaire* (1851).

The small holding peasants form a vast mass, the members of which live in similar conditions but without entering into manifold relations with one another. Their mode of production isolates them from one another instead of bringing them into mutual intercourse. The isolation is increased by France's bad means of communication and by the poverty of the peasants. Their field of production, the small holding, admits of no division of labour, in its cultivation, no application of science, and, therefore, no diversity of development, no variety of talent, no wealth of social relationships. Each individual peasant family is almost self-sufficient; it itself directly produces the major part of its consumption and thus acquires its means of life more through exchange with nature than in intercourse with society. A small holding, a peasant and his family; alongside them another small holding, another peasant and his family. A score of these make up a village, and a few score of villages make up a Department. In this way, the great mass of the French nation is formed by simple addition of homologous magnitudes, much as potatoes in a sack form a sack of potatoes. In so far as millions of families live under economic conditions of existence that separate their mode of life, their interests and their culture from those of the other classes, and put them in hostile opposition to the latter, they form a class. In so far as there is merely a local identification among these small holding peasants, and the identity of their interests begets no community, no national bond and no political organization among them, they do not form a class. They are consequently incapable of enforcing their class interests in their own name, whether through a parliament or through a convention. They cannot represent themselves, they must be represented . . .

9f Three generations of radical language

Letter of A. Yates of Coventry, in *Red Republican*, 7 September 1850.

The principles enumerated in the *Red Republican* are just what the mass of the people require to be made thoroughly acquainted with, and without which I verily believe that if this country were to be revolutionized tomorrow, in twelve months hence our position would be little, if anything, superior to that which the brave but too confiding Proletarians of France is at the present time. The Lords of the soil, the lords of the tall chimneys, the swindling usurers, profit mongers and priests, would combine and resort to any and every stratagem to cheat us out of the fruits of our victory . . . The people have so long been accustomed to part with four-fifths of their earnings to tax-eaters and profit-mongers, that now they appear to bear it with the same indifference that a Jerusalem pony bears his burden . . . [With Knowledge] the funeral dirge of kingcraft, priestcraft and lordcraft and all other devilish crafts . . . will speedily be sung.

Part Two

Class and conflict–action

1 Peace and Peterloo

The movement of parliamentary reform stretched back to Wilkes, Wyvill and Major Cartwright (1740–1842) in the 1770s and to the artisans of the London and provincial corresponding societies who studied Paine in the 1790s. But the French wars and the tightening of the government's grip on public and political order, sent the movement underground. Not until the founding of the Hampden clubs in 1812 (1a) with their claims for manhood suffrage rooted in the ancient laws of England, and Cartwright's missionary tours on their behalf, did a reform movement of working- and middle-class radicals come out into the open. Samuel Bamford, a Lancashire weaver, whose remarkable autobiography spans these years, became the secretary of one such club (1b), and Cobbett's *Political Register* (1c) became their intellectual diet. (For Cobbett's political radicalism, see p. 8.) But economic unrest grew and the Government, fed by spy reports of arming and drilling (1d), and alarmed by the Spa riots in London which seemed to substantiate them, suspended habeas corpus in 1817. Radical leaders scattered; Cobbett fled the country. Working-class radicalism again re-formed itself the following year into a network of provincial societies, the Political Protestants (1e), who systematically criticized Old Corruption in their class meetings. Working-class unrest culminated in a Manchester meeting of 1819 to hear Henry Hunt (1773–1835) which was charged by the local yeomanry: Peterloo (1f). It was a massacre that was neither to be forgiven nor forgotten.

Suggestions for further reading

E. P. Thompson, *The Making of the English Working Class* (1963); R. J. White, *Waterloo to Peterloo* (1957).

1a Hampden clubs

F. D. Cartwright, *Life and Correspondence of Major Cartwright* (1826), ii, pp. 24–6, 44–6.

Its first public meeting took place at the Thatched House Tavern, 20th April, 1812, Walter Fawkes, Esq. in the chair. It was then '*Resolved*—That a society be now instituted, which shall have for its object the securing to the people the free election of their Representatives in the Commons House of Parliament.

'That such society be called the Hampden Club.

'That by the laws and statutes of this realm the subject has settled in him a fundamental right of property, and that he is not compelled to contribute any tax, or other charge, not set by common consent in Parliament.

'That according to Sir Edward Coke, the members of the House of Commons ought to be general inquisitors of the realm for the maintenance and execution of the laws, and for the redress of divers mischiefs and grievances.

'That according to the first statute of Westminster, anno 3 Edw.1 A.D. 1275, because electors ought to be free, no great man (haut homme), or other by force of arms, nor by malice, shall disturb any from making free election.

'That according to the celebrated declaration of King William for restoring the laws and liberties of England, article 18th, "all elections of parliament men ought, to be free, to be made with an entire liberty, without any sort of force, or the requiring the electors to choose such persons as shall be named to them".

'That according to the constitutional position of the late Lord Camden, "Taxation and representation are inseparable".

'And that Parliament should be of a continuance agreeable to the English constitution.

'*Resolved*—That it appears to the members of this club, that the present corrupt practice of the government of this country, etc, differs most widely from the principles of its constitution. That this deviation from the fundamental laws of the land, and the want of identity which in this country ought to subsist between the representative and the represented, are in a great degree the cause of those evils under which the nation is suffering; and that, therefore, a reform of the representation in the Commons House of Parliament is alike necessary to the constitutional independence of the Crown, the liberties of the people, and the safety of the country.

'That the members of the Hampden Club pledge themselves to use every exertion in county meetings, and in all other meetings warranted by the constitution, in conjunction with their countrymen, to induce the House of Commons to take this important subject into their early and serious consideration, and to restore to the country her real constitution and ancient laws.

'That it is the determination of this Club to confine their resolutions and exertions strictly to the procuring a reform in the representation of the people.'

It was in vain that several of Major Cartwright's friends endeavoured to discourage him from attempting another political tour early in the year 1813 . . . he set forward on the 17th of January, and completed his journey on the 15th of February.

Speaking of his proposal that others should follow his example in this respect, 'I do not', he says, 'feel the force of Sir John's objection to travelling about; English gentlemen are perpetually travelling. In the thing itself, there is nothing extraordinary. Some go to see lakes and mountains. Were it not as allowable to travel for seeing the actual condition of a starving people? Some make journeys to examine the ruins of abbeys and castles, that they may publish drawings and dissertations. Would it not be as laudable to visit the ruins of the constitution, of national prosperity and happiness, that by the very act they may do much towards repairing that constitution, and recovering that prosperity and happiness?

. . . What is the simple case? In a limited tour I discover in the mass of the middle and working classes, a very general sense of wrong and misery, and a very general disposition to petition for a reform of that house, the corruption of which was generally supposed to be the cause; but diffident of that knowledge and of the best mode of applying for redress or the best form of a petition.' . . .

During a journey of only twenty-nine days, the 'travelling reformist' visited Lutterworth, Hinckley, Leicester, Loughborough, Chesterfield, Sheffield, Huddersfield, Wakefield, Leeds, Preston, Wigan, Liverpool,

Bolton, Manchester, Stroud, Bath, Shepton-Mallet, Bridgewater, Taunton, Wellington, Bristol, Calne, Marlborough, Newbury, Hungerford, Abingdon, and Reading.

1b The early reform movement

S. Bamford, *Passages in the Life of a Radical* (1841), chapter 2.

A series of disturbances commenced with the introduction of the Corn Bill in 1815, and continued with short intervals, until the close of the year 1816. In London and Westminster riots ensued, and were continued for several days, whilst the bill was discussed; at Bridgeport, there were riots on account of the high price of bread; at Biddeford there were similar disturbances to prevent the exportation of grain; at Bury, by the unemployed, to destroy machinery; at Ely, not suppressed without bloodshed; at Newcastle-on-Tyne, by colliers and others; at Glasgow, where blood was shed, on account of the soup kitchens; at Preston, by unemployed weavers; at Nottingham, by Luddites, who destroyed thirty frames; at Merthyr Tydvil on a reduction of wages; at Birmingham, by the unemployed; at Walsall by the distressed; and December 7th, 1816, at Dundee, where, owing to the high price of meal, upwards of one hundred shops were plundered. At this time the writings of William Cobbett suddenly became of great authority; they were read on nearly every cottage hearth in the manufacturing districts of South Lancashire; in those of Leicester, Derby and Nottingham; also in many of the Scottish manufacturing towns. Their influence was speedily visible; he directed his readers to the true cause of their sufferings—misgovernment; and to its proper corrective—parliamentary reform. Riots soon became scarce, and from that time they have never obtained their ancient vogue with the labourers of this country. . . . instead of riots and destruction of property, Hampden clubs were now established in many of our large towns, and the villages and districts around them. Cobbett's books were printed in a cheap form; the labourers read them, and thenceforward became deliberate and systematic in their proceedings. . .

One of these clubs was established in 1816, at the small town of

Middleton, near Manchester; and I . . . was chosen secretary. The club prospered; the number of members increased; the funds raised by contribution of a penny a week, became more than sufficient for all out-goings; and taking a bold step, we soon rented a chapel which had been given up by a society of Kilhamite Methodists. This place we threw open for the religious worship of all sects and parties, and there we held our meetings on the evenings of Monday and Saturday in each week . . .

On the first of January, 1817, a meeting of delegates from twenty-one petitioning bodies, was held in our chapel, when resolutions were passed declaratory of the right of every male to vote, who paid taxes; that males of eighteen should be eligible to vote; that parliaments should be elected annually; that no placeman or pensioner should sit in parliament; that every twenty thousand of inhabitants should send a member to the house of commons; and that talent, and virtue, were the only qualifications necessary. Such were the moderate views and wishes of the reformers in those days, as compared with the present: the ballot was not insisted upon as a part of reform. Concentrating our whole energy for the obtainment of annual parliaments and universal suffrage, we neither interfered with the house of Lords; nor the bench of bishops; nor the working of factories; nor the corn laws; nor the payment of members; nor tithes; nor church rates; nor a score of other matters, which in these days have been pressed forward with the effect of distracting the attention, and weakening the exertions of reformers . . .

It was not until we became infested by spies, incendiaries, and their dupes—distracting, misleading, and betraying, that physical force was mentioned amongst us. After that our moral power waned; and what we gained by the accession of demagogues, we lost by their criminal violence, and the estrangement of real friends.

1c The impact of Cobbett

W. Cobbett, *Political Register*, 2 August 1817.

The effects of No. 18 [2 November 1816] were prodigious. It occupied the conversation of all the acting men in the kingdom. The whole town was in *a buzz*. The labouring classes of people seemed as if they had never heard a word on politics before. The effect on their minds was like what might be expected to be produced on the eyes of one bred up in the dark, and brought out, all of a sudden, into broad daylight . . . In town and country, there were, in two months, more than *two hundred thousand* of this one Number printed and sold; and this, too, in spite of all the means which the Government, the Church, the Military and Naval Half-Pay, and all the innumerable swarms of Tax-Gatherers and Tax-Eaters, were able to do to check the circulation . . .

Early in December, Mr. Becket, the Under Secretary of State to Lord Sidmouth, said, in answer to a proposition for silencing me in some *very atrocious* manner, 'No: he must be *written down*'. Accordingly, up sprang little pamphlets at Norwich, at Romsey, at Oxford, and at many other places, while in London, there were several, one of which could not cost less than *two thousand guineas* in advertising and in large and expensive *placards*, which were pulled down, or effaced, the hour they were put up, and which were replaced the next hour as one wave succeeds another in the sea. At last, after all the other efforts of this kind, came 'ANTI-COBBETT' . . . written 'by a Society of *Gentlemen*', amongst whom, I was told, were CANNING, W. M. GIFFORD and SOUTHEY. . . Not content with advertisements in three hundred newspapers; not content with endless reams of placards; the managers of this concern actually sent out *two hundred thousand* circular letters, addressed to persons by name, urging them to circulate this work amongst all their tradesmen, farmers, work people, and to give it their strong recommendation; and this they were told was *absolutely necessary* to prevent a *bloody revolution*! . . .

1d Provocation and suppression, 1817

S. Bamford, *Passages in the Life of a Radical* (1841), pp. 37–8.

At dusk on the evening of Tuesday the 11th of March, the day after the blanket meeting, a man dressed much like a dyer was brought to my residence by Joseph Healey, who had found him enquiring for me in the lower part of the town. The stranger said he had something of a private and important nature to communicate . . . that he was deputed, by some persons at Manchester to propose that, in consequence of the treatment which the blanketeers had received at the meeting and afterwards, 'a Moscow of Manchester' should take place that very night. The man paused and looked at us severally. I intimated that I knew what he meant, and desired him to go on. He said it would entirely depend on the co-operation or otherwise of the country people; that other messengers had been sent to every reform society within twenty miles of the town; that if the answers were favourable to the project, the light of the conflagration was to be the signal for the country people to come in—and, in such case the Middleton people were requested to take their station on St. George's field. He said the plan had been arranged by a meeting held at Manchester; that the whole force would be divided into parties, one of which was to engage the attention of the military and draw them from their barracks; another was to take possession of the barracks and secure the arms and magazine; another was to plunder and then set fire to the house of individuals who were marked out; and a fourth was to storm the New Bailey and liberate the prisoners, particularly the blanketeers confined there. I said it was a serious thing to undertake, and that an answer could not be returned from Middleton until some friends had been consulted.

Suspension of habeas corpus

ibid., chapter 7.

Personal liberty not being now secure from one hour to another, many of the leading reformers were induced to quit their homes, and seek concealment where they could obtain it. Those who could muster a few pounds, or who had friends to give them a frugal welcome, or who had trades with which they could travel, disappeared like swallows at the close of summer, no one knew whither. The single men stayed away altogether; the married ones would occasionally steal back at night to their wan-cheeked families, perhaps to divide with them some trifle they had saved during their absence—perhaps to obtain a change of linen or other garment for future concealment—but most of all, as would naturally be the case, to console, and be consoled by their wives and little ones . . .

But with all precautions, it did sometimes happen, that in such moments of mournful joy the father would be seized, chained, and torn from his family before he had time to bless them or to receive their blessings and tears. Such scenes were of frequent occurrence, and have thrown a melancholy retrospection over those days. Private revenge or political differences were gratified by secret, and often false information handed to the police. The country was distracted by rumours of treasonable discoveries, and apprehensions of the traitors, whose fate was generally predicted to be death or perpetual imprisonment. Bagguley, Johnson, Drummond, and Benbow, were already in prison at London; and it was frequently intimated to me, through some very kind relations in law, that I and some of my acquaintances would soon be arrested . . . It seemed as if the sun of freedom were gone down, and a rayless expanse of oppression had finally closed over us. Cobbett, in terror of imprisonment, had fled to America; Sir Francis Burdett had enough to do in keeping his own arms free; Lord Cochrane was threatened, but quailed not; Hunt was still somewhat turbulent, but he was powerless—for he had lost the genius of his influence when he lost Cobbett, and was now almost like Samson shorn and blind. The worthy old Major remained at his post, brave as a lion—serene as an unconscious child; and also, in the rush and tumult of that time, almost as little noticed. Then, of our country reformers, John Knight had disappeared; Pilkinton was out of the way somewhere, Bradbury had not yet been heard of; Mitchell moved in a sphere of his own, the extent of which no man knew save himself; and Kay and Fitton were seldom visible beyond the circle of their own village;—whilst to complete our misfortunes, our chapel keeper, in the very tremor of fear, turned the key upon us and declared we should no longer meet in the place.

Our Society, thus houseless, became divided and dismayed; hundreds slunk home to their looms, nor dared to come out, save like owls at nightfall, when they could perhaps steal through bye-paths or behind hedges, or down some clough, to hear the news at the next cottage. Some might be seen chatting with and making themselves agreeable to our declared enemies; but these were few, and always of worthless character. Open meetings thus being suspended, secret ones ensued; they were originated at Manchester, and assembled under various pretexts. Sometimes they were termed 'benefit socieities'; sometimes 'botanical meetings'; 'meeting for the relief of the families of imprisoned reformers', or 'of those who had fled the country'; but their real purpose, divulged only to the initiated, was to carry into effect the night attack on Manchester, the attempt at which, had before failed for want of arrangement and co-operation.

1e The Political Protestants

Black Dwarf, 16 August 1818.

RULES AND RESOLUTIONS OF THE POLITICAL PROTESTANTS.

We, the Members of this Institution, wishing not to invade the rights of any man, or set of men, are at the same time determined not to consent to the invasion of our own rights. Therefore, we do most solemnly protest against the scandalous, wicked, and treasonable, influence, which the Borough Merchants have established in the People's House of Commons. Being firmly convinced, that if such corrupt and hateful influence had not existed; which has operated to the total subjugation of our rights in that House, and converted it into a perfect mockery of representation, our unfortunate country would not have been cursed with a twenty-five years war—with a thousand millions of debt—with seventy millions of annual taxes—

with ruined manufactories and commerce—with a standing army of one hundred and forty thousand men kept up in time of peace—with two millions of paupers, and twelve millions of annual Poor Rates—a Corn Bill, to prevent the people of England eating cheap bread; and thousands of British subjects perishing by hunger, and many thousands more escaping to America, to avoid such horrid misery!—A troop of Spies and Informers sent out to persuade a set of poor men who were but half fed, half clad, and consequently half mad, to commit acts of outrage, that they might have the advantage of hanging them!—With Gagging Bills—Dungeon Bills—Imprisonment without trial;—and lastly, an infamous Bill of Indemnity, to protect our seat-selling tyrants from being brought to justice for all their satanic deeds, these are the fruits of the Borough Mongering influence!

We, bitterly lamenting the condition of our plundered and insulted Country, have resolved to unite ourselves under the denomination of POLITICAL PROTESTANTS; for the purpose of sincerely protesting against the mockery of our indisputable right to a real Representation; and to use every means in our power, which are just and lawful, to rescue the House of Commons from the all-devouring influence of the Borough Merchants, and restore it to the people, agreeable to Magna Charta, and the spirit of the Constitution; and that nothing shall ever cause us to cease in our exertions, until we are fully and fairly represented in the People's House.

We sincerely believe, that political ignorance has been the cause of all our national misery and degradation, and that nothing but a firm and extensive Union of the people to promote and diffuse a correct knowledge of our immutable rights, can possibly protect our Country either from absolute despotism on the one hand or a dreadful Revolution and anarchy on the other. We shall, therefore, meet once a week, in small classes, not exceeding twenty in each Class, and subscribe One Penny each, for the purpose of purchasing such means of information as may be required; in which way we exhort all Friends to radical Reform throughout the Kingdom to associate.

The Leaders of each Class shall hold a Meeting once a Month, to report the progress of the Institution; and in order to do away all ground of accusation against our proceedings, we declare that we will not have any secret transactions whatever, and that our Meeting, our Books and Accounts, of every description, shall at all times be laid open for the inspection of the Magistrates or others, who may request the same.

Hull, July 20, 1818.

1f Peterloo

Evidence of J. B. Smith and of Rev. E. Stanley, in F. Bruton (ed.), *Three Accounts of Peterloo* (1921).

It seemed to be a gala day with the country people who were mostly dressed in their best and brought with them their wives, and I saw boys and girls taking their father's hand in the procession . . . At length Hunt made his appearance in an open barouche drawn by two horses, and a woman dressed in white sitting on the box. On their reaching the hustings which were prepared for the orator, he was received with enthusiastic applause; the waving of hats and flags; the blowing of trumpets; and the playing of music. Hunt stepped on to the hustings, and was again cheered by the vast assemblage. He began to address them . . . About this time there was an alarm among the women and children near the place where I stood, and I could also see a part of the crowd in motion towards the Deansgate side, but I thought it a false alarm, as many returned again and joined in the huzzas of the crowd. A second alarm arose, and I heard the sound of a horn, and immediately the Manchester Yeomanry appeared . . . I heard the order to form three deep, and then the order to march. The trumpeter led the way and galloped towards the hustings, followed by the yeomanry . . .

. . . Their sabres glistened in the air, and on they went, direct for the hustings . . . As the cavalry approached the dense mass of people, they used their utmost efforts to escape: but so closely were they pressed in opposite directions by the soldiers, the special constables, the position of the hustings, and their own immense numbers, that immediate escape was impossible. . . .

On their arrival at the hustings a scene of dreadful confusion ensued. The orators fell or were forced off the scaffold in quick succession; fortunately for them, the stage being rather elevated, they were in great degree beyond the reach of the many swords which gleamed around them. Hunt fell—or threw himself—among the constables, and was driven or dragged, as fast as possible, down the avenue which communicated with the magistrates' house; his associates were hurried after him in a similar manner. By this time so much dust had arisen that no accurate account can be given of what further took place at that particular spot. The square was now covered with the flying multitude; though still in parts the banners and caps of liberty were surrounded by groups. The Manchester Yeomanry had already taken possession of the hustings, when the Cheshire Yeomanry entered on my left in excellent order, and formed in the rear of the hustings . . .

The Fifteenth Dragoons appeared nearly at the same moment, and paused rather than halted on our left, parallel to the row of houses. They then pressed forward, crossing the avenue of constables, which opened to let them through, and bent their course towards the Manchester Yeomanry. The people were now in a state of utter rout and confusion, leaving the ground strewed with hats and shoes, and hundreds were thrown down in the attempt to escape. The cavalry were hurrying about in all directions, completing the work of dispersion . . . I saw nothing that gave me an idea of resistance, except in one or two spots where they showed some disinclination to abandon the banners; these impulses, however, were but momentary, and banner after banner fell into the hands of the military power . . .

During the whole of this confusion, heightened at its close by the rattle of some artillery crossing the square, shrieks were heard in all directions, and as the crowd of people dispersed the effects of the conflict became visible. Some were seen bleeding on the ground and unable to rise; others, less seriously injured but faint with the loss of blood, were retiring slowly or leaning upon others for support . . . The whole of this extraordinary scene was the work of a few minutes.

S. Bamford, *op. cit.*, chapter 35.

In ten minutes from the commencement of the havock, the field was an open and almost deserted space. The sun looked down through a sultry and motionless air. The curtains and blinds of the windows within view were all closed. A gentleman or two might occasionally be seen looking out from one of the new houses before-mentioned, near the door of which, a group of persons, (special constables), were collected, and apparently in conversation; others were assisting the wounded, or carrying off the dead. The hustings remained, with a few broken or hewed flag-staves erect, and a torn and gashed banner or two drooping; whilst over the whole field, were strewed caps, bonnets, hats, shawl, and shoes, and other parts of male and female dress; trampled, torn, and bloody. The yeomanry had dismounted—some were easing their horses' girths, others adjusting their accoutrements; and some were wiping their sabres. Several mounds of human beings still remained where they had fallen, crushed down and smothered. Some of these were still groaning—others with staring eyes, were gasping for breath, and others would never breathe more. All was silent save those low sounds, and the occasional snorting and pawing of steeds. Persons might sometimes be noticed peeping from attics and over the tall ridgings of houses, but they quickly withdrew, as if fearful of being observed, or unable to sustain the full gaze, of a scene so hideous and abhorrent.

2 Combinations and combination acts, 1815–25

Trades unions could always be prosecuted at common law for conspiracy. But as part of the backlash against radicalism in the 1790s, Pitt passed the Combination Acts of 1799 and 1800, which allowed magistrates to sentence unionists summarily to three months in prison. It was thought that this would be a more prompt and certain method of controlling trades unionism than a common law prosecution. The hope was to suppress dangerous economic protest, just as controls on the press, on arming, on meetings and the occasional suspension of *habeas corpus*, were used to suppress political protest.

However, the correspondence between Manchester magistrates and the Home Office in 1817 and 1818 showed that trades union organization was effective and coming openly into contact with political radicalism (2a). This united activity among the textile trades was formalized in the Philanthropic Society of summer 1818 (2b), perhaps the first general union of trades, and with connections in Nottingham, Birmingham and Liverpool. The alarm (and correspondence) of magistrates and Home Office grew, and the Home Office pressed its justices to employ the combination acts. (These extracts from the Home Office papers are quoted from A. Aspinall (ed.), *Early English Trade Unions*, 1949.)

But the Combination Acts were increasingly seen as ineffective, for what prosecutions there were against trades unions were usually brought under the old common law; as inappropriate, since political economy favoured free trade and no government interference in the working of the market; and ultimately, as unjust. Francis Place (1771–1854), the radical London tailor who organized much of the period's 'pressure from without', together with Joseph Hume (1777–1855), the radical MP, secured a Committee of Enquiry in 1824 into the working of the Acts (2c). The Committee heard that men were harassed if they refused to accept lower wages (evidence of William Temple), were prosecuted if they resisted jointly (evidence of Alexander), but that masters could and did combine to cut wages (evidence of Ravenhill), and the men could not prosecute them in return (evidence of Place). The Select Committee recommended (2d) that the Combination Acts and the offending common law should both be repealed, and though certain controls over trades unions were re-enacted the following year, the legal status of trades unionism was not again in doubt. But what was ominous for the future was the intellectual gulf between the adherents of the new middle-class political economy, and working men. It was a gulf revealed in the Place Papers (2e) and soon to be reinforced by working-class attacks on capitalism (see Part I, nos 5–7).

Suggestions for further reading

For a wider range of Home Office material, as well as for its introduction, see A. Aspinall (ed.), *Early English Trade Unions* (1949); M. D. George, 'The Combination Laws Reconsidered', *Economic History*, 1927.

2a The politicization of distress

HO 42/178, quoted in A. Aspinall, *op. cit.*, pp. 253–7.

James Norris, J.P. to Viscount Sidmouth *Manchester, 29 July 1818*

About six weeks ago the bricksetters and their labourers together with the joiners and carpenters first turned out for an advance. The former got what they wanted; the latter one-half of what they wanted. Just as the latter people obtained their object, the *dyers* turned out and were out for about a fortnight or three weeks. They adopted a practice for the first time here of parading two and two through the public streets almost every day—certainly conducting themselves with great order, but still the practice being novel, it tended to alarm. My brother magistrates and myself did not think it right on this account to interfere in their practice in order that the lower classes might see distinctly that we kept aloof from any question between them and their employers as to the advance of wages, and in order that they might pay a greater respect to any judgement which we might be called upon to pronounce in case the masters proceeded against any of them under the Combination Act. No case however was at any time brought before us, and the dyers, who, it was generally imagined by the public, had not been so well paid as many other classes, ultimately obtained their prices. About a week before the dyers returned to work the spinners almost throughout the whole of the town and neighbourhood on one day struck for an advance, having previously given their employers notice that they would do so a fortnight before, and thus a number of at least 10,000 hands were in one day turned loose on the town and created no small degree of alarm. . . . The spinners, from their working in such large numbers together, have a much better opportunity of effectually fulfilling their objects of combinations, and have undoubtedly from the beginning carried on such a system of intimidation against those who are willing to work, that the masters have not been able to break through it, nor to bring any case before the magistrates. The difficulty the masters have is that of identity. Four or five hundred or perhaps one or two thousand assembling from different factories and at the hour of work, viz. 4 or 5 o'clock in the morning, go to a factory at the other end of town where they are not known, and so carry off by force or intimidation, though without any violent breach of the peace, the hands who might be disposed to go to work—and the parties assembled being strangers, the masters have in no one instance that I have heard of been able to identify persons, so that no case can be made out under the Combination Act. This is certainly a most unfortunate circumstance, because a few strong examples might have the effect of encouraging those to go to work who are willing but who under these circumstances dare not.

The system of support from one trade to another is carried on to an amazing extent, and they regularly send delegates out to the different towns who are in work to receive their subscriptions. There is no doubt however that, notwithstanding this support, they suffer considerably from privation, but still there is no appearance of their going to work at the old prices, and the masters, I believe, are generally pertinacious, and with great reason, because the spinners, averaging them throughout the mills in Manchester, gain 30*s*. per week each hand; and the larger [the] family a man has, the better for him, because he can employ his children. There can be little doubt but that the spinners have sent their emissaries to different towns in the country, so that all the towns in the neighbourhood are equally well acquainted with what the body of spinners are doing here, and at any day if they thought it conducive to their ends, the whole neighbourhood might be in the same condition. The example of turning out is from all these circumstances spreading most widely, and I believe the weavers (who certainly are the most suffering part of our labouring classes) have come to a determination to seek an advance, and committees are now forming amongst them for that purpose, and several large meetings near the neighbouring towns have been held with this view. I trust the masters will take their case into consideration, and if possible afford them the increase desired, in order that so very large a body as the weavers are in this County may not be added to the extensive number already idle.

In two instances since the spinners have been out we have had riots in this town, but I consider each of them to have been accidental and not premeditated. In the first instance it was an attack upon the beadles of the town . . . The latter instance occurred on Monday evening last on the *accident* of a fire. A body of about 500 had got together evidently with a view to take advantage of the fire and breed a disturbance, but fortunately it did not succeed. . . .

I have already stated to your Lordship that the men out of employ assemble in considerable bodies at the outskirts of the town, and are evidently acting much in concert and under very excellent organization. Whether there may ultimately be anything political in their intentions and movements I am not able to state to your Lordship, but your Lordship will perceive how easy a matter it might be for the disaffected in this part, and of which I am sorry to say I think we have too many amongst the lower classes to throw politics into the way of these men and convert what at present appears but a turn-out into an engine for alarming the Government of the country and producing a new order of things under the stale idea of a reform, and to insinuate at this time into the minds of these men that this will be about the time for removing all their grievances, as they would term them, by means of a general rising.

I am sorry to inform your Lordship that from all I can learn, Messrs. Drummond, Baguley, Ogden, Knight, and in short, all the men who disturbed the public peace last year, have been most active for several months past in disseminating amongst the lower orders at meetings convened for the purpose in the different lesser townships in the neighbourhood the most poisonous and alarming sentiments with respect to the government of the country, and have continually inculcated the idea of a general rising, and although I do not by any means think that the system of turning out in the different trades is connected with this idea, or that the sentiment itself has taken root in the minds of the mass of the population, yet I am disposed to think that this idea gains ground and that in consequence the working classes have become not only more pertinacious but more insolent in their demands and demeanour, particularly with reference to the spinners who have no reason on earth to ask an advance of wages except that they think it is one way of coming at the property of their employers. Several inflammatory handbills have been addressed to the public from the press of Ogden . . .

They are certainly much bolder grown than they were last year, and if they can avail themselves of the present temper of the working people to throw this populous district into disorder, and I might, I think, truly add, rebellion, they certainly will attempt it. The opportunity is but too favourable, but I am not prepared to add that I think their plan is at all organized at present. The impression on the minds of a number of our most respectable merchants, etc. is that an attempt of this sort will certainly ultimately take place, and I trust whenever it does, we shall be prepared to meet it. Most undoubtedly, if these people continue to travel about the country and disseminate the principle alluded to, it must in the end gain considerable strength in the public mind and feeling . . .

HO 79/3/208–10, quoted in A. Aspinall, *op. cit.*, p. 264.

Henry Hobhouse to James Norris *Whitehall, 4 August 1818. Private.*

You cannot be more fully impressed than Lord Sidmouth is, with the propriety of the magistrate forbearing to interfere in questions between master and servant so long as the peace is unbroken, but it is impossible for the Secretary of State to contemplate with indifference the danger likely to result to the public weal from the existence, in such a population as that of the south-eastern part of Lancashire, of large bodies of men without the visible means of subsistence, and exposed to the harangues of the disaffected demagoguism who are known to be ever alive to the means of doing mischief in that quarter of England . . .

2b General union

C. Cave, Printer, Exchange Buildings, Manchester, handbill, 19 August 1818; HO 42/181, quoted in A. Aspinall, *op. cit.*, pp. 273–4.

Manchester handbill, 19 August 1818

As a *meeting of Deputies* from the under-mentioned TRADES from Manchester, Stockport, Ashton-under-Lyne, Oldham, Bury, etc., etc., etc.

Calico printers, dyers and dressers, hatters, blacksmiths, jenny spinners, cotton weavers, bricklayers, fustian cutters, colliers, sawyers, shoemakers, slubbers, mule spinners, machine makers, etc.

The following Address and Resolutions were unanimously agreed to.

At a general meeting of trades convened to take into consideration the distressed state and privations to which the working class of society are reduced by their avaricious employers reducing wages to less than sufficient to support nature or purchase the bare necessaries for our existence, with great economy and hard labour; therefore, to render redress in such cases of distress to any body or party reduced as aforesaid,

RESOLUTIONS

First—That there be a Union of all Trades called the PHILANTHROPIC SOCIETY, to be held in Manchester on the second Monday in every month, when all TRADES shall send a *delegate* with proper credentials for admission.

Second—That every trade be recommended to raise a FUND amongst themselves for the general benefit of all trades joined in this Union, and in particular any trade that may be engaged in resisting oppression, or to alleviate distress, and to enable the labouring part of the community to live in comfort and decency.

Third—That any trade feeling the necessity of an advance of wages, that trade shall be bound to give notice to a meeting of delegates convened for that purpose; and their concurrence being obtained, all other trades will support them.

Fourth—That if any trade be under the necessity of leaving their employ through the oppression of their employers, they shall first call the general representatives together and inform them, provided that such representatives be not overpowered with too much business at one time, that they may be prepared for supporting the cause and provide for the same; in short, no trade shall leave their employ without first calling the other trades together and then act by and with their consent in taking the most favourable time for resistance.

Fifth—That any body of workmen being oppressed or illegally used, this Society will support them in obtaining legal redress.

Sixth—That all printing of notices, etc. with all delegations, or any other necessary expenses, shall be paid out of their separate funds.

Seventh—That a Committee of eleven persons be chosen by ballot, out of the different trades who form this Society, and shall be regularly enrolled on the list kept for that purpose. The Committee to go out by regular rotation every month, so that the whole may be changed every three months.

Eighth—That in order to preserve decorum in this Society or meeting of representatives, no person shall be allowed to advance any political or religious argument, under a forfeit of 3*d*. for the first offence, and 6*d*. for the second, which must be paid the night it is forfeited.

Ninth—That there shall be an Auxiliary Society of the different trades in each town; that each trade shall have its own by-laws, and each auxiliary to act in conjunction with the Resolutions of the central Philanthropic Society.

Tenth—That the representatives be empowered to alter or amend, add or diminish any Rule or Rules for the benefit of this Society, provided it does not infringe upon or act against any trade or division belonging to the general Philanthropic Society.

HO 79/3 269–70, quoted in A. Aspinall, *op. cit.*, p. 276.

Henry Hobhouse to the Rev. C. W. Ethelston Whitehall, 24 August 1818
Confidential

. . . The grand desideratum in your country at present seems to be a want of spirit in the master manufacturers to make use of the means which the law affords them in the Combination Act for the suppression of the conspiracy which has existed for so many weeks, and appears to be gradually spreading.

If the law had been early and spiritedly enforced, there can be no doubt that great good would have resulted from it. Even yet, much benefit would arise from resorting to the Act, and I regret to see it almost a dead letter while conspiracy is increasing on every side. No means should be spared of exhorting the masters to their duty in this respect. It is impossible to doubt that they are in possession of abundant proofs if they would but bring them forward.

HO 42/180, quoted in A. Aspinall, *op. cit.*, p. 286.

Colonel Fletcher to Henry Hobhouse *Bolton-le-Moors, 4 September 1818*
. . . The danger of a committee dictating what wages must be paid, is manifest, and if [it] should be submitted to, a worse than universal suffrage would succeed. It would introduce a mob oligarchy, bearing down all the better orders of society, and would quickly be succeeded by universal anarchy . . .

HO 42/181, quoted in A. Aspinall, *op. cit.*, pp. 304–5.

James Norris to Viscount Sidmouth *Manchester, 11 October 1818*
I wished to acquire what information I could respecting the General Union of Trades before I again troubled your Lordship. I am happy now to be able to inform you that from all the information I can acquire, the General Union, so far at least as respects this district, is broken up. Delegates from Nottingham, Birmingham and Liverpool were here about a month ago, but they came after the spinners had gone in, and found the latter, I believe, so happy in being again employed, that it broke their own spirit and they left here in disgust . . .

I am informed that the plan of the General Union *certainly* originated in Nottingham . . . Shoemakers, tailors and other trades had joined in the Union, but I believe for the present at least it is broken up. The spinners' submission, with the imprisonment of Baguley, etc., have mainly contributed to this happy event . . .

2c The working of the Combination Acts

Evidence of William Temple, a cotton spinner from Stockport, *Select Committee on Artisans and Machinery* (1824), fifth report.

On Wednesday the 13th, I believe it was, that my master came to me, and asked me whether I was determined to quit his employ on the Saturday, the 16th; Yes, I said, unless he would give me what would enable me to increase the support of my family. I said, so long as I could get more wages elsewhere as there were other factories giving at that time a penny halfpenny to twopence a hundred more than him; he was giving 3½ per hundred [hanks].

The result was, I left his service on Saturday; and he said, I must not consider myself as his servant again. On Monday the 18th, he sent my name with 20 more, round to the masters not to employ me and the rest . . . I went to Mr. Jesse Howard, and asked him if he would give me employment, he asked me my name and I told him; and he said, I have got your name upon a list from Mr. Smith, and must not employ you. I got advice from an attorney; I commenced an action against Mr. Smith . . . for damages, for depriving me of employment elsewhere; the result of it was, he got a Bench warrant against me, both for Lancashire and Cheshire, under the Combination and Conspiracy Law. Lancashire was, on account of the factory being on that side of the water, and the Cheshire, for raising subscriptions for individuals when out of employ; I went to Lancaster, expecting the action to be brought, and I was arrested, and I had ten days to procure bail for 200£. I did procure it, and was liberated; and had then to make the best of my road to Chester, having been arrested on the 15th of August, for the purpose of liberating my bail; and upon arriving at Chester, I surrendered my bail there of 200£ when I traversed the case to the ensueing assizes; and bail was levied on me for 400£, myself in 200£ and sureties in 100£ each. I laid in prison till the 14th of December, before that bail could be procured. I was liberated on bail on the 14th of December, then I had to appear at Lancaster at the ensueing assizes. It was put to me, if I would plead guilty, I might be discharged at the bar; I did so, in consequence of my bail at Chester. I made my way to Chester again, where I was tried, and after a trial of six hours, I was found guilty . . . of conspiring, confederating, combining, and agreeing for the price of my labour.

What was your sentence?—Twelve months imprisonment in Chester castle . . . Do you mean to state, you were sentenced to twelve months imprisonment for telling your master, alone, that you would leave his employ, if he did not give you higher wages?—I do.

Evidence of John Alexander, boot and shoe maker, *Select Committee on Artisans and Machinery* (1824), third report.

As you have been in the situation of secretary, are you sufficiently acquainted with their proceedings, to be able to inform the Committee of any instances in which the journeymen shoemakers have struck to raise wages?—I do not know of any instance since I have been in London, where they have struck for an advance of wages. I know of many instances in which they have struck to repel reductions; I know there has not been an instance in the city of London, nor I believe not more than one or two in country during that time, where the men have struck for an advance of wages . . . There is one instance within my knowledge, of Mr. Algar in Lombard Street; two years ago, next summer, he reduced his wages; he formerly gave 7*s.* for making boots, and 4*s.* 6*d.* for making shoes, and he reduced his shoes to one half of that money, that is to 2*s.* 3*d.*; the men were not willing to work for him at that, and they refused it.

How many of those men might there be?—I think there might be about six or seven . . . Mr. Algar took them up for combination; he summoned them before the Lord Mayor . . . He charged them with conspiring or combining to advance their wages; and that the men would not work, unless the whole of them got the wages they formerly had had . . . The Lord Mayor remarked, that it was a very hard case, but the law was imperative, and he must send them for two months, I think it was two months, to the house of correction, or fourteen days with hard labour; and he gave them their choice, and they chose the fourteen days . . . The society supported their families during the time they were at hard labour . . .

Evidence of Mr George Ravenhill, a hat manufacturer, *Select Committee on Artisans and Machinery* (1824), second report.

. . . I believe as far as I can recollect it, that the masters considered the combination, on the part of the journeymen, to be illegal, and that they in consequence determined to prosecute the men for the combination . . .

Then you and the other masters acted under the impression, that it was legal for you to combine to prosecute the men for demanding higher wages, though it was not legal for the men to combine to demand higher wages?—That, I believe, was the impression on the minds of the masters.

Evidence of Francis Place, tailor, *Select Committee on Artisans and Machinery* (1824), first report.

Is it within your knowledge, that masters in this town have combined against the men?—Yes, on many occasions.

Have you ever known a master prosecuted by the men, for combination?—No; I believe it would be nearly impossible to prosecute a master to conviction. To prosecute at all, money must be raised; to raise money there must be a combination among the men, and then they may be prosecuted by the masters. If, as the law now stands, the men were to prosecute the masters, there would be a cross prosecution. The Combination Law compels the men to give evidence against one another, and thus the prosecution may almost always be effectual. No law compels the masters to give evidence against one another; thus it is almost impossible ever to convict a master . . .

You think, therefore, that the Combination Laws press on the men and not upon the masters?—They are unequal and unjust.

Are the feelings of irritation, which you state generally to exist between the masters and the men, chiefly occasioned by the existence of those laws?—I have no doubt of it.

Do you think that if these laws were repealed, that irritation would subside?—It would gradually subside . . .

Is not money always subscribed to support a strike, and would that be the case if the law were repealed?—It has always been the case; it would no longer be necessary if the law were repealed; if the men could legally combine, disputes would seldom occur, but when they did, they would be settled by compromise between the parties. Workmen dread a strike . . .

Is not the workman much more in the power of the master, than the master is in the power of the man?—Whatever there is of power, is with the master.

Evidence of Rev. T. R. Malthus, *Select Committee on Artisans and Machinery* (1824), sixth report.

What is your opinion of the efficiency of those laws?—I think they are not efficient; and that they would be unjust if they were efficient.

And therefore it is your opinion it would be better they should be repealed?—Certainly.

Evidence of Peter Gregory of Coventry, *ibid.*

The laws operate entirely to the disadvantage of the working class of society . . .

2d The Report of the Select Committee

The Report of the Select Committee on Artisans and Machinery (1824), pp. 589–91.

I

That it appears, by the Evidence before the Committee, that Combinations of workmen have taken place in England, Scotland and Ireland, often to a great extent, to raise and keep up their wages, to regulate their hours of working, and to impose restrictions of the masters, respecting apprentices or others whom they might think it proper to employ; and that, at the time the Evidence was taken, Combinations were in existence, attended with Strikes or suspension of work and that the Laws have not hitherto been effectual to prevent such Combinations.

2

That serious breaches of the peace and acts of violence, with strikes of the workmen, often for very long periods, have taken place, in consequence of, and arising out of the combinations of workmen, and been attended with loss to both the masters and the workmen, and with considerable inconvenience and injury to the community.

3

That the masters have often united and combined to lower the rates of their workmens' wages, as well as to resist a demand for an increase, and to regulate their hours of working; and sometimes to discharge their workmen who would not consent to the conditions offered to them; which have been followed by suspension of work, riotous proceedings and acts of violence.

4

That prosecutions have frequently been carried on, under the statute and the common law, against the workmen, and many of them have suffered different periods of imprisonment for combining and conspiring to raise their wages, or to resist their reduction, and to regulate their hours of working.

5

That several instances have been stated to the Committee, of prosecutions against masters for combining to lower wages, and to regulate the hours of working; but no instance has been adduced of any master having been punished for that offence.

6

That the laws have not only not been efficient to prevent Combinations, either of masters or workmen; but, on the contrary have, in the opinion of many of both parties, had a tendency, to promote mutual irritation and distrust, and to give a violent character to the Combinations, and to render them highly dangerous to the peace of the community.

7

That it is the opinion of this Committee, That masters and workmen should be freed from such restrictions, as regard the rate of wages and the hours of working, and be left at perfect liberty to make such agreements as they may mutually think proper.

8

That, therefore, the statute laws that interfere in these particulars between masters and workmen, should be repealed; and also, that the common law, under which a peacable meeting of masters or workmen may be prosecuted as a conspiracy, should be altered . . .

2e Place's prophecy

Place Papers, B.M. Add. Mss. 27798, ff. 12–24.

Repeal of the combination acts: manipulation and the manipulated.

In 1814, therefore, I began to work seriously to procure a repeal of the laws against combinations of workmen, but for a long time made no visible progress . . .

On the 12th February (1824), Mr. Hume made his motion, and obtained his Committee . . .

The workmen were not easily managed. It required great care and pains and patience not to shock their prejudices, so as to prevent them doing their duty before the Committee. They were filled with false notions, all attributing their distresses to wrong causes, which I, in this state of the business, dared not attempt to remove. Taxes, machinery, laws against combinations, the will of the masters, the conduct of magistrates, these were the fundamental causes of all their sorrows and privations. All expected a great and sudden rise of wages, when the Combination Laws should be repealed; not one of them had any idea whatever of the connection between wages and population. I had to discuss everything with them most carefully, to arrange and prepare everything . . .

Place to Sir F. Burdett, 25 June 1825, B.M. Add. Mss. 27798, f. 57.

Combinations will soon cease to exist. Men have been kept together for long periods only by the oppression of the laws; these being repealed, combinations will lose the matter which cements them into masses, and they will fall to pieces. All will be as orderly as even a Quaker could desire. He knows nothing of the working people who can suppose that, when left at liberty to act for themselves, without being driven into permanent associations by the oppression of the laws, they will continue to contribute money for distant and doubtful experiments, for uncertain and precarious benefits.

3 Rural unrest

In the mid 1820s, Cobbett toured southern England on horseback, reporting on its cultivation, the standard of living of its labourers, and the decline of its traditional practices such as living-in. New money and new urban styles, he claimed, were disrupting the placid stable rural economy (3a). The explosion he forecast occurred in 1830 when the rural proletariat of the arable south and east of England rose in the Swing riots. They demanded higher wages and an end to the threshing machine which destroyed their winter employment (3b). They reinforced their demands with rick-burning. Though the local gentry were often sympathetic, the government's Special Commissions were savage, and hung nine men and transported nearly 500 others. Cobbett angrily insisted that Swing had its roots deep in hunger and oppression (3c) which would be remedied only by parliamentary reform. Years later, Joseph Arch (1826–1919), founder of the agricultural worker's union, looked back (3d) on his village childhood with bitterness at the discipline exercised by parson and squire.

Suggestions for further reading

For *Cobbett's Rides*, see the Penguin edition (1967), edited by G. Woodcock; for Swing, T. and B. Hammond, *The Village Labourer* (1911); and E. Hobsbawm and G. Rudé, *Captain Swing* (1969).

3a The destruction of the rural economy

W. Cobbett, *Rural Rides* (1967 edn), pp. 226–9.

Reigate, Thursday evening, 20 October, 1825.

Having done my business at Hartswood to-day about eleven o'clock, I went to a *sale* at a farm, which the farmer is quitting. Here I had a view of what has long been going on all over the country . . .

Everything about this farm-house was formerly the scene of *plain manners* and *plentiful living*. Oak clothes-chests, oak bed-steads, oak chests of drawers, and oak tables to eat on, long, strong, and well supplied with joint stools. Some of the things were many hundreds of years old. But all appeared to be in a state of decay and nearly of *disuse*. There appeared to have been hardly any family in that house, where formerly there were, in all probability, from ten to fifteen men, boys, and maids: and, which was the worst of all, there was a *parlour*! Aye, and a *carpet* and *bell-pull* too! One end of the front of this once plain and substantial house had been moulded into a '*parlour*'; and there was the mahogany table, and the fine chairs, and the fine glass, and all as bare-faced upstart as any stock-jobber in the kingdom can boast of. And there were the decanters, the glasses, the 'dinner-set' of crockery ware, and all just in the true stock-jobber style. And I dare say it has been '*Squire* Charington and the *Miss* Charingtons; and not plain Master Charington, and his son Hodge, and his daughter Betty Charington, all of whom this accursed system has, in all likelihood, transmuted into a species of mock gentlefolks, while it has ground the labourers down into real slaves. Why do not farmers now feed and *lodge* their work-people, as they did formerly? Because they cannot keep them *upon so little* as they give them in wages. This is the real cause of the change. There needs no more to prove that the lot of the working classes has become worse than it formerly was. This fact alone is quite sufficient to settle this point. All the world knows, that a number of people, boarded in the same house, and at the same table, can, with good food, be boarded much cheaper than those persons divided into twos, threes, or fours, can be boarded. This is a well-known truth: therefore, if the farmer now shuts his pantry against his labourers, and pays them wholly in money, is it not clear, that he does it because he thereby gives them a living *cheaper* to him; that is to say, a *worse* living than formerly? Mind he has a *house* for them; a kitchen for them to sit in, bed rooms for them to sleep in, tables, and stools, and benches, of everlasting duration. All these he has; all these *cost him nothing*; and yet so much does he gain by pinching them in wages that he lets all these things remain as of no use, rather than feed labourers in the house. Judge, then, of the *change* that has taken place in the condition of these labourers! And, be astonished, if you can, at the *pauperism* and the *crimes* that now disgrace this once happy and moral England.

The land produces, on an average, what it always produced; but, there is a new distribution of the produce. This 'Squire Charington's father used, I dare say, to sit at the head of the oak-table along with his men, say grace to them, and cut up the meat and the pudding. He might take a cup of *strong beer* to himself, when they had none; but, that was pretty nearly all the difference in their manner of living. So that *all* lived well. But the '*Squire* had many *wine-decanters* and *wine-glasses* and 'a *dinner set*', and a '*breakfast set*', and '*desert knives*;' and these evidently imply carryings on and a consumption that must of necessity have greatly robbed the long oak table if it had remained fully tenanted. That long table could not share in the work of the decanters and the dinner set. Therefore, it became almost untenanted; the labourers retreated to hovels, called cottages; and, instead of board and lodging, they got money; so little of it as to enable the employer to drink wine; but, then, that he might not reduce them to *quite starvation*, they were enabled to come to him, in the *king's name*, and demand food *as paupers* . . .

This is not only the natural progress, but it has been the progress in England. The blame is not justly imputed to 'SQUIRE CHARINGTON and his like; the blame belongs to the internal stock-jobbing system. There was no reason to expect, that farmers would not endeavour to keep pace, in point of show and luxury, with fund-holders, and with all the tribes that *war* and *taxes* created. Farmers were not the authors of the mischief; and *now* they are compelled to shut the labourers out of their houses, and to pinch them in their wages, in order to be able to pay their own taxes; and, besides this, the manners and the principles of the working class are so changed, that a sort of self-preservation bids the farmer (especially in some counties) to keep them from beneath his roof.

I could not quit this farm-house without reflecting on the thousands of scores of bacon and thousands of bushels of bread that had been eaten from the long oak-table which, I said to myself, is now perhaps, going, at last, to the bottom of a bridge that some stock-jobber will stick up over an artificial river in his cockney-garden. '*By* —— *it shant*', said I, almost in a real passion, and so I requested a friend to buy it for me . . .

3b Swing: in Norfolk

The magistrates of North Walsham, 24 November 1830, HO52/9, p. 156, quoted in E. Hobsbawm and G. Rudé, *Captain Swing* (1969).

The *Magistrates* in the Hundreds of *Tunstead* and *Happing*, in the County of Norfolk, having taken into consideration the disturbed state of the said Hundreds and the Country in general, wish to make it publicly known *that it is their opinion* that such disturbances principally arise from the use of Threshing Machines, and to the insufficient Wages of the Labourers. The Magistrates therefore beg to *recommend* to the Owners and Occupiers of Land in these Hundreds to *discontinue the use of Threshing Machines, and to increase the Wages of Labour* to Ten Shillings a week for able bodied men, and that when task work is preferred, that it should be put out at such a rate as to enable an industrious man to earn Two Shillings per day.

The Magistrates are determined to enforce the Laws against all tumultuous Rioters and Incendiaries, and they look for support to all the respectable and well disposed part of the Community; at the same time they feel a full conviction that *no severe measures will be necessary*, if the proprietors of Land will give proper employment to the Poor on their own Occupations, and encourage their Tenants to do the same.

3c The rural war

Cobbett's *Political Register*, 27 November 1830.

> 'With regard to this war, Lord Grey said . . . "I can only promise that the state of the country shall be made the object of our immediate, our diligent and unceasing attention . . . To relieve the distress which now so unhappily exists in different parts will be the first and most anxious end of our deliberations; but I here declare . . . that it is my determined resolution, wherever outrages are perpetrated, or excesses committed, to suppress them with severity and vigour (cheers). Severity is, in the first instance, the only remedy which can be applied to such disorders with success; and, therefore, although we are most anxious to relieve the distress of the people who are suffering, let them be well assured they shall find no want of firm resolution upon our part. (hear, hear) . . . Their first object would be to examine into the nature of the existing distress, and then into the disturbances consequent upon that distress, and, as there was every reason to believe, upon the instigation of persons whom that distress did not affect . . . The danger with which the country was threatened was to be the first subject of consideration, and must be met with a prompt and determined hand." (Hear, hear, hear).'

This must certainly be an assembly of the bravest men in the whole world! Observe how they cheered every time the word *resolution*, *determination*, *severity* or *vigour*, occurred! And, the '*prompt and determined hand*' seems to have fairly *entranced* their Lordships. But, now, let us inquire *cooly* into this matter. Let us fairly state the case of those who are carrying on this war. Lord Grey proposes to inquire into the '*nature* of the *existing distress*'. These words are enough to make one despair of him and his measures. Just as if the distress was *temporary*, and had now arisen from some *special cause*! . . . One would as soon expect them to propose an *inquiry* into the cause of the dirt in London streets. The one is just as notorious and as obvious as the other . . .

Forty-five years ago, the labourers all brewed their own beer, and that now none of them do it; that formerly they ate meat, cheese, and bread, and they now live almost wholly on potatoes; that formerly it was a rare thing for a girl to be with child before she was married, and that now it is as rare that she is not, the parties being so poor that they are compelled to throw the expense of the wedding on the parish; that the felons in the jails and hulks live better than the honest labouring people, and that these latter commit thefts and robbery, in order to get into the jails and hulks, or to be transported; that men are set to draw waggons and carts like beasts of burden; that they are shut up in pounds like cattle; that they are put up at auction like Negroes in Jamaica; that married men are forcibly separated from their wives to prevent them from breeding . . . It is no *temporary cause*, it is no *new* feeling of discontent that is at work; it is a deep sense of grievous wrongs; it is long harboured resentment; it is an accumulation of revenge for unmerited punishment . . . it is a natural effect of a cause which is as obvious as that ricks are consumed by fire, when fire is put to them . . .

But if this excite our astonishment, what are we to say of that part of Lord Grey's speech in which he speaks of 'instigators'? . . . What! can these men look at the facts before their eyes; can they see the millions of labourers everywhere rising up, and hear them saying that they will '*no longer starve on potatoes*'; can they see them breaking threshing-machines; can they see them gathering together and demanding an increase of wages; can they see all this, and can they believe that the *fires* do not proceed from the same persons; but that these are the work of some invisible and almost incorporeal agency! . . .

The *motive* of it is, however, evident enough to men who reflect that every tax-eater and tithe-eater, no matter of what sort or size he or she is, is afraid to believe, and wishes the nation not to believe, that *the fires are the work of the labourers*. And *why* are they so reluctant to believe this, and so anxious that it should be believed by nobody? Because the labourers are *the millions* (for, mind, *smiths*, *wheelwrights*, *collar-makers*, *carpenters*, *bricklayers*, all are of one mind); and because, if *the millions be bent upon this work*, who is to stop it? Then to believe that the labourers are the burners, is to believe that they must have been urged to the deeds by desperation, proceeding from *some grievous wrong*, real or imaginary; and to believe this is to believe that the burnings will continue, until the *wrong be redressed*. To believe this is to believe that there must be such a change of system as will take *from the tax and tithe-eaters a large portion of what they receive, and give it back to the labourers*, and believe this the tax and tithe-eaters never will, until the political Noah *shall enter into the ark*! . . . [The labourers] look upon themselves as engaged in a *war*, with a *just object* . . . Is this destructive war to go on till all law and all personal safety are at an end? . . . The truth is, that, for many years past, about *forty-five millions a year* have been *withheld from the working-people of England*; about five or six millions have been doled back to them in *poor-rates*; and the forty millions have gone to keep up *military academies, dead-weight, standing-army, military asylums, pensions, sinecures*, and to give to parsons, and to build new palaces and pull down others, and to pay loan-mongers and all that enormous tribe; and to be expended in various other ways not at all necessary to the well-being of the nation.

These *forty millions a year* must now *remain with the working people* . . . And what is to be the *result* of all this? Why, a violent destruction of the whole fabric of the Government, or a timely, that is, an *immediate* and *effectual* remedy; and there is no remedy but *a radical reform of the Parliament*. . . .

3d Village discipline

The Life of Joseph Arch by himself (1898 edn), pp. 10–55.

Because my father had refused to sign for 'a small loaf and a dear one', he could not get any work whatever for eighteen weeks. He tried hard to get a job, but it was useless; he was a marked man, and we should have starved if my mother had not kept us all by her laundry work.

It was a terrible winter . . . Those who owned and held the land believed, and acted up to their belief as far as they were able, that the land belonged to the rich man only, that the poor man had no part or lot in it, and had no sort of claim on society. If the poor man dared to marry and have children, they thought he had no *right* to claim the necessary food wherewith to keep himself and his family alive. They thought, too, every mother's son of them, that, when a labourer could no longer work, he had lost the right to live. Work was all they wanted from him; he was to work and hold his tongue, year in and year out, early and late, and if he could not work, why, what was the use of him? It was what he was made for, to labour and toil for his betters, without complaint on a starvation wage. When no more work could be squeezed out of him he was no better than a cumberer of other folk's ground, and the proper place for such as he was the churchyard, where he would be sure to lie quiet under a few feet of earth, and want neither food nor wages any more. A quick death and a cheap burying—that was the motto of those extortioners for the poor man past work . . .

Numbers of people used to go to the rectory for soup, but not a drop of it did we touch. I have stood at our door with my mother, and I have seen her face look sad as she watched the little children toddle past, carrying the tin cans, and their toes coming out of their boots. 'Ah, my boy,' she once said, 'you shall never, never do that. I will work these fingers to the bone before you have to do it!' She was as good as her word—*I never went to the rectory for soup* . . .

I remember a thing which made my mother very angry. The parson's wife issued a decree, that the labourers should sit on one side of the church and their wives on the other. When my mother heard of it she said, 'No, "those whom God hath joined together let no man put asunder," and certainly no woman shall!'

I can also remember the time when the parson's wife used to sit in state in her pew in the chancel, and the poor women used to walk up the church and make a curtsey to her before taking the seats set apart for them. They were taught in this way that they had to pay homage and respect to those 'put in authority over them', and made to understand that they must 'honour the powers that be,' as represented in the rector's wife. You may be pretty certain that many of these women did not relish the curtsey-scraping and other humiliations they had to put up with, but they were afraid to speak out. They had their families to think of, children to feed and clothe somehow; and when so many could not earn a living wage, but only a half-starving one, when very often a labouring man was out of work for weeks at a stretch,—why, the wives and mothers learned to take thankfully whatever was doled out to them at the parsonage or elsewhere, and drop the curtsey expected of them, without making a wry face. A smooth face and a smooth tongue was what their benefactors required of them, and they got both . . .

My proud little spirit smarted and burned when I saw what happened at the Communion service.

First, up walked the squire to the communion rails; the farmers went up next; then up went the tradesmen, the shopkeepers, the wheelwright, and the blacksmith; and then, the very last of all, went the poor agricultural labourers in their smock frocks. They walked up by themselves; nobody else knelt with them; it was as if they were unclean—and at that sight the iron entered straight into my poor little heart and remained fast embedded there. I said to myself, 'If that's what goes on—never for me!' I ran home and told my mother what I had seen, and I wanted to know why my father was not as good in the eyes of God as the squire, and why the poor should be forced to come up last of all to the table of the Lord. My mother gloried in my spirit . . .

There was no chapel in our village, but when I was about fourteen years of age some dissenters began to come over from Wellsbourne. They used to hold meetings in a back lane. When the parson got wind of it, he and his supporters, the farmers, dared the labourers to go near these unorthodox Christians. If we did, then goodbye to all the charities; no more soup and coals should we have. And it was no idle threat. If that was not religious persecution I should like to know what was! They knew they had the labourers under their thumbs, and so they put the screw on when it pleased them . . .

The teaching in most of the village schools, then, was bad almost beyond belief. 'Much knowledge of the right sort is a dangerous thing for the poor', might have been the motto put up over the door of the village school in my day. The less book-learning the labourer's lad got stuffed into him, the better for him, and the safer for those above him, was what those in authority believed and acted up to . . . These gentry did not want him to know; they did not want him to think; they only wanted him to work. To toil with the hand was what he was born into the world for, and they took precious good care to see that he did it from his youth upwards. Of course he might learn his catechism; that, and things similar to it, was the right, proper, and suitable knowledge for such as he; he would be the more likely to stay contentedly in his place to the end of his working days . . .

When they [the agricultural labourers] did start a sick benefit fund . . . the parsons, the farmers, and the leading men of the parish did their very best to put it down, to stamp it out with their despotic heels. The parson refused point blank to preach a sermon in aid of funds for it . . . That a labourer, who had fallen out of work through illness, should be supported, even for a time, from a common fund over which the rectory had no direct control, was gall and wormwood to the parson. Worse still, the labourer's wife would not be so ready to come to the rectory back-door, humbly begging for help. Worse and worse still, she and the children might slip out of the yoke of Church attendance altogether, if rectory charity were no longer a necessity. No; this sick club was the thin edge of a bad wedge, and it must be pulled out and broken up without delay.

We labourers had no lack of lords and masters. There were the parson and his wife at the rectory. There was the squire, with his hand of iron overshadowing us all. There was no velvet glove on that hard hand, as many a poor man found to his hurt. He brought it down on my father because he would not sign for a small loaf and a dear one; and if it had not been for my mother, that hand would have crushed him to the earth, maybe crushed the life right out of him. At the sight of the squire the people trembled. He lorded it right feudally over his tenants, the farmers; the farmers in their turn tyrannised over the labourers; the labourers were no better than toads under a harrow. Most of the farmers were oppressors of the poor; they put on the iron wage-screw, and screwed the labourers' wages down, down below living point; they stretched him on the rack of life-long abject poverty.

4 Political unionism

Although Cobbett continued to write and Hunt to talk, the political reform movement died away after the Six Acts. But in the late 1820s the campaigns for Catholic Emancipation and reform of parish government (see p. 150) brought London artisans, shopkeepers and dissenters together in radical discussion groups. Meanwhile economic distress deepened and Thomas Attwood (1783–1856), a Birmingham banker, formed the Birmingham Political Union to agitate for parliamentary reform in order to end economic mismanagement (4a). A working-class version of it was started in London when the political and parish radicals captured a projected general trades union for political reform, the National Union of the Working Classes (4b). Its aims were a mixture of Painite radicalism ('The Rights of Man') and Owenite economics but the extravagance of its politics horrified conservatives, and the implications of its economics appalled Place (4c).

So some six months later, respectable middle-class radicals, headed by Place and Hume, formed the National Political Union (4d), which, like the BPU, firmly rejected the notion of class; it was a union of People against the Aristocracy. Where the NPU worked for the Reform Bill, the NUWC wanted universal suffrage; where the leaders of the NPU advocated political economy, the leaders of the NUWC rejected it for a socialist alternative. Inevitably, they distrusted each other (4e). It was a tension repeated in many cities, including Birmingham where working-class radicals broke away from the BPU for specifically class reasons (4f). Yet their detailed political demands were very similar—attacking taxes, aristocracy, monopolies and an Established Church (4g and 4h).

The middle-class political unions fell away with the passing of the Reform Act, the working-class unions with the rise of trades unions at the end of 1833. But in 1836, former NUWC members came together in the London Working Men's Association to press for universal suffrage and the repeal of the newspaper duties, though unlike the NUWC, the LWMA deliberately limited its numbers (4i). One of their manifestoes in 1837 (4j) showed how traditional their political radicalism remained. Yet it was the LWMA that a year later drew up the Charter.

Suggestions for further reading

For the unionism of 1831–2, see D. Frazer in J. Ward (ed.), *Popular Movements* (1970); D. Rowe, 'Class and radicalism in London 1831–2', *Historical Journal*, 1970; on the middle-class side, see J. Hamburger, *Intellectuals in Politics*, 1965, and W. E. Thomas, 'Francis Place and working class history', *Historical Journal*, 1962; D. Rowe has edited a selection of the Place Papers in *London Radicalism 1830–1843*.

4a The Birmingham Political Union

Resolutions at a meeting of the Birmingham Political Union, 1830 pamphlet.

At a most numerous and respectable Meeting of the Merchants, Manufacturers, Tradesmen, Mechanics, Artizans, and other inhabitants of the Town of Birmingham, held at Mr. Beardsworth's Repository, on Monday morning the 25th of January 1830, the following Resolutions were entered into.

George Frederick Muntz Esq. in the chair.
Resolved unanimously:

1.—That the ruinous depression of the trade of the town of Birmingham has been progressively increasing for the last four years, and has now arrived at an extent never before equalled . . .

2.—That, in the opinion of this meeting, the general distress which now afflicts the country, and which has been so severely felt at different periods during the last 15 years, is entirely to be ascribed to the gross mismanagement of public affairs; and that such mismanagement can only be effectually and permanently remedied by an effectual reform in the Commons House of Parliament; and this meeting is also of opinion that for the legal accomplishment of this great object, and the further redress of public wrongs and grievances, it is expedient to form a general Political Union between the lower and middle classes of the people in this town . . .

4b The National Union of the Working Classes

In Spring 1831 some carpenters applied to the British Association, the leading London Co-operative society, for help in setting up a general union of trades, 'The Metropolitan Trades Union'. They were quickly joined by the working-class radicals, the 'Rotundists', and then by the parish radicals, who together captured the union for political radicalism. It became the NUWC, with nearly 2,000 members in London organized in small classes, studying Paine, Owen and the penny Unstamped, and with its headquarters at the Rotunda. It founded some and established contact with dozens of other working-class unions through the country. Its numbers fell away with the surge in trades unionism in late 1833.

From trades union to political union

F. Place, B.M. Add. Mss. 27791, f. 280.

Its projectors in the first instance wished to form a trades union for the purpose of raising wages and reducing the hours of working with a view to the ultimate object the division of property among the working people, but the persons they called to their assistance under the circumstances of the times, and the general agitation caused by the Reform Bill, at once converted it into a Political Union, leaving the proceedings of working men's trades unions as a secondary object . . .

Resolutions of the meeting 26 April 1831

Penny Papers for the People, 27 May 1831.

1. Resolved, that the Working Classes of Great Britain and Ireland must obtain their rights *as men*, before they can possess them *as workmen*, or enjoy the produce of their own labour.

2. That wherever the producing classes have influence at elections for members of Parliament, they should strenuously exert it to procure the return of friends of the people, without being duped by Whig or Tory . . .

THE RIGHTS OF MAN

I. The end of society is the PUBLIC GOOD, and the institution of government is to secure to EVERY INDIVIDUAL, the enjoyment of his rights.

II. The rights of Man in society, are liberty—equality before the laws—security of his person—and the full enjoyment of the produce of his labours.

III. Liberty is that power which belongs to a man of doing everything that does not infringe upon the rights of another . . .

IV. The law is the free and solemn expression of the public will:—it ought to be the same for all, whether it protects or punishes;—it cannot order but what is just and useful;—it cannot forbid but what is hurtful . . .

VIII. A people have always the right of revising, amending, and changing their constitution:—one generation cannot subject to its laws future generations.

IX. Every adult member of society, has an equal right to nominate those who legislate for the community; thereby concurring through his representatives in the enactment of the laws.

X. Oppression is exercised against the social body, when ONE of its members is oppressed:—oppression is exercised against EACH MEMBER, when the social body is oppressed.

XI. When a government violates the rights of the people resistance becomes the most sacred, and the most indispensable of duties.

OBJECTS OF THE NATIONAL UNION

1. The objects of the NATIONAL UNION are,—First, to avail itself of every opportunity, in the progress of society, for the securing, by

degrees, those things specified in the preceding declaration of the Rights of Man.

2. To obtain for every working man, unrestricted by unjust and partial laws, the full value of his labour, and the free disposal of the produce of his labour.

3. To support, as circumstances may determine, by all just means, every fair and rational opposition made by societies of working men (such societies being part of the Union), against the combination and tyranny of masters and manufacturers; whenever the latter shall seek, unjustly, to reduce the wages of labour, or shall institute proceedings against the workmen; the character of which proceedings, in the estimation of the Union, shall be deemed vexatious and oppressive.

4. To obtain for the nation an effectual reform in the Commons House of the British parliament: the basis of which reform shall be annual parliaments, extentions of the suffrage to every adult male, vote by ballot, and, especially, NO PROPERTY QUALIFICATION for members of parliament; this Union being convinced, that until intelligent men from the productive and useful classes of society possess the right of sitting in the Commons House of Parliament, to represent the interests of the working people, justice in legislation will never be rendered unto them.

5. To inquire, consult, consider, discuss and determine, respecting the rights and liberties of the working people, and respecting the just and most effectual means of securing all such rights.

6. To prepare petititions, addresses and remonstrances to the crown, and both Houses or either House of Parliament, respecting the preservation of public rights, the repeal of bad laws, and the enactment of a wise and all-comprehensive code of good laws.

7. To promote peace, union and concord among all classes of people and to guide and direct the public mind, into uniform, peaceful, and legitimate operations . . .

8. To collect and organize the peaceful expression of public opinion, so as to bring it to act upon the House of Parliament, in a just and effectual way.

9. To concentrate into one focus a knowledge of moral and political economy, that all classes of society may be enlightened by its radiation . . .

4c Another version of the NUWC

Bristol Job Nott, 6 June 1833.

Summary report and digest of the speeches of radical orators. A meeting was held at ——, at which Mr. B—— acted as Chairman and made the following energetic speech: 'Police, bloody, brutal, Whigs, murder, bludgeons, massacre, scalps, savage ambition, rights, liberties, constitution, violation, spoliation; brickbats, pokers, spits, toasting forks, broomsticks, cabbage stumps, rotten eggs; caps of liberty, flags, banners, death's heads and crossbones, union'.

Messrs. G—— and H—— seconded a resolution to the following effect—'Whigs, villains, monsters, hippopotami, salamanders, murderers, manglers and Muscovites; No faith, defiance, hatred, detestation, abhorrence, revenge; courage, union, order, peace, love; justifiable homicide, manslaughter for ever!'

Mr. L—— spoke in the following energetic manner—'England, glory, pride, power, debt, misery, starvation; bayonets, standing army, tithes, bloody Ghenghis Khan, Tamerlane, Barbarossa, Nero, Caligula, Marcius, Sylla, Brutus, Liberty, Fraternity, Equality, destruction, reformation, excitation, agitation, reservation, reason, light of nature, window taxes, taxes off candles, wheat a shilling a bushel, taxes off newspapers; Carlile, Hetherington, glass bottles, flint stones, smashification, blunderbusses, raw head and bloody bones, Terrific Register, daggers, fire, havoc, death or liberty; patience, petition, carbines, gunpowder, peace, fury, blood, obedience, revenge, party, slaughter, chaos, order, smoke'.

The views of the NUWC, according to Place

F. Place, B.M. Add. Mss. 27791, ff. 48–9, undated, probably about October 1831.

Everything which was produced belonged to those who by their labour produced it and ought to be shared among them, that there ought to be no accumulation of capital in the hands of anyone to enable him to employ others as labourers, and thus by becoming a *master* make slaves of others under the name of workmen . . . They denounced everyone who dissented from these notions as a *political economist*, under which appellation was included the notion of a bitter foe to the working classes, enemies who deserved no mercy at their hands . . . The whole body of the working people should on a day to be named cease to labour at any kind of employment for others, and refuse to be again employed for a month.

4d The National Political Union

Sir Francis Burdett, Bart., M.P., chairman; placard in Place, B.M. Add. Mss. 27791, f. 46, 31 October 1831.

This is not a Union of the Working Classes, nor of the Middle Classes, nor of any other Class, but of all Reformers, of the masses and of the millions.

The *National Political Union*, is essentially a Union of the People, and is the first instance on record of the Nation breaking through the trammels of class, to associate for the Common interest in a Common cause.

The first blessing of Reform therefore is already produced; among those who struggle for it, a brotherhood is established, and recurrence made to a manlier and more genuine intercourse between the Rich and the Poor.

If the People associate, the interests of the People must inevitably prosper: With the Reform Bill, which 199 Lords and Bishops have rejected, and with the preservation of peace and order, are the interests of the People bound up. If then the People associate, the Reform Bill, and all its happy consequences, cannot be denied them, nor can peace and order be infringed . . .

Whoever, then, is for Reform! for Reform, without Bristol Riots! for Reform, with all its benefits peacefully and therefore *certainly* attained! for Reform, in a word, with the People's House of Commons! let him enroll his name at the *Crown and Anchor Tavern*, Strand, in the *National Political Union*.

4e The NUWC and the NPU

The National Union of the Working Classes, reported in *Poor Man's Guardian*, 3 December 1831.

Mr. Watson:

. . . he proceeded to notice the announcement of a new publication called the *Union*. It was very strange this individual should put forward his reasons for uniting with the National Political Union. Could they not put them forward themselves? (hear). If they wanted our assistance why did they not come to us? (Cheers). We will unite with them, but on these conditions—Universal Suffrage, Vote by Ballot, and no Property Qualification. (Cheers) But, no they would have a union of their own, half of the council to be chosen from the working classes; but were they chosen here? No, but from individuals of their own union. And had they put forth their declaration of sentiments? No. They want representation, but for whom? Shopkeepers, not for the poor (Hear). But this writer wants us to merge into the Political Union. Should we do that, and leave ourselves slaves and stepping-stones to others? (No, no, and cheers).

4f The need for separate working-class unions

Arthur S. Wade, *Poor Man's Guardian*, 17 November 1832.

To Thomas Attwood, Esq., On the conduct of the Birmingham Political Council respecting the formation of a Midland Union of the Working Classes.

Sir—

In a newspaper report of the recent proceedings of the Council of the Birmingham Political Union, I perceive that some member of the Council asserted that . . . no sufficient reasons had been adduced for the formation of a Union of the Working Classes. It appeared to me that the reverse was the case; but that such a remark may not be urged in future, I will submit the five following reasons for the necessity of a Working Class Union—

1. Because the leaders in other Unions, being men of property living upon the rental of land, the interest of money, or the profits of trade, have separate and distinct interests from the working man: for example, he who lives on the rental of land has an interest opposed to the abolition of the corn laws, and the abolition of every other monopoly that would diminish his income; he who lives on the interest of money has a great predilection for paper schemes, bubble speculations, cheap productions, and depreciated labour; he who lives on the profits of trade has an interest in obtaining labour as cheap as possible and selling it at the dearest rate; and, as all of these individual interests are opposed to the best interests of the productive classes, I ask you are those persons so fit and proper to represent them as the working classes themselves?

2. That as the majority of those who have taken an active part in these unions are men of property, they have an interest in securing the representation of property rather than of human beings. As a proof of this, men of property, from time immemorial, have always secured the power to make laws, and always protected their own interests, reckless of the consequences; the effects of which you may this day

behold in the extreme wealth on the one hand, and the destitution and starvation of the artizans of your own town on the other.

3. Believing that the wretched condition of the working classes, especially in the manufacturing districts, is principally to be ascribed to the improvement and inventions which have superseded manual labour, and thereby forced the unemployed into competition for employment; and knowing that masters and capitalists have an interest in still further increasing the powers of wood and iron, if they can procure them cheaper than human labour, I think that they are not the most proper persons, either in or out of Parliament, to take into consideration a question with reference to the proper disposal of these powers so as to benefit the working classes.

4. Because they who move in a sphere above the working classes, or who consider themselves independent of useful labour, have an interest in securing for themselves, families, and connexions, places and situations in the army, navy, church and excise, and thus become identified with the aristocracy in increasing the public burthens, and, consequently, such persons are not fit to represent the interests of the working man.

5. Since there is sufficient intelligence amongst the working classes to discuss, too, questions connected with their best interests, and a growing disposition to acquire further knowledge, they ought to be free to communicate with their brethren on their rights and liberties, without being subject to the dictation or control of those persons whose interests are the reverse of their own. . . .

4g The middle-class radical platform

R. Detroisier in Place, B.M. Add. Mss. 27796, ff. 146–7, 11 July 1832.

The pledges suggested by the National Political Union, to test the suitability of parliamentary candidates.

I. *Parliamentary reform.* This includes

1. Shortening the duration of Parliaments.

2. Voting by Ballot. . . .

II. *Law reform.* This includes a thorough revision of all laws—common, statute, civil, criminal, ecclesiastical, local, parliamentary, and municipal . . .

III. *Financial reform.* This includes reduction of taxes to the greatest possible extent; reduction of all over-paid salaries and pensions, as well as payment of every kind, from the highest office in the state to the lowest; the total abolition of all sinecures, all useless offices, and all unearned pensions . . .

IV. *Trade reform.* This includes the abolition of ALL monopolies, and more especially the Corn Law monopoly; the free admission of all sorts of produce for manufacturers, and indeed of free trade in every respect . . .

V. *Church reform.* This includes—

1. Equalization to a great extent of the church establishment. Every dignitary of the church preaches poverty and wallows in wealth. Great wealth being condemned as incompatible with *the true* religion, none of its ministers should therefore be wealthy.

2. Ceasing to compel any one to pay for the maintenance of any particular doctrine he does not approve.

3. Abolition of tithes in the fairest way and in the shortest time possible.

VI. *Abolition of slavery.* This includes the freedom of every person, of every colour, and every shade of colour; holding of persons in slavery is UNJUST, atrocious, and cruel . . .

VII. *Taxes on knowledge.* These are the stamp duty on newspapers, the excise duty on paper, and the duty on advertisements . . .

4h Cold Bath Fields—a statement of grievances

Quoted in Place, B.M. Add. Mss. 27797, ff. 11–16.

A small group of men within the NUWC, led by Lee and Mee, who held Spencean ideas on property, called a public meeting at Cold Bath Fields in May 1833 to discuss a General Convention, or a people's parliament. Within minutes, they were charged by the police. In the scuffle, a policeman was stabbed to death, and some fifty people were wounded.

We therefore, the unrepresented classes of the Metropolis enumerate the most prominent of the evils under which we are now suffering.

1. Individual appropriation of the soil, which is the natural right of all; from whence arises that odious impost on the first necessary of life, the tax upon corn.

2. The law of Primogeniture, by which the spurious portion of society are fastened like leeches upon the industry of the country.

3. The Funding System which has created a thousand millions of debt and deluged the world with human blood.

4. Hereditary and exclusive legislation passed by a corrupt and selfish few which has produced and maintained among others the following National Curses.

I.	An Hereditary Monarchy, costing at least £3 million	per annum
II.	A Civil List of Male and Female Pensioners £1 million	do
III.	113 privy councillors costing £600,000	do
IV.	A Law Church Establishment costing £9 millions	do
V.	A Debt requiring for interest alone £35 millions	do
VI.	A Standing Army costing £7 millions	do

To these may be added Enclosure Laws—Mortmain Laws—Game Laws—Stamp Laws—Trespass Laws—Subletting Laws and Excise Laws—Empressment for Sailors—Tithe Exactions—with expensive erections of Palaces—Prisons—Churches—Barracks—Workhouses. Monopolies in Commerce—Monopolies in Trade—Taxes on Knowledge—Taxes on houses—Taxes on the light of heaven; with a thousand other fertile sources of oppression through the medium of indirect taxation on the labour and industry of the productive classes of the community.

4i Address of the London Working Men's Association

William Lovett, *Life and Struggles* (1876), 1967 edn, pp. 83–4.

In forming Working Men's Associations, we seek not a mere exhibition of numbers unless, indeed, they possess the attributes and character of *men*! and little worthy of the name are those who have no aspirations beyond mere sensual enjoyments, who, forgetful of their duties as fathers, husbands, and brothers, muddle their understandings and drown their intellect amid the drunken revelry of the pot-house—whose profligacy makes them the ready tools and victims of corruption or slaves of unprincipled governors, who connive at their folly and smile while they forge for themselves the fetters of liberty by their love of drink.

We doubt not that the excessive toil and misery to which the sons of labour are subject, in the absence of that knowledge and mental recreation which all just governments should seek to diffuse, are mainly instrumental in generating that intemperance, the debasing influence of which we perceive and deplore. But, friends, though we possess not the political power to begin our reformation at the source of the evil, we cannot doubt the efficacy of our exertions to check by precept and example this politically-debasing, soul-subduing vice.

Fellow-countrymen, *when we contend for an equality of political rights*, it is not in order to lop off an unjust tax or useless pension, or to get a transfer of wealth, power, or influence, for a party; *but to be able to probe our social evils to their source, and to apply effective remedies to prevent, instead of unjust laws to punish*. We shall meet with obstacles, disappointments and it may be with persecutions, in our pursuit; but with our united exertions and perseverance, we must and will succeed.

And if the teachers of temperance and preachers of morality would unite like us, and direct their attention to the *source* of the evil, instead of nibbling at the effects, and seldom speaking of the cause; then, indeed, instead of splendid palaces of intemperance daily erected, as if in mockery of their exertions—built on the ruins of happy home, despairing minds, and sickened hearts—we should soon have a sober, honest and reflecting people . . .

Who can foretell the great political and social advantages that must accrue from the wide extension of societies of this description acting up to their principles? Imagine the honest, sober and reflecting portion of every town and village in the kingdom linked together as a band of brothers, honestly resolved to investigate all subjects connected with their interests, and to prepare their minds to combat with the errors and enemies of society—setting an example of propriety to their neighbours, and enjoying even in poverty a happy home. And in proportion as home is made pleasant, by a cheerful and intelligent partner, by dutiful children, and by means of comfort, which their knowledge has enabled them to snatch from the ale-house, so are the bitters of life sweetened with happiness.

Think you a corrupt Government could perpetuate its exclusive and demoralizing influence amid a people thus united and instructed? Could a vicious aristocracy find its servile slaves to render homage to idleness and idolatry to the wealth too often fraudulently exacted from industry? Could the present gambling influences of money perpetuate the slavery of the millions, for the gains or dissipation of the few? Could corruption sit in the judgement seat—empty-headed importance in the senate-house—money-getting hypocrisy in the pulpit—and debauchery, fanaticism, poverty, and crime stalk triumphantly through the land—if the millions were educated in a knowledge of their rights? No, no, friends; and hence the efforts of the exclusive few to keep the people ignorant and divided. Be ours the task, then, to unite and instruct them; for be assured the good that is to be must be begun by ourselves.

The objects of the Association

ibid., pp. 76–7.

1. To draw into one bond of *unity* the *intelligent* and *influential* portion of the working classes in town and country.

2. To seek by every legal means to place all classes of society in possession of their equal political and social rights.

3. To devise every possible means, and to use every exertion, to remove those cruel laws that prevent the free circulation of thought through the medium of a *cheap and honest press*.

4. To promote, by all available means, the education of the rising generation, and the extirpation of those systems which tend to future slavery.

5. To collect every kind of information appertaining to the interests of the working classes in particular and society in general, especially statistics regarding the wages of labour, the habits and condition of the labourer, and all those causes that mainly contribute to the present state of things.

6. To meet and communicate with each other . . .

7. To publish their views and sentiments in such a form and manner as shall best serve to create a moral, reflecting, yet energetic public opinion; so as eventually to lead to a gradual improvement in the condition of the working classes, without violence or commotion.

8. To form a library of reference and useful information; to maintain a place where they can associate for mental improvement, and where their brethren from the country can meet with kindred minds actuated by one great motive—that of benefiting politically, socially, and morally, the useful classes. Though the persons forming this Association will be at all times disposed to co-operate with all those who seek to promote the happiness of the multitude, yet being convinced from experience that the division of interest in the various classes, in the present state of things, is too often destructive of that union of sentiment which is essential to the prosecution of any great object, they have resolved to confine their members as far as practicable to the working classes. But as there are great differences of opinion as to where the line should be drawn which separates the working classes from the other portions of society, they leave to the Members themselves to determine whether the candidate proposed is eligible to become a Member.

4j The LWMA demands reform

The Rotten House of Commons, an address from the London Working Men's Association, 1837.

Fellow-Countrymen,—Have you ever enquired how far a just and economical system of government, a code of wise and just laws, and the abolition of the useless persons and appendages of State, would affect the interests of the present 658 members of the House of Commons? . . .

Is the *Landholder*, whose interests lead him to keep up his rents by unjust and exclusive laws, a fit representative for working men?

Are the whole host of *Money-makers*, *Speculators*, and *Usurers*, who live on the corruptions of the system, fit representatives for the sons of labour?

Are the immense number of *Lords*, *Earls*, *Marquises*, *Knights*, *Baronets*, *Honourables*, and *Right Honourables*, who have seats in that house, fit to represent our interests? many of whom have the certainty before them of being the *hereditary legislators* of the other house, or are the craving expectants of place or emolument; persons who cringe in the gilded circle of a court, flutter among the gaieties of the ball-room, to court the passing smile of Royalty, or whine at the Ministers of the day; and when the interests of the people are at stake, in the Common, are often found the revelling debauchees of fashion, or the duelling wranglers of a gambling-house.

Are the multitude of *Military* and *Naval Officers* in the present House of Commons, whose interest it is to support that system which secures them their pay and promotion, and whose only utility, at any time, is to direct one portion of our brethren to keep the other in subjection, fit to represent our grievances?

Have we fit representatives in the multitude of *Barristers*, *Attorneys*, and *Solicitors*, most of them seeking places, and all of them having interests depending on the dissensions and corruptions of the people? . . .

Is the *Manufacturer* and *Capitalist*, whose exclusive monopoly of the combined powers of wood, iron, and steam enables them to cause the destitution of thousands, and who have an interest in forcing labour down to the minimum reward, fit to represent the interests of working men?

Is the *Master*, whose interest it is to purchase labour at the cheapest rate, a fit representative for the *Workman*, whose interest it is to get the most he can for his labour?

Yet such is the only description of persons composing that house, and such the interests represented, to whom we, session after session, address *our humble petitions*, and whom we in our ignorant simplicity imagine will generously sacrifice their hopes and interests by beginning the great work of political and social reformation.

Working men, inquire if this be not true, and then if you feel with us, stand apart from all projects, and refuse to be the tools of any party, who will not, as a *first and essential measure*, give to the working classes *equal political and social rights*, so that they may send their own representatives from the ranks of those who live by labour into that house, to deliberate and determine along with *all other interests*, that the interests of the labouring classes—of those who are the foundation of the social edifice—shall not be daily sacrificed to glut the extravagance of the pampered few. If you feel with us, then you will proclaim it in the workshop, preach it in your societies, publish it from town to village, from county to county, and from nation to nation, that there is no hope for the sons of toil, till those who feel with them, who sympathize with them, and whose interests are identified with theirs, have *an equal right to determine what laws shall be enacted or plans adopted for justly governing this country*.

5 The freedom of the press

From November 1816, when Cobbett dedicated his *Twopenny Trash* to the 'ragged radicals' (see above, p. 94), a working-class press was an essential part of the working-class protest. The *Black Dwarf* and the *Republican* joined the *Register* in lacerating aristocratic government with its taxes, pensions and sinecures (see above, p. 8). So in the Six Acts following Peterloo, the government limited what could be said in the popular press by tightening up the law of criminal libel (5a) and priced what could be said beyond the pockets of the poor, by maintaining a fourpenny stamp on newspapers and a stringent definition of what comprised a newspaper. The first of these controls, that of criminal libel, was challenged by Carlile during the 1820s. He and his shopmen were repeatedly imprisoned but survived on local subscription (5b) and local sellers. The second of these, the newspaper stamp, was challenged in the 1830s by the Unstamped, the illegal underground penny papers, headed by Hetherington and the *Poor Man's Guardian* (5c). These papers were fanned out from London and the NUWC to Land's End, Lancashire and Lowestoft, arguing the right of working men both to the vote and to the produce of their labour (see above, pp. 49 ff). Over a thousand people were imprisoned for selling the Unstamped, but ultimately their sales far surpassed those of the stamped press, and in 1836 the government reduced the duty to a penny, but strengthened its penal powers over the press.

A cheap press was now more accessible, but government retained control over what could be said and sold, and under prodding from the clergy, the 1840s saw a revival of prosecutions for blasphemy, in particular against Hetherington (5d), and the secularists Robert Southwell and G. J. Holyoake. Blasphemy, it was argued, dissolved the moral consensus which was society's cement.

Suggestions for further reading

For the earlier period, see W. Wickwar, *The Struggle for the freedom of the Press, 1819–1832* (1928); then, P. Hollis, *The Pauper Press* (1970), for the 1830s; and E. Royle's *Radical Politics 1790–1900, Religion and Unbelief* (1971), for the debate on blasphemy.

5a The Six Acts

60 G3 c.9

Whereas Pamphlets and printed Papers containing Observations upon Public Events and Occurrences, tending to excite Hatred and Contempt of the Government and Constitution of these Realms as by Law established, and also vilifying our holy Religion, have lately been published in great Numbers, and at very small Prices; and it is expedient that the same should be restrained . . .

Medusa, 1 January 1820.

Ministers may narrow the channel of information, but they cannot recall that stream of light which has been shed into every village, hamlet and workshop of the kingdom . . . The attempt to prevent the diffusion of political knowledge among the People, is merely the continuation of the war against liberty and knowledge which commenced with the French Revolution. Knowledge is the great instrument by which the rights of the People are to be acquired, and of course it is against this powerful engine all the efforts of tyranny are directed . . . All their efforts will prove abortive. An appetite has been created for information which must and will be satisfied.

Pamphlets and printing

Carlile to Hunt, *Republican*, 22 February 1822.

Be assured that it is pamphlet vending that is destined to work the great necessary moral and political change among mankind. The Printing Press may be strictly denominated a Multiplication Table, as applicable to the mind of man. The art of printing is a multiplication of mind . . . Pamphlet vendors are the most important springs in the machinery of Reform. See how they are persecuted: and yet you would denounce them as unworthy of the support of the public . . . We want more pamphlet vendors and fewer talkers in the cause of Reform . . .

5b Supporters of a free press

Some subscriptions from Halifax to Richard Carlile, *Republican*, 4 October 1822.

	s. d.
Not a lover of Oppression	0. 6.
Richard Brook, a Republican and Materialist	5. 0.
James Penny (Millbridge,) a Republican and Materialist	2. 6.
The honest Inquirer, J. G.	1. 0.
Benjamin Ormerod	5. 0.
A. Machan	2. 6.
One who dislikes Religious Persecution	5. 0.
J. S. an Enemy to all Priests, and not afraid of Devils	5. 0.
Thomas Hanson (Millbridge)	1. 0.
J. C. a well-wisher to your good cause	4. 0.
Joseph Binns	1. 0.
W. Hampson, a Free-thinker	1. 6.
An old Veteran	0. 6.
Henry Swin	1. 0.
J. J. a once deluded Fanatic	1. 0.
The existence of mind or soul independent of organization is a nonentity, however it may serve the purposes of Priestcraft, or a salvo for bigotted Tyranny	5. 0.
Old Ben Dalton	1. 0.
George Hurst	1. 0.
D. C. Common Sense	1. 0.
A Friend to Humanity	0. 6.
Geo. Row	0. 6.
Jos. Smith	1. 0.

	s. d.
James M'Lean	1. 0.
James Mills, The vermin that most annoy mankind, are Kings and Priests, and they that are with them joined	1. 0.
Geo. Johnson, a Friend to Reform	1. 0.
Joseph Cockin	0. 6.
J. Smith, and may the happy time soon arrive, when a majority of the British People shall prefer Truth to Falsehood, and pure Reason to baneful Fanaticism	1. 0.
J. C. Maculey, an open Deist	1. 6.
Richard Brown, (Lockwood)	1. 0.
James Brook, a Christian, but an hater of persecution	0. 6.
A Friend and Tinner	1. 0.
M. a Friend 6*d.* and Wm. Bowker 6*d.*	1. 0.
M. L. an Enemy to Tyranny and Oppression	2. 6.
Joseph G. a Friend to Reason	1. 0.

	s. d.
Thomas Fawcett, a Knaresborough Elector	1. 0.
A Friend to Truth	1. 0.
Micah Wright, once a Fanatic but now a Materialist	5. 0.
W. L. P. H.	2. 0.
William Willis 1*s.* and William Wilson 1*s.*	2. 0.
John Buckley, a Republican of Long Royd Bridge, a detester of Priestcraft from the high Church Dignitary, to the smooth-faced Hypocritical canting 'do put some money in the plate' Methodist Parson, in short a real disciple of Mirabaud	1. 0.
J. R. (A Churchwarden)	1. 0.
J. D. Rhodes, a Republican and Materialist	1. 0.
John Shaw, a Republican	1. 0.
W. H., a Philanthropist	2. 0.
J. R.	2. 6.
An Enemy to Persecution	1. 0.

5c The Unstamped press

Poor Man's Guardian, 30 July 1831.

WANTED

Some hundreds of POOR MEN out of employ, *who have* NOTHING TO RISK, some of those *unfortunate wretches* to whom DISTRESS has made a PRISON a desirable HOME.

An HONEST and moral way of finding *head* and *gaol shelter*, and moreover, of EARNING THE THANKS OF THEIR FELLOW COUNTRYMEN, now presents itself to such *patriotic* ENGLISHMEN as will, *in defiance* of the most ODIOUS 'LAWS' of a most ODIOUS TYRANNY, imposed upon an *enslaved* and *oppressed people*, to sell to the poor and the ignorant

THE POOR MAN'S GUARDIAN,

A Weekly 'Newspaper' for the People,
Published contrary to 'Law' to try the Power of 'Might against Right'. N.B. A subscription is opened for the *relief, support,* and *reward* of all such persons as may become VICTIMS of the *Whig Tyrants.*

Joshua Hobson of Huddersfield, 6 August 1833, reported in *Man,* 18 August 1833.

GENTLEMEN OF THE BENCH—I appear at your request, to state to you why I took upon myself to break what you are pleased to call the law. I was induced to publish the *Voice of the West Riding,* because a paper was wanted to support the rights and interests of the order and class to which it is my pride to belong, it being notorious that their just privileges were not only left unadvocated, but absolutely denied. The object of the paper was to teach the productive classes the means by which they might extricate themselves from their degraded state of thraldom, and place society upon a basis where every individual member of the social brotherhood should enjoy his just rights and no more. Its object was also the exposure and reformation of local as well as national abuse. To drag the tyrant and hypocrite from their den of infamy, and to show up the hideous monsters to the gaze and virtuous indignation of every good man in the community—to teach the sanctified knaves they could not with impunity practise those vices which they affect so loudly to condemn—to learn the oppressors of the poor that though they might for a time pass unnoticed, and be allowed to practise their unholy deeds unmolested, yet there was a point which they could not pass, when the Argus eyes of the great moral corrector should be directed upon them, and every movement and action of their lives watched and noted for adoption by others if virtuous, or rejection if vicious. I contend, further, that the printing and publishing such a paper, is not a violation of any moral principle, but, on the contrary, one of the most virtuous actions that man can do, that of doing good to his species.

5d Blasphemy

State Trials (new series), iv, cols 5670–9.

In 1840, Hetherington was prosecuted and imprisoned for selling *Haslam's Letters to the Clergy*, in which the Old Testament was denounced as immoral.

The Attorney General:
. . . As the law now stands, there can be no doubt that to assail with obloquy, and to insult the holy Scriptures of the Old and New Testament, which we believe to contain the revealed will of God, is a crime for which punishment may, and ought to be, inflicted. There are two grounds on which it seems to me that such an act may be properly made the subject of penal visitation. In the first place, it wounds and shocks the feelings of those who are entitled to the protection of the law, not only for their persons and property, but for everything belonging to them which contributes to their enjoyment and comfort. However, the great mischief of this act arises from its tendency to dissolve the foundation of the moral obligations on which society rests. The vast bulk of the population depend entirely on revelation; and, if a doubt could be raised among them that the Ten Commandments were given by God from Mount Sinai, men would think they were at liberty to steal, women would consider themselves absolved from the restraints of chastity . . . The civil magistrate is not to interfere with private opinion or with philosophical speculation; but he is called upon to repress what directly leads to crime, as much as to punish crime when actually committed. Now, gentlemen, can there be a doubt that in a Christian country the effect must be the most pernicious of a publication which, without investigation to be examined, or reasoning to be refuted, broadly asserts that the Bible is a compound of filth, blasphemy and nonsense; that its author was an idiot; and that it ought to be burned to prevent posterity from knowing that we believed in such abominable trash? . . .

What other course can be pursued? This is poison to which no antidote can be administered, and you can only strive to prevent its further distribution. What could a *Paley* or a *Watson* do against *C. J. Haslam*, if there be such a man in existence? The author of such a work does not reason, and cannot be reasoned with. He is to be punished, not refuted.

6 Parish radicalism

The parish was the primary unit of local government, and the vestry was its committee of management which levied the rate. The vestry was frequently corrupt and closed, so radicals who wished to cut back on the rate had first to control the vestry. They therefore worked for Hobhouse's Bill (passed in 1831) to permit all rate-payers to elect the members of the vestry. The Whigs backed Hobhouse's bill in return for support of their own reform bill, and so parish and parliamentary reform became inseparable (6a and 6b). Parish reformers entered the political unions and provided the parliamentary reform movement with its grass roots organization. With the passing of both bills, the parish radicals next attacked assessed taxes which fell particularly heavily on shopkeepers; despite some misgivings, the working-class radicals of the NUWC gave them their support (6c).

Suggestions for further reading

There is no full account, but see F. Sheppard, *Local Government in St. Marylebone, 1688–1835* (1958).

6a The Vestries Act and the Reform Act

J. Brooke, *The Democrats of Marylebone* (1839).

Amongst the most violent in favour of the Reform Bill were those who had been struggling for parochial representation . . . they were chiefly instrumental in convening the metropolitan meetings . . . for petitioning the House of Lords to pass the Reform Bill . . . The chief strength of the reform party lay amongst the small shopkeepers, the minor rate-payers and the Dissenters . . . In the parish of St. Marylebone, a parochial committee, appointed at a public meeting of the rate-payers, exercised a powerful influence among the parishioners . . . In St. Pancras too, a number of district public-house clubs, calling themselves parochial committees, held weekly meetings . . . These committees, assisted by the influential ultra local representatives, stood prominently forward on all great political questions, and thereby drew around them the discontented and turbulent political spirits of the locality . . .

The ultra-party had in fact assumed almost exclusively a political character in Marylebone, even prior to the passing of the Reform Act. Taking an active share in the political agitation of the period, the question of local taxation had become, in their view, magnified into one of national liberty. The complaints against the pressure of the poor rates had, in a great degree, given place to charges of despotism against the aristocracy, and thence to a demand from the Legislature for the rights of the people . . . The meetings held in favour of the Vestries Bill were . . . generally the very same persons who constituted the open air and other Reform Bill demonstrations . . . These men, therefore . . . had as much in view a political as a parochial object; indeed, the majority of the leaders of the ultra reform party were and are more notorious for their violence in politics than celebrated for their services in the management of parochial affairs.

6b The great procession

J. Powell's account, B.M. Add. Mss. 27790, ff. 39–47.

John Powell, a young clerk, took on board a Thames steamer a copy of the *Sun* of 8 October 1831 announcing the loss of the Reform Bill in the House of Lords.

When the paper with a black border was seen in my hand, the passengers rushed towards me, I was instantly mounted on a chair, and compelled to read the debate through from beginning to end . . . . A kind of meeting followed in which most of the persons declared their determination to return to town that evening, to stir in their respective parishes, and above all to pay no taxes unless measures were taken to carry an efficient Reform Bill . . .

Our first object was to visit leading reformers in the different parishes to suggest the matter [of a procession and petition] to them . . . We were successful and on Sunday night became assured that the proposal would be supported by many at several parish meetings on Monday and Tuesday . . . In Clerkenwell, my own parish . . . we were 10,000 strong . . . We had a large body from the parish of St. Mary Islington. In St. James Westminster and the adjoining parishes, we were after some difficulty successful . . . The southern parishes, the last of which was St. Mary Newington managed their own business in the same way . . . The most formidable part of the procession came perhaps from the parishes which create the great borough of Marylebone viz. Marylebone, Paddington and Pancras . . .

The numbers of the procession were variously estimated by the newspapers from 70,000 to 300,000 . . . No such things has occurred either before or since, for the class of persons comprising the procession were respectable house-keepers and superior artizans, the bone and muscle of a nation . . .

6c Assessed taxes, a cause for class co-operation?

The NUWC, reported in the *Poor Man's Guardian*, 2 November 1833.

Mr. Mee observed that a spirit of resistance had for a long time shown itself in many parts of London, and particularly in Marylebone, against the payment of the Assessed Taxes. It was for the meeting to consider if such resistance was justifiable and worthy of their countenance and support . . . Was it not a well known fact that throughout all the Metropolitan boroughs many persons had been disenfranchised because they had not paid those obnoxious rates? . . . This abominable tax was a barrier to the best class of house-keepers, the working shopkeeper, who approximated the closest to the character of an operative (hear) . . . Here, then, would be the benefits of the repeal of those rates; these honest men would be enabled to exercise their franchise, and he would wish to impress on the minds of every working man, that it was only from the class of shopkeepers he had just alluded to that the operative can hope peacefully to gain his rights, which were the rights of every man throughout the country; namely, universal suffrage, vote by ballot and no property qualification (cheers) . . . On the other hand, the working classes must endeavour to impress on the minds of the middle classes, who now sought their assistance, the necessity of their cooperation with us in our endeavours to procure justice for all. We have, and will assist them to procure their rights, and we have a right to expect their assistance to procure ours (hear) . . .

Mr. Jackson observed that the middle and working classes had combined to procure the Reform Bill for the benefit of the former. They were now called upon again to assist the shopkeeper to get rid of an unrighteous impost, the Assessed Taxes, and herein they would only be carrying out the principles of the Union—'All for Each and Each for All'. He trusted the shopkeeper would be guided by that maxim, as it could only be by the united endeavours of both these classes that the whole of the people could be peaceably invested with their rights in society . . . In fact, the middling classes would soon find that until they united with the working classes and procured universal suffrage, vote by ballot, and short parliaments, no relief would ever be obtained from the government (hear) . . .

Mr. Taylor was of opinion that the working classes ought not too readily come forward to assist the shopkeepers; the working classes had assisted them to gain the Reform Bill, but he was sorry to say they had not exhibited any wish to return them the favour. The middle class men, too, often make the working men their tools. The working men had been the sacrifice for their benefit, and he thought they ought to wait until the middle class applied to them, and not to be such serviles as to be at their beck and call whenever it might serve their purpose . . .

7 Co-operation, 1820–35

Owen taught (see above, p. 27) that working men did not receive the value of their labour because they were forced to sell it for a money wage, and that competition, or the working of the market, ensured that the money wage was an artificially low wage. His followers explored three methods of bypassing the market economy —the co-operative store, the labour exchange and the co-operative community. All of these sought to eradicate competition and the middle man who stood between working men as producers and working men as consumers.

In 1821, some printers led by George Mudie, started the Co-operative and Economical Society which sponsored an artisan community at Spa Fields (7a), several of whose members subsequently formed the First London Co-operative Society in 1824. In 1828 came the founding of the Brighton Co-operative Trading Society and by 1830 there were some 300 co-operative stores, co-ordinated by the British Association for the Promotion of Co-operative Knowledge (7b), buying food at wholesale price and saving the profits to promote communities. From there it was an obvious step to engage unemployed men to produce goods for the stores, and from that to a labour exchange (7c and 7d) to which men brought their goods and were paid in labour notes with which they purchased other goods. It caught up notions of the just price, the labour theory of value and self-employment; it meant the end of political parasites and competitive economics. Regular co-operative congresses, from 1831 to 1835, brought all these strands of Owenism together. The dignity this offered working men is poignantly illustrated in a letter to the *Crisis* (7e), the leading Owenite paper.

The labour exchange was to widen into the Grand National Consolidated Trades Union; and like political unions, co-operation as a method of class help was to recede before trades unionism.

Suggestions for further reading

See J. F. Harrison, *Robert Owen and the Owenites* (1969); S. Pollard, 'Nineteenth Century Co-operation', in A. Briggs and J. Saville (eds), *Essays in Labour History* (1959); S. Pollard and J. Salt (eds), *Robert Owen, prophet of the poor* (1971).

7a Co-operation at Spa Fields

The Economist, 1 December 1821.

Several families have taken possession of the [Co-operative and Economical] Society's premises in Spafields . . . The rooms are charged at from two shillings to four shillings per week each, including taxes, and including the use of the large dining-room, stores, kitchen, cellars etc. Many of the private apartments are large and handsome.

A scale for the expenses of living, according to the number in each family respectively, was also agreed upon . . . The congregating members had resolved on making one common stock of the whole of their several incomes; but it has been deemed expedient to depart from that arrangement . . . because . . . such a feature in the establishment might operate to prevent persons from joining the society, not yet prepared to act so extensively upon its principles. It is, however, finally resolved, that support shall be continued to the members during loss of employment and in sickness and old age, and that their families shall continue to receive all the benefits of the institution, in cases of the death of parents.

The scale of expenses for living is as follows:—

A man, his wife, and five children	£1. 2. 6*d*. per week.
. . . .	
one child	16. 3½*d*.
. . . .	
Single man	14. 5*d*.

. . . The fund so to be accumulated . . . will be applied in reduction of the scale of expenses for living, or in purchasing materials etc. for the employment of members within the society, or it will be equally divided amongst the members, as may from time to time be determined.

The produce of the industry of the children belongs to the society . . . The children are to sleep in general dormitories, and are to be under constant superintendence night and day. The greatest attention, of which the circumstances of the parents will admit, will be paid to their training and education.

The society can now execute orders in carving and gilding, and for boots, shoes, gentlemen's clothes, dress-making and millinery, umbrellas, hardware (including stoves, kettles etc.) cutlery, transparent landscape window-blinds, and provisions. All the articles will be furnished of the best qualities, according to price, which will be uniformly moderate. In a short time, schools will be opened . . . on very moderate terms.

7b The early co-operative movement

William Lovett, *Life and Struggles* (1876), pp. 33–7 in the 1967 edn.

I think it was about the close of the year 1828 that the first of those trading associations was established at Brighton . . . and its success was such that between four and five hundred similar associations were very soon established in different parts of the country. The members of those societies subscribed a small weekly sum for the raising of a common fund, with which they opened a general store, containing such articles of food, clothing, books etc. as were most in request among working men; the profits of which were added to the common stock. As their funds increased some of them employed their members; such as shoemakers, tailors, and other domestic trades: paying them journeymen's wages, and adding the profits to their funds. Many of them were also enabled by these means to raise sufficient capital to commence manufacturers on a small scale; such as broadcloths, silk, linen, and worsted goods, shoes, hats, cutlery, furniture etc. Some few months after I had given up my shop in May's Buildings, I was induced to accept the situation of storekeeper to the 'First London Association' . . . Like many others, I was sanguine that those associations formed the first step towards the social independence of the labouring classes, and I was disposed to exert all my energies to aid in the work. I was induced to believe that the gradual accumulation of capital by these means would enable the working classes to form themselves into joint stock associations of labour, by which (with industry, skill, and knowledge) they might ultimately have the trade, manufactures, and commerce of the country in their own hands . . .

. . . As our association was the first formed in London, it was looked up to for information and advice from all parts of the country. This, entailing much labour, led to the formation of another society, entitled 'The British Association for Promoting Cooperative Knowledge'. As also, several societies had commenced manufactures on a small scale, they were anxious for some depot, or place in London, where their productions might be deposited for sale to the public, or for exchange with one another. This desire induced the British Association to take a large house in 19, Greville Street, Hatton Garden, the first floor of which was fitted up as a cooperative bazaar, the lower portion being occupied by our First London Association . . .

. . . Those societies from the establishment of which so much had been expected, were, however, in the course of three or four years mostly all broken up, and with them the British Association. The chief, or, at the least, the most prominent causes of their failure were religious differences, [with Mr. Owen,] the want of legal security, and the dislike which the women had to confine their dealings to one shop. . . . When Mr. Owen first came over from America he looked somewhat coolly on those 'Trading Associations', and very candidly declared that their mere buying and selling formed no part of his grand 'co-operative scheme'; but when he found that great numbers among them were disposed to entertain many of his views, he took them more in favour, and ultimately took an active part among them . . .

I am satisfied . . . that much good resulted from the formation of those co-operative trading associations, notwithstanding their failure. Their being able to purchase pure and unadulterated articles of food; their manufacturing and exchanging with one another various articles which they were induced to make up in their leisure hours, or when out of employment; the mental and moral improvement derived from their various meetings and discussions, were among the advantages that resulted from them.

G. Skene, secretary of the BAPCK, in the *Cooperator*, 22 February 1830.

The grand aim of cooperative societies is *not* to combine to raise the wages of its members by buying at wholesale prices and selling the same for ready money . . . but, on the contrary, to raise a capital sufficient to purchase and cultivate land and establish manufactories of such goods as the members can produce for themselves, and to exchange for the production of others; likewise to form a community, thereby giving equal rights and privileges to all.

7c Mutual exchange

Crisis, 30 June 1832.

Now hundreds of thousands of persons of *all* the various trades in existence, rise each morning without knowing how or where to procure employment. They can EACH produce MORE than they have occasion for themselves, and they are EACH IN WANT OF EACH OTHER'S SURPLUS PRODUCE . . . the tailor being in want of shoes, the tinman in need of clothes etc. etc. The usual course . . . has been to convert their stock into money, by disposing of it to a money-lender, or middle-man, and then exchanging this money for the articles they may require, either with the producer, or most generally to another middle man . . . thus being entirely dependent on the middle-man—who always obtains a profit by retaining a part of the produce for himself . . . Now there is no necessity for this middle-man, producers can do without him—they merely want to come in contact with each other, and they can exchange their respective produce to their mutual advantage . . . They have only to fix upon a place where all their surplus produce can be deposited, to be exchanged for produce of a similar value . . . This system is not only applicable to individuals but to [Co-operative Societies] . . . It should embrace *all* the various species of manufacture . . . so that there should be no necessity to have recourse to any but their own market for anything they may require . . .

The end of competitive economics

B. Warden, *Poor Man's Guardian*, 10 March 1832.

Sir,

. . . I hope a mighty revolution will soon take place in the moral and physical condition of the *only* useful classes in Society by the *universal* establishment of Labour Exchanges in which the producers will have money . . . of their own in the shape of Labour Notes. If the working classes have a grain of sense they will look to this subject . . . they will then in reality work for themselves, for if the rich and idle will have carriages, they must pay the men who really make these things, and not the master. In the Labour Exchange no *profit* can be made on the labour of the journeyman. Here no competition can enter . . . Let the gardener, the agriculturist, and the butcher begin to unite with their fellow workmen in forming Co-operative *Employment* Societies. Let them Exchange rather than sell the produce of Labour, and then the haughty aristocrat will soon be obliged to feel that those who are idle are indeed the most dependent and useless class in the community . . .

Exclusive dealing and the GNCTU

Crisis, 19 April 1834.

The best means of creating a new market for the productions of useful industry, [is] by enabling the working classes themselves to be *consumers* . . . as well as *producers*. This can only be done by their forming arrangements to prevent the profits of their toil from going out of the circle of the productive classes into that of the unproductive classes. For this end, each Trade Society must open shops and offices for dealing with each, and profitably employing their unemployed: no Unionist to lay out his money at any other places but these, for all the articles they can supply. Provisions being the first thing needful, let the Bakers Union open shops . . . butchers shops . . . gardeners, cheesemongers, and other provision dealers. The tailors and shoemakers . . . may also open shops for the sale of their articles in the same manner . . . By these means the producers of real wealth will be enabled to keep the greater part of the circulating medium in their own hands . . . The industrious classes will then become what they ought to be, namely, a distinct people from the idle and useless . . .

7d Stores and societies

Co-operative congress at Liverpool, reported in *Crisis*, 27 October 1832.

Mr. Pare of Birmingham . . .

Exchanges . . . were now beginning to be much facilitated by the issue of labour exchange notes, and the establishment of Equitable Labour Exchange Banks . . . The workmen delivered their goods at the store, and received in exchange notes, calculated from the value of one hour's labour, which was taken at sixpence and upwards, including the cost of the raw materials, and with these notes he could procure an equal value of other commodities of which he might be in want, from the store where all sorts of goods were displayed, with their price in labour and materials ticketed upon them, and the consequence was that they were no longer obliged to wait till some second party got money enough to pay for the goods, but deposited them, and received their value at once in exchange goods . . . The co-operative system was thus calculated to embrace the whole of society, and there was no doubt that if properly followed up it would produce the best effects on all classes. (Loud applause) . . .

Mr. Wilson, a delegate from Halifax, stated that in May 1829, he and eight other persons laid down a shilling each, and with this nine shillings, and £5 lent by his brother, they commenced business in a small room in a back entry. Their numbers had increased; they now occupied a large shop at £27 per annum rent, and were now worth £240, and had begun to find labour for some of their members (Hear, hear). Sixteen other societies had commenced since then in the neighbourhood . . .

Mr. Carson observed that . . . at Lamborough Green, in this county, a place so noted for vice and immorality, that it was hardly safe for a respectable man or woman to go there at any time, one of these societies had been established, and within two or three months they had a well-stocked shop, a school and reading rooms, and instead of going to the public house at night to fight and drink, they went to the reading room, and as they got power, acquired the knowledge which enabled them to use it properly. (Applause) . . . There were now not fewer than 700 societies of this nature throughout the country, and they were daily increasing. At Brighton, there was a female co-operative society, consisting of milliners and satin-stick makers, who had clubbed together and got a shop of their own, at which, when any of them were out of employ they went and worked at baby-linen and other articles, thus preserving themselves from penury and want, and the temptation to crime arising from those evils (Hear, hear). Co-operative societies were formed to redeem working men from a state little better than slavery;—the only difference between the masters and men was capital, and the men having the knowledge and the means had now found out that they could produce capital . . . The workmen were now creating wealth for themselves, and the means of exchanging it . . . Goods were now being brought to the Labour Exchange in London in wagon loads; upwards of 250 shops had already bills in the window, saying 'Equitable Exchange notes taken here,'—and even the bills at some of the play houses had at the bottom of them this notice, 'Mr. Owen's notes received here'. (Hear, hear).

Mr. Edmund Taylor, the representative of a society of 3,000 members at Bickacre, stated that a very few months ago, the first pound was laid down towards an establishment which now rented green fields, orchards, etc. to the amount of £600 per annum, besides a muslin and silk printing concern. They had two printing machines, and between fifty and sixty printing tables, which would soon be in full operation; they had between thirty and forty journeymen calico printers constantly at work, and were beginning to enjoy comforts and advantages to which they had hitherto been strangers. (Hear, hear) . . .

7e The impact of Owen

Crisis, 17 May 1832.

A letter from H. D. of Islington.

I am a poor man, Mr. Owen, and hitherto have been a most discontented one. From the hour in which I first reflected on the comparative misery of my own fate, with that of the rich and great, I have been dissatisfied . . . envious of their comforts and unmindful of my own . . . When the painted and gorgeous carriage of the higher orders has whirled by me at the corner of the street, dashing the dirt of its wheels in the face of a poor weary man, proud even in his adversity, I will own to you that I have cursed its possessor in my heart, with a double loathing at the thought of my own wretched home, my coarse and scanty meal, my coarse and stained apparel . . . The change my whole being has undergone since I heard you, most respected Sir, advocate the people's cause, and teach him the heart-reviving lesson, *TO RESPECT HIMSELF* . . .

As I walked from the doors of the institution on the days of the Congress there, a noble pride swelled within me, for I had heard from some of the mouths of the labouring and neglected classes, arguments and sentiments that would have done honour to both Houses of Parliament. I said within myself 'And I also am of this order of society; I am no drone to eat the honey of the hive, and contribute nothing to this store'. I feel my own importance, and that I am equally a man with him who turns his head haughtily away, with contemptuous frowns as I civilly make way for him, and who thinks himself my superior because he wears a finer coat than mine—chance ushered him into the world in the castle of a nobleman, whilst I, (as unconscious as himself) first drew my breath in the hovel of a labourer . . .

8 Trades unionism 1825–40: the wage question

Trades unionism meant two things after the repeal of the Combination Acts—the attempt to maintain and occasionally to advance wages; and the campaign to limit the hours of factory children (and therefore of adults), the Short Time movement (see below, section 9).

The *Trades Newspaper* was founded in 1825 to fight any attempt to re-impose the Combination Acts; it repeatedly argued that only union would stop wages from being cut whenever there was surplus labour (8a). The first wave of unionism came as the slump of 1826 receded. John Doherty (1799–1854), an Irish cotton spinner, organized the Lancashire spinners in 1829, and took them into a general union with other trades, the National Association for the Protection of Labour, in 1830 (8b). It survived until 1832.

The second wave of unionism came in 1832–4. William Benbow, a London bookseller and veteran of the years of Peterloo, publicized a Grand National Holiday, or general strike (8c), which would bring the non-producers to their knees. It entered Chartist strategy. In Birmingham, the Builders' Union developed an elaborate federated and hierarchical structure (8d) with which to resist new methods of employment, and under Owen's influence its paper, the *Pioneer*, systematically advocated industrial syndicalism as the most certain way of winning working-class rights. Political agitation, in the style of the *Poor Man's Guardian*, it thought was futile (8e). In the Midlands, masters tried to smash the unions by imposing 'the document' on their workers, forcing them to renounce their union. In Derby this led (8f) to a protracted and bitter lock-out during the winter of 1833. The masters' views were widely shared by middle-class commentators (8g). Meanwhile in London the emergence of the GNCTU brought co-operative techniques to trades union demands; lock-outs and strikes could and should be sustained by co-operative stores, self-employment and moral improvement (8h and i). In the face of the masters' hostility, it lasted less than a year. The harshest attack on unionism was the trial and transportation of the Dorchester labourers in April 1834. George Loveless in his account (8j) showed how the traditional bonds of the rural economy were being broken by capitalist farming on the one side, and dissent on the other; he and his fellow unionists had quite deliberately adopted proletarian weapons.

The third outburst of trades unionism came at the end of the 1830s with a series of strikes, by engineers, typefounders and then by the Glasgow cotton spinners, which was notorious for its violence (8k and l). A select committee investigated the outrages of unionism, and in his evidence, Doherty emphasized that unions were primarily defensive and turned to strikes only in desperation (8m). Frederick Engels, colleague of Marx, surveying working-class activity in 1844, pointed out that power remained firmly with the masters (8n) but that the masters were right to suspect trades unionism as dangerous to their society.

Suggestions for further reading

See G. D. H. Cole, *Attempts at General Union, 1818–1834* (1953); W. Oliver, 'The GNCTU of 1834', *Economic History Review*, 1964; and in general, S. and B. Webb, *A History of Trade Unionism* (1894).

8a The need for union

W. Longson, *Trades Newspaper*, 30 October 1825.

When two or three employers out of fifty—(and it can be no libel on the human character to suppose three bad in fifty)—I say, that when these two or three reduce workmen's wages, they can and will undersell all the others:—those others perceive the means whereby they are undersold: well, the price of the whole of their manufactured foods is depreciated in the same proportion that those two or three have enabled themselves to reduce their goods by defrauding the workmen of a portion of their wages. All the well-disposed masters are thus obliged to reduce wages in their own defence. The unprincipled again reduce wages, which again lays the whole of the masters under the same necessity as before of a general reduction. Now, it is evident, that to counteract the source of all this mischief, it is not necessary that there be a union of workmen to oppose the whole of the masters; but to leave the employ of a few unprincipled ones, who cause, or force the others to reduce. . . A few, or even the whole operatives, employed by any of these *grinding masters*, cannot, by leaving his employ, oblige him to be contented with the general rate of profits, because in every trade there is a redundancy of hands; and from the redundancy these masters can immediately obtain workmen in the place of those who refuse the wages he offers. So that those who would contend with such oppressors, have no alternative but submission or starvation, unless they be in Union.

When a master will withhold from his workmen, from 20 to 30 per cent of the wages paid by other masters, for the same labour, will any man have the hardihood to face me down, that the workmen ought to be compelled and starved into submission to this barefaced robbery? Were some of these petty tyrants to hold a dagger's point against a workman's breast, and compel him, by a menace of instant death, to sell his labour upon such terms, everybody would call it a robbery: but is not hunger as sharp and dreadful an instrument of death as a dagger? . . . Surely he that will have more profits than others by defrauding the hireling of his wages, ought not to have the power of starving his men into such unjust, degrading, and ruinous submission. And there is no other way of depriving him of this destructive power, but by other workmen supporting his, till he consent to pay the common rate of wages . . .

8b Doherty and general union

Doherty's *United Trades Co-operative Journal*, 21 August 1830.

General Union—a call to the operative spinners of Manchester.

It is vain, it is childish for men to complain of the consequences of reducing wages, so long as they do not attempt to apply a remedy to the evil. What does it avail to denounce and reprobate an employer as an unprincipled and greedy tyrant while you do not attempt to check his wicked career. Singly and alone the workman cannot be a match for his employer, but united and supported by thousands of his fellow-labourers he is much more than a match for them. This then is the means by which the working classes may yet save themselves from all the horrid consequences of poverty, pauperism, ignorance and crime. It is by Union only that you can hope to stand . . . The law allows you to unite.

The National Association for the Protection of Labour

United Trades Co-operative Journal, 10 July 1830.

Agreed to by the meeting of Delegates held in Manchester . . . on the 28th, 29th and 30th June, 1830.
Resolved 1. That the miserable conditions to which, by repeated and unnecessary reductions of wages, the working people of this country are reduced, urges upon this meeting the imperative necessity of adopting some effectual means for preventing such reductions and securing to the industrious workman a just and adequate remuneration for his labour.

2. That to accomplish this necessary object a Society shall be formed consisting of the various organized Trades throughout the kingdom.

3. That this Society be called 'The National Association for the Protection of Labour'.

4. That the funds of this Society shall be applied only to prevent

reductions of wages, but in no case to procure an advance. Any trade considering their wages too low may exert themselves to obtain such advance, as they may think necessary and can obtain it by their own exertions.

8c The Grand National Holiday

William Benbow, *Grand National Holiday, and Congress of the Productive Classes* (1832).

We are the people, our business is with the people, and to transact it properly, we must take it into our own hands. The people are called upon to work for themselves! . . . We chalk down to them a plan; woe to them if they do not follow in its traces!

The holiday signifies a *holy* day, and ours is to be of holy days the most holy . . . Our holy day is established to establish plenty, to abolish want, to render all men equal! In our holy day we shall legislate for all mankind; the constitution drawn up during our holiday, shall place every human being on the same footing. Equal rights, equal liberties, equal enjoyments, equal toil, equal respect, equal share of production: this is the object of our holy day—of our sacred day—of our festival! . . .

The grounds and necessities of our having a month's Holiday, arise from the circumstances in which we are placed, we are oppressed in the fullest sense of the word; we have been deprived of every thing; we have no property, no wealth, and our labour is of no use to us, since what it produces goes into the hands of others. We have tried everything but our own efforts . . . Our Lords and Masters have proposed no plan that we can adopt; they contradict themselves, even upon what they name the source of our misery. One says one thing, another says another thing. One scoundrel, one sacrilegious blasphemous scoundrel, says 'that over-production is the cause of our wretchedness'. Over-production, indeed! when we half-starving producers cannot, with all our toil, obtain anything like a sufficiency of produce. It is the first time, that in any age or country, save our own, *abundance* was adduced as a cause of want. Good God! where is this abundance? Abundance of food! ask the labourer and mechanic where they find it. Their emaciated frame is the best answer. Abundance of clothing! the nakedness, the shivering, the asthmas, the colds and rheumatisms of the people, are proofs of the abundance of clothing! Our Lords and Masters tell us we produce too much; very well then, we shall cease from producing for one month, and thus put into practice the theory of our Lords and Masters.

Over-population, our Lords and Masters say, is another cause of our misery. They mean by this, that the resources of the country are inadequate to its population. We must prove the contrary, and during a holiday take a census of the people, and a measurement of the land, and see upon calculation, whether it be not an unequal distribution, and a bad management of the land, that make our Lords and Masters say, that there are too many of us. Here are two strong grounds for our Holiday; for a CONGRESS of the working classes . . .

We shall then by our consultations, deliberations, discussions, holiday and congress, endeavour to establish the happiness of the *immense majority* of the human race, of that far *largest* portion called the *working classes*. What the few have done for themselves, cannot the many do for themselves? Unquestionably . . .

Committees of management of the working classes must be forthwith formed in every city, town, village and parish throughout the United Kingdom. . . They must call frequent meetings, and shew the necessity and object of the holiday . . .

We suppose that the people are able to provide provisions and funds for one week; during this week they will be enabled to enquire into the funds of their respective cities, towns, villages and parishes, and to adopt means of having those funds, originally destined for their benefit, now applied to that purpose . . .

When all the details of the above plan are put into execution, the committee of each parish and district, shall select its wise men to be sent to the National Congress . . .

The object of the Congress: that is what it will have to do. To reform society, for 'from the crown of our head to the sole of our foot, there is no soundness in us'. We must cut out the rottenness in order to become sound. Let us see what is rotten. Every man that does not work is rotten; he must be made to work in order to cure his unsoundness. Not only is society rotten; but the land, property, and capital is rotting. There is not only something, but a great deal rotten in the state of England . . .

8d The Operative Builders' Union

Pioneer, 21 September 1833.

The Union was founded in Manchester in 1831 as a federation of associated building trades to fight the new methods of contracting which interposed a middleman contractor between employer and journeyman. In 1833 it was infiltrated by Owenite ideas on co-operation and education. At its height it was 40,000 strong.

The service and deplorable condition to which the producers of wealth, throughout Great Britain and Ireland, have been reduced by competition with machinery and with each other, and the utter impossibility of any permanent improvement being effected for their benefit while this competition shall be permitted to be continued; have elicited the following proposals, as a certain, speedy, and effectual mode of giving a new direction to the industry of the building classes, and as a means of placing them and their children, and their children's children, in a state of permanent independence.

UNION

To the United Working Builders of Great Britain and Ireland

Proposals for the Establishment of a National Association for Building, to be called 'THE GRAND NATIONAL GUILD OF BUILDERS:' *to be composed of Architects and Surveyors, Masons, Carpenters and Joiners, Bricklayers, Plasterers, Slaters, Plumbers, Glaziers, and Painters, Whitesmiths, Quarry-men, and Brickmakers.*

OBJECTS OF THE UNION.

1. The general improvement of all the individuals forming the building class; insuring regular employment for all.
2. To ensure fair remuneration for their services.
3. To fix a reasonable time for labour.
4. To educate both adults and children.

5. To have regular superior medical advice and assistance, and to make provision for the comfortable and independent retirement of the aged and infirm.

6. To regulate the operations of the whole in harmony, and to produce a general fund sufficient to secure all these objects.

7. To insure a superiority of building for the public at fair and equitable prices.

8. To obtain good and comforable dwellings for every member of the Union; extensive and well-arranged workshops; places of depot for building materials; provisions and clothing; halls for the meeting of the Lodges and Central Committees; schools and academies for the instruction of adults and children in morals and the useful sciences.

9. And also the establishment of Builders' Banks in the various districts in which the Grand District Lodges shall be established.

MEANS OF EFFECTING THE OBJECTS OF THE UNION

Capital at least £15,000 in one or more shares of 5s. from each member of the Union, already sufficient in numbers to effect these objects.

1. Each class of the builders to be composed of men who have served five years' apprenticeship, and are above eighteen years of age . . .

2. . . . The Lodges to meet weekly.

3. The *Local Lodges* to elect their Central Committee of local management. The Central Local Committees to superintend the building business of their localities, and to sit daily.

4. Ten Central Committees to constitute a DISTRICT. Two delegates from Central Committee to form a District Committee . . . The District Committees to meet quarterly, to receive the reports of the Local Central Committee, regulate the proceedings, and audit the accounts of the district.

5. Each *District Committee* to elect a delegate to form a GRAND NATIONAL COMMITTEE in London. . . The Grand National Committee to meet annually, to deliberate and decide upon the general interests of the union.

8e The argument for syndicalism

Pioneer, 28 December 1833; 31 May 1834.

And since we know that no government can be founded in right, except it be representative of the interest it is established to govern, and composed of parties thoroughly understanding the interests of the governed, we of the LABOURER'S INTEREST, feel assured that a government working in any degree of perfection for our good, must be composed of men who either labour themselves, or have laboured—who legislate solely for labour—THE BASIS OF SOCIETY . . .

In virtue of these conclusions, we have determined that REFORM shall commence from within. . . . We feel that to regulate trade, or the several branches of labour by which we live, will most speedily regulate government. These are the 'means' we adopt for the 'end' and we hold them to be more powerful than petitioning . . .

Every trade has its internal government in every town; a certain number of towns comprise a district, and delegates from the districts form the Annual Parliament; and the King of England becomes President of the Trades Unions!

Universal suffrage is the fundamental principle of a trade union, where every brother is understood to have a voice in the management of the common affairs of the trade. But it is a universal suffrage which begins with the elements of government, and not, like the democratic principle of the *Guardian* and his friends, with the universal business of political legislation. If the populace of this country were fully enlightened upon every subject of political economy, or even if they were possessed of general knowledge and practical experience in the management of complex business, we should think it high time to claim on their behalf an immediate participation in the government of state affairs; but we are at present so miserably divided in opinion upon some of the most simple and elementary principles of politics and morality, that it is utterly impossible that unanimity of counsel in general politics could be secured by an appeal to the voice of the people.

. . . Their eyes are so short-sighted that they look only to partial release—the diminution of taxation, the separation of church and state, the revision of the pension list, and such other milk-and-water favours; and, when they have received these boons, pray where are they? Is the power of private capital and monopoly in any wise impaired? Is the system of commercial competition paralysed? And finally have the working classes obtained any practical knowledge by merely scrutinizing the measures of government and dictating to their representatives in Parliament? No, none of these objects are gained. There is only one way of gaining them, and that is by a general association of the people for the purpose of initiating themselves into the practice of conducting those affairs in which they HAVE SOME EXPERIENCE. The Unions are of all other modes the only mode by which universal suffrage can safely be obtained, because it is obtained by practise, or in the language of the trade, by apprenticeship. Nothing but experience can conduct any system of policy with success, and experience of government is better acquired by commencing with the management of simple business in which we are skilled by partial experience, than in launching into an ocean of business without a chart to guide or a gale of wind to lend us an impulse.

We conceive that it is a very difficult thing so to organize the people as to make them act with unanimity upon the single subject of labour and trade . . . Beside such is our opinion of the growing power and intelligence of a Trade Union, that we are thoroughly convinced that, when it is sufficiently organized and conducted in an orderly and business-like manner, it will gradually draw into its vortex all the commercial interest of the country, and, in so doing, it will become by its own self-acquired importance, a most influential, we might almost say dictatorial, part of the body politic. When this happens, we have gained all that we want: we have gained universal suffrage; for if every member of the Union be a constituent, and the Union itself becomes a vital and influential member of the state, it instantly erects itself into a House of Trades, which must supply the place of the present House of Commons, and direct the commercial affairs of the country, according to the will of the trades who compose the associations of industry.

This is the ascendency scale by which we arrive to universal suffrage. Our sanguine and enthusiastic friends of the old republican school, however, expect it to come down as a favour from the legislators, to be granted to our humiliating and degrading intercession, or petition, or extorted by our thundering or blustering threats. We expect no such thing, or if even it come in this way, it is not the present generation that shall witness the concession. And when it is made the people have just to begin and serve the apprenticeship of Trades Unions in order to qualify themselves for action; and while they are under training for government, they will consign the affairs of the country into the hands of a few who will merely treat them as they are now served by the reigning oligarchy. The difference between our mode of obtaining universal suffrage and the old radical model is that ours is gained in a noble and independent manner, without any fawning, crouching, humbling, petitioning, and praying, nay without even a threat or an angry word; the other is got by condescending to the most abject prostration of spirit; and when it is got we must take just the very steps we are now taking, that is, to unite the working men and teach them to manage individual trades. . . We are practical men; that is, we advocate the system of training men by practise as well as theory; whereas the republican system is the advocate of mere theory only; a system which involves the working man in all the mazes of political economy, without giving him an opportunity of exerting his bodily activity in the management of that productive industry which is the basis of all national wealth, and of all individual happiness . . . we adopt the system of the division of labour . . . The Trade Union system of the division of labour brought to bear upon the great field of social policy; the old republican system is the old-fashioned Jack-of-all-trades system which would make every man Jack of all trades and master of none . . .

8f The Derby turn-out

Pioneer, 14 December 1833.

At a meeting of the Masters and Manufacturers, held at the King's Head Inn, Derby, on Monday, the 25th of November, 1933,

It was resolved,

That this meeting acknowledges the right of workmen to give or withhold their labour, and asserts the equal right of masters to give or withhold employment; and that, when workmen unite to impose terms upon their employers, the latter must either submit to that dictation or resist it by a similar union.

That experience at Leeds, Manchester, Sheffield, Huddersfield, Wakefield, Leicester, and Liverpool, has proved that the principles of the Trades' Union are injurious to the interests of the masters, by putting a stop to their several trades; to the commerce of the country, by the suspension of work, and consequent inability to execute domestic or foreign orders; and ultimately to the members themselves.

That, to regulate the price and hours of labour, to abolish piece-work, and to substitute day-work in lieu of it (thus placing the industrious and skilful upon the same level with the idle and unskilful workmen); to dictate to the masters whom they shall or shall not employ, and the number of apprentices or learners they shall be allowed to take; and, in case of disobedience to the mandate of the Union, to withdraw his work-people simultaneously from the service of the party disobeying, and prevent any other workmen from entering his employ; are notoriously the objects and practice of the Trades' Union.

That these objects have not only been unequivocally displayed by acts in the towns above referred to, and by similar proceedings in other places, but are avowed and advocated in the *Pioneer, or Trades' Union Magazine*.

That the members of the Union are bound by a secret oath, and their admission is accompanied by mystical ceremonies, calculated and designed to impose upon and overawe the minds of credulous and unsuspecting men, and render them the unconscious slaves and ready tools of their more crafty leaders.

That the Derby Branch of the Trades' Union is yet in its infancy, but that its principles and objects are identical with those exhibited in other towns; and some of its members have not hesitated to declare that they are only waiting until the increase of its numbers and the augmentation of its funds shall enable it to act with more decisive effect.

That, as great numbers of the workmen in Derby have joined the Trades' Union, with a view to control their employers, and for purposes which the latter believe to be destructive to their interests and utterly subversive of that free agency which the Unionists claim for themselves, those employers are compelled by necessity to unite in their own defence, and do now resolve, unanimously,

That each of them will immediately cease to employ every man who is a member of the Trades' Union, and will not receive or take back into his service any man who continues to be a member of that Union, or of any other Union having similar objects.

That this resolution is adopted on the deliberate conviction that a prompt, vigorous, and persevering resistance to the Trades' Union is absolutely necessary, to protect the just rights of the masters, to preserve the commerce of the country, and to secure the true interests of the workmen themselves.

THOMAS BRIDGETT & CO.
BODEN & MORLEY
WRIGHT & BAKER
WILLIAM TAYLOR
JOHN JOHNSON
S. J. WRIGHT
JOSEPH HALL
ROBERT WARD
JOSEPH COOPER & SON
JOHN ADIN
RALPH FROST
J. & C. S. PEET
WILLIAM FROST
JOSEPH GASCOYNE
THOMAS COOPER
WILLIAM MOSEDALE
RICHARD MACCONNEL
ED. FALCONER
THOS. TUNALEY, JUN.
JOHN RAWLINS

8g From the other side

Blackwood's Edinburgh Magazine, March 1834.

Let us not deceive ourselves; the great contest between the working classes and their employers, between capital and numbers . . . is approaching, and cannot be averted. [The] . . . Reform Bill has rendered it inevitable. . . . It is the sense, the bitter and universal sense of this deception of which they have been the victims, which has produced the present general spread of Trades' Unions; in other words, of immense association of working men, to obtain, by a simultaneous strike over all parts of the country, and the terror which the display of physical strength can hardly fail to produce, those extraordinary practical advantages which the general condition of the labour market will not permit them to obtain, but which were falsely held out to them as the immense boon which they would certainly obtain by the change in the Constitution of Parliament.

E. Tufnell, *The Character, Object and Effects of Trades Unions* (1834), pp. 105, 125.

[Unions] are alike hurtful to the workmen, who form them; to the capitalists, who are the object of their hostility, and to the public in general, who more remotely feel their effects . . . Were we asked to give a definition of a Trade Union, we should say it was a Society whose constitution is the worst of democracies—whose power is based on outrage—whose practice is tyranny—and whose end is self-destruction.

8h The founding of the GNCTU: resolutions of a conference held in London, 13–19 February 1834

Pioneer, 8 March 1834.

The GNCTU developed out of the trade groups which had organized themselves around the Labour Exchange, and it enrolled those artisans, particularly the tailors, who were trying to 'equalize' the conditions between the honourable and dishonourable portions of the trade (8i). At its height it was some 11,000 strong in London, 16,000 strong in the provinces; but several major unions, including the builders, were suspicious of Owen's conciliatory attitude towards the masters and refused to join; and after a series of unsuccessful strikes had drained its resources, the GNCTU collapsed in summer 1834.

The paramount necessity of a unity of action by the Unions, on well-defined plans, is rendered evident by the state of our brethren in Derby, . . . It must be a matter of deep regret to all of us that no arrangements have yet been made, calculated for the permanent profitable employment of turned-out operatives of that place: as it appears to this committee that, had the Unions been consolidated, they would have placed those men ere this, by one simultaneous movement, beyond the reach of their merciless oppressors. . . .

But in the isolated state in which the Unions at present remain, not one of them can depend with certainty upon the efficient aids of the other, in any great struggle in which they may be compelled to engage by the blind opposition of their employer.—It is only by a concentration of their force upon objects of a permanent nature: in fact, it is only by their showing to the world that the producers of real wealth and knowledge can, if they choose, make themselves a distinct and separate body from those who produce neither, that the just demands of industry will be universally allowed and conceded. It is earnestly to be desired that measures will emanate from this meeting proportionate to the accomplishment of these aims.

The committee deem it here proper to observe that they do not consider a consolidation of the funds of the different Trades' Unions necessary, or even expedient. All that they contend for on this head is, that a unity of action should be maintained throughout them;—that they should all be under the same regulations as regards their general government and organization;—and that a perfect agreement should exist among them as to the modes of levying and disposing of all sums collected for the relief of members on occasions of emergency, and where, otherwise, a detached society might fall victims to their oppressors for want of means to enter upon arrangements of permanent stability, to procure which it is not to be expected that the casual donations and subscriptions of the benevolent will be found adequate.

Proposition 1.—The first proposition of this committee is, therefore, that as many different Trades' Unions as possible do mutually agree, under a perfect understanding with each other, to maintain a unity of action in all their proceedings, with respect to their general laws and government, and also with regard to the levying and disposing of all funds raised for objects of presumed permanent utility.

Proposition 2.—As land is the source of the first necessaries of life, and as without the possession of it the producing classes will ever remain in a greater or less degree subservient to the money capitalists, and subject to the deterioration of the money value of their labour consequent upon the fluctuations of trade and commerce, this committee advise that a great effort should now be made by the Unions to secure such portions of it on lease as their funds will permit, in order that, in all such instances as the case of the Derby turned-outs—and which are now becoming frequent,—where the men cannot be otherwise profitably and permanently employed, they may be so employed in rearing the greater part, if not the whole, of their subsistence, under the direction of practical agricultural superintendents,—which arrangements would not have the effect of lowering the price of labour in any trade, but, on the contrary, would rather tend to increase it by drawing off the at present superfluous supply in manufactures. . . .

Proposition 3.—The committee would, nevertheless, earnestly recommend in all cases of strikes and turn-outs, where it is practicable, that the men be employed in the making or producing of all such commodities as would be in demand among their brother unionists, or any other parties: and that to effect this, each lodge should be provided with a work-room or shop, in which those commodities may be manufactured on account of such lodge which shall make proper arrangements for the supply of the necessary materials.

Proposition 4.—That great advantages would accrue to unionists by the formation, in each district lodge, of a fund for the support of the sick and aged, and for defraying the funeral expenses of deceased members on a principle similar to that of benefit societies.

Proposition 5.—That in all cases where it be practicable, each district or branch lodge should establish within its locality one or more depots for provisions, and articles in general domestic use; by which means the working-man may be supplied with the best commodities, at little above whole-sale prices, and he would then not be exposed as at present, to the extortions and adulterations of petty retailers and dealers.

Proposition 6.—That each lodge do make arrangements for furnishing the means of mental improvement to their members, and for the cultivation of good habits among them, by affording them every facility for meeting together for friendly conversation, mutual instruction, and rational amusement or recreation; which arrangements might be rendered in a short period infinitely more enticing and agreeable than the delusive, pernicious and dearly-bought gratifications sought in the tap-room or the gin-shop.

Proposition 7.—As a very large number of females among the industrious classes are exposed to great hardships and oppression in the disposal of their labour, by the competition for employment, which at present exists amongst them, and as our union would be manifestly incomplete without their goodwill and co-operation . . .

we should offer them every encouragement and assistance to form themselves into lodges, for the protection of their industry, in every city or town where it is practicable. . . . For the first time in the history of the world, we see men awakening to a true sense of their dignity and their power—men, who but a short time since were unconscious of either,—who knew not that their labour was the mine of wealth from which society derived all the principal necessaries, comforts, and luxuries of civilized life,—but who had foolishly looked upon the produce of their toil as 'forbidden fruit', which it would be presumptuous in them even to *think* of enjoying!—At length their 'eyes are opened:'—they no longer imagine themselves as ordained by nature to be slavish drudges of society,—doomed to incessant toil—not to satisfy their own reasonable wants, but the vitiated extravagance of the Non-Producers, or, those whom they have mistakingly called their 'betters'—No longer will the working-man be told that there must be 'lower orders' in society. *The truth is out!* They know that all men are equal in the eyes of Nature, and that all have an equal right to her spontaneous bounties. . . . They would earnestly call upon their brethren here assembled, nobly to resolve, before they depart to their homes, upon such measures as, after calm enquiry and full investigation, shall seem best fitted to give the working men of this kingdom their just rights, and the full reward of their industry, by putting an end to the necessity of their competing with each other in the disposal of their labour to the non-producers; as, until that be done, they may in vain expect to be more than partially relieved from their distresses:—in fine, to resolve upon such measures as shall offer and afford to the productive classes a complete emancipation from the tyranny of capital and monopoly.

8i The tailors' strike: the demand for equalization

Poor Man's Guardian, 3 May 1834.

To the masters: 25 April 1834

SIR—By direction of the Friendly Society of Operative Tailors, I have to acquaint you, that in order to stay the ruinous effects which a destructive commercial competition has so long been inflicting upon them, they have resolved to introduce certain new Regulations of Labour into the Trade, which Regulations they intend should commence from Monday next; and I beg herewith to enclose you a copy of them.

As the demands there specified are of so reasonable a nature; and as, moreover, they are unquestionably calculated for the ultimate benefit of employers, as well as employed, the Society confidently hope that you will accede to them, and that henceforward a mutual confidence may be sustained between masters and men, and that their interests may be no longer separated, and opposed to each other.

It only remains for me to add, that your workmen, members of this Society, will cease to be employed by you, should you decline to act upon the new regulations; and further, I think it right to apprize you that, in that case, they will no longer consider it necessary to support your interest; but will immediately enter into the arrangements prepared by the Society for the employment of such Members for the benefit of the Society.

I am, sir, your most obedient humble servant,

JOHN BROWNE

Secretary of the Grand Lodge of Operative Tailors.

REGULATIONS

No Brother shall be allowed to work more than ten hours per day from the third Monday in the month of April to the last Saturday in the month of July; nor more than eight hours per day the remaining eight months of the year; and for such labour the remuneration shall be 6*s*. per day for the ten hours labour, which is to be performed between the hours of seven o'clock in the morning, and six o'clock in the evening; and 5*s*. per day for the eight hours labour, to be performed between the hours of eight o'clock in the morning, and five o'clock in the evening, out of which time, in either case, he shall leave his employer's premises one hour for refreshment. Nor shall any Brother work for an employer anywhere but on his (the employer's) premises, which shall be healthy and convenient, or on any other terms than by the day or hour. And no Brother shall be allowed to solicit employment, or to work for less than the regular wages within four miles of Covent Garden.

8j The Tolpuddle 'Martyrs'

G. Loveless, *The Victims of Whiggery* (1838)

In 1834 some agricultural labourers in Dorset tried to resist wage-cutting by forming themselves into a Friendly Society. They were tried and transported for taking an illegal oath. Not until 1838 were they brought back. Loveless became a delegate to the Chartist convention in 1839.

In the year 1831–2, there was a general movement of the working classes for an increase of wages, and the labouring men in the parish where I lived (Tolpuddle) gathered together, and met their employers, to ask them for an advance of wages, and they came to a mutual agreement, the masters in Tolpuddle promising to give the men as much for their labour as the other masters in the district. The whole of the men then went to work, and the time that was spent in this affair did not exceed two hours. No language of intimidation or threatening was used on the occasion. Shortly after we learnt that, in almost every place around us, the masters were giving their men money, or money's worth, to the amount of ten shillings a week—

we expected to be entitled to as much—but no—nine shillings must be our portion. After some months we were reduced to eight shillings per week. This caused great dissatisfaction and all the labouring men in the village, with the exception of two or three invalids, made application to a neighbouring magistrate . . . I was one nominated to appear, and when there we were told that we must work for whatever our employers thought fit to give us, as there was no law to compel masters to give any fixed sum of money to their servants. In vain we remonstrated that an agreement was made . . .

From this time we were reduced to seven shillings per week, and shortly after our employers told us they must lower us to six shillings per week. We consulted together what had better be done, knowing it was impossible to live honestly on such scanty means. I had seen at different times accounts of Trade Societies; I mentioned this, and it was resolved to form a friendly society among the labourers, having sufficiently learned that it would be vain to seek the redress either of employers, magistrates, or parsons. I inquired of a brother to get information how to proceed, and shortly after, two delegates from a Trade Society paid us a visit, formed a Friendly Society among the labourers, and gave us directions how to proceed. This was about the latter end of October, 1833. On the 9th of December, 1833, in the evening, Edward Legg (a labourer), who was witness against us on our trial, came and desired to be admitted into the Society.

Nothing particular occurred from this time until the 21st of February, 1834, when placards were posted up at the most conspicuous places, purporting to be cautions from the magistrates, threatening to punish with seven years transportation any man who should join the Union. This was the first time that I heard of any law being in existence to forbid such societies. I met with a copy, read it, and put it into my pocket. February the 24th at day break, I arose to go to my usual labour, and had just left my house, when Mr. James Brine, constable of the parish, met me and said, 'I have a warrant for you, from the magistrates' . . . Accordingly I and my companions walked in company with the constable to Dorchester, about seven miles distant, and were taken into the house of a Mr. Woolaston, magistrate . . . Legg was called upon to swear to us, and we were instantly sent to prison . . .

In this situation the chaplain of the prison paid us a visit, to pour a volley of instruction in our ears, mixed up, however, in the cup of abuse. After upbraiding us and taunting us with being discontented and idle, and wishing to ruin our masters, he proceeded to tell us that we were better off than our masters, and that government had made use of every possible means for economy and retrenchment to make all comfortable. He inquired if I could point out anything that might be done to increase the comfort of the labourer. I told him I thought I could; and began to assure him that our object was not to ruin the master, but that, for a long time, we had been looking for the head to begin, and relieve the various members down to the feet; but finding it was of no avail, we were thinking of making application to our masters, and for them to make application to their masters, and so up to the head; and as to their being worse off than ourselves, I could not believe it, while I saw them keep such a number of horses for no other purpose than to chase the hare and the fox. And besides I thought gentlemen wearing the clerical livery, like himself, might do with a little less salary. 'Is that how you mean to do it?' said he. 'That is one way I have been thinking of, Sir'.—'I hope the Court will favour you, but I think they will not; but I believe they mean to make an example of you'. And saying this he left us.

On the 15th March, we were taken to the County-hall to await our trial . . . As to the trial, I need mention but little; the whole proceedings were characterized by a shameful disregard of justice and decency; the most unfair means were resorted to in order to frame an indictment against us; the grand jury appeared to rack heaven and earth to get some clue against us, but in vain; our characters were investigated from our infancy to the then present moment; our masters were inquired of to know if we were not idle, or attended public-houses, or some other fault in us; and much as they were opposed to us, they had common honesty enough to declare that we were good labouring servants, and that they never heard of any complaint against us; and when nothing whatever could be raked together, the unjust and cruel judge, John Williams, ordered us to be tried for mutiny and conspiracy, under an act 38 Geo. 3, cap. 123, for the suppression of mutiny amongst the marines and seamen, several years ago, at the Nore. The greater part of the evidence against us, on our trial, was put into the mouths of the witnesses by the judge . . . I shall not soon forget his address to the jury in summing up the evidence: among other things, he told them, that if such Societies were allowed to exist, it would ruin masters, cause a stagnation in trade, destroy property,—and if *they should not find us guilty, he was certain they would forfeit the opinion of the grand jury*. I thought to myself, there is no danger but we shall be found guilty, as we have a special jury for the purpose, selected from among those who are most unfriendly towards us—the grand jury, landowners, the petty jury, land-renters. Under such a charge, from such a quarter, self-interest alone would induce them to say, 'Guilty' . . .

At the time when so much incendiarism was prevailing in so many parts of the kingdom, a watch was set in our parish for the protection of property in the night, and I and my brothers, among others, were chosen to watch some property. Will any reasonable man believe, if we had been rioters, that we should have been so chosen? . . . But the secret is this: I am from principle, a Dissenter, and by some, in Tolpuddle, it is considered the sin of witchcraft; nay, there is no forgiveness for it in this world nor that which is to come; the years 1824–5 are not forgotten, and many a curious tale might be told of men that were persecuted, banished and not allowed to have employ if they entered the Wesleyan Chapel at Tolpuddle . . .

8k Unions and intimidation: Glasgow cotton spinners

Evidence of A. Alison Esq., Sheriff of Lanarkshire, *Select Committee on Combinations* (1838), qus 1851–6.

I do not think there has been a single instance of a combined trade in Glasgow having had a strike in which intimidation did not begin the day after . . . The public acts of the cotton-spinners' association were, in a peculiar manner, brought under my notice, in consequence of the strike which took place in April 1837; . . . In the beginning of May, . . . I received information that large threatening crowds had assembled in the neighbourhood of Oak Bank Factory, a cotton-factory in the neighbourhood of Glasgow. The information was, that they had been going on for some days; at the time, I was confined to bed, but as soon as I was able to go out, I went myself to see them; I saw a crowd of some 600 to 800 persons assembled in the road; the new hands at that time were leaving the work; it was four o'clock in the afternoon, and I was informed by persons in the crowd, that they had marched through Glasgow with music at their head, in military order; I went up to the door of the factory and I saw several persons come out wounded, with blood streaming down their faces upon their clothes, upon their waistcoat, and neckcloth, from wounds which, I was informed, had been inflicted by the crowd.

Had those wounded persons come out of the factory?—They had. When I saw them they were walking out of the factory; some of them had fresh blood upon them from wounds that had been inflicted that day or the day before; but I saw, I suppose, ten or a dozen persons with blood upon them. In consequence of this I called a meeting of the magistrates, and we issued a proclamation dissuading the people from going out for fear of dangerous consequences. . . .

Thus it ceased in that quarter; but they began again immediately after on the other border of the Clyde, in the Calton, which was the great manufacturing quarter in Glasgow, and continued there, with hardly any intermission, for about 10 days. Every evening there were crowds of persons assembled, in addition to the regular guards appointed to every factory, which, at that period, amounted to between 300 and 400. Every factory had from six to fifteen persons stationed as guards at the gates, to observe the new hands going out and in, to cajole them, and to get them to leave their employment; if necessary, to use violence to induce them, but by all means to get quit of them. The crowds of persons at Mile End varied from 500 to 2,000 every evening; they surrounded almost every mill; and for the next 10 days I can describe the city as being in a state almost of insurrection. I had constant applications for military from all the people, but I told them I was extremely unwilling to employ soldiers; that I knew that any accident would be attended with most disastrous consequences, and I would not let them go out unless I was by their side, but I recommended to them, if possible to endeavour to make prisoners; and I was convinced that by the application of the law to prisoners, a pacification would be gained far better than by the employment of the military.

81 Masters and men in Norwich

Evidence of Mr. Robberds, 22 September 1838, to the Assistant Commissioners on the Handloom Weavers, *P.P. England* (1840), xxiii, pp. 339–41.

Having ascertained that manufacturers in other parts of the Kingdom were selling camlets at lower prices than I could charge, and that they were enabled to do this by the lower rate of wages which they paid for weaving, I announced to my weavers, about the middle of last May, that from that time I should reduce the scale by which they were paid. Soon after I had taken this step, some men, styling themselves a deputation from the Weavers' Committee, came to speak to me on the subject. I inquired if they were camlet weavers, and having been answered in the negative, I stated that I had nothing to say to them, and would hear nothing from them; that I knew of no Weavers' Committee; that the regulation of wages was a question to be decided between me and my workmen, and that I should allow no other parties to interfere. On this they withdrew, and I afterwards agreed to explain to two of my weavers, attended by a third person, the circumstances which rendered the proposed alteration necessary.

The rate of wages which I offered is still considerably higher than that given to the hand-loom weavers of Yorkshire, whose average earnings are not more than 12*s*. a-week, while, at my reduced rate, regular and industrious workmen can bring in from 15*s*. to 20*s*. per week, and their wives and sons (of a competent age) from 12*s*. to 15*s*. more.

The committee, however, although there were no camlet weavers among them, would not allow my hands to take my work. A watch was stationed from six in the morning till twelve at night at each end of the street on which my manufactury is situated, to observe all that was done, and to intimidate those who were willing to take work. There were many who stated both to me and others that they were anxious to be employed, but dared not, on account of the threats used against them. At length a few ventured to brave the danger, but some, as they were carrying away their work, were assailed in the open streets, and forced to bring it back, others who reached their homes in safety, were there beset by riotous mobs, and compelled to return the materials unwrought, and in two instances houses where the work was in progress were broken open during the night, and the goods destroyed on the loom.

Wherever I could obtain sufficient evidence, the offenders were taken before the magistrates, and in most of these cases the committee undertook their defence. Some of the parties were convicted of assaults, and fined, but the fines were immediately paid (no doubt by the committee) and the parties at liberty to repeat the same outrages. Some underwent short terms of imprisonment, and others were bound over to keep the peace which they were among the first to break. . . . All these proceedings were of no avail, intimidation and violence, escaping thus almost with impunity, were carried to greater lengths. The dispute began to be rendered subservient to the purposes of party. One of the most useful members of the court of Guardians was turned out by the parish which he represented, because he disapproved of the conduct of the weavers, and candidates for municipal honours sought to acquire popularity by courting the promoters of these disturbances. Subscriptions were collected for their support, to which publicans and small tradesmen were the principal contributors, some deluded by the idea that a high rate of wages would enable the working classes to spend more freely, and others influenced by the fear of becoming marked men, and losing their customers. Those who refused to give any money, or in any manner discountenanced the proceedings of the weavers, were abused as under price men, and every possible effort was made to injure them in their business. Thus encouraged, the committee issued hand-bills, announcing that they had sufficient funds to maintain the camlet weavers for several months, and it was generally understood that they received an allowance of 3*s*. each per week.

In the meantime I had commenced preparations for making my camlet by the power-loom, and passed some weeks in Yorkshire for that purpose. On my return from that district, towards the end of August, I found my weavers generally dissatisfied with the conduct of the committee, and severely pinched by starving so long on 3*s*. per week, when they might have been earning at least five times as much. Many of them applied to me for work. I told them I should give them none unless they went publicly to the magistrates stating that they were willing to be employed on my terms, and claiming efficient protection for themselves and the materials intrusted to them. They at once complied with these conditions, and an additional police force was engaged to guard both by day and night the houses of those who might take work. But before these arrangements were completed, a body of nine or ten men attacked the house of a weaver named Wells. . . . Their apprehension . . . and the vigilant observation of the police produced an immediate calm. More weavers than I could employ came for work, and those who obtained it have been unmolested. My business is now proceeding quietly on my own terms, and offers have been made me to take even lower wages than I am paying.

But the consequences of these proceedings have been very injurious to the working classes. Not only have they lost the circulation among them of at least £1,000 in wages, but three months of idleness and delusive excitement have deteriorated all their habits. Many of them will never recover from the effects of their privations. One old man who had for many years maintained himself decently, and for whom I had ordered work, came to thank me for it, but, he added, 'I must give up. I have been obliged to sell everything, and starvation has brought me so low that I can do no more. I must go home to my parish, and for this I have to thank the silk weavers' committee'.

The necessary and inevitable result of such transactions will, however, be the introduction of the power-loom into this city.

8m Defence and desperation

Evidence of John Doherty to the *Select Committee on Combinations* (1838), qus 3378–92, 3455–60.

When was the last general strike?—In 1829 . . . I believe invariably . . . they have arisen from the masters offering reductions, or in some other way interfering with the wages of the operative.

What, generally speaking, is the result of strikes by workmen?—In general they have been unsuccessful. Partial strikes are more frequently successful; but I am not aware of any general strike being entirely successful.

Do men enter upon a strike willingly?—No, they do not, very far from it; they enter upon it with the utmost reluctance . . . They believe, that if they did not strike, the evil which is opposed at that time would be oftener repeated and would fall heavier upon them . . . Men must naturally be averse to strikes. In the first place, there is the loss of employment for a time at any rate, there is the probable consequence of their ultimate discharge, and their entire loss of employment, and if they take an active part, of endless unceasing persecution. I mean not only being kept out of employment by the master they have left, or are about to leave, but all the other masters (for it sometimes extends throughout the whole country) are adverse to them. There is therefore the unwillingness of the workmen from those causes, and there is a great reluctance on their part from the fear of what it brings upon their wives and families at home whenever there is a strike.

There were several objects of the Spinners Association; the main object was to prevent reduction of wages; and next . . . to procure an Act of Parliament to lessen the hours of labour in factories . . .

You do not deprecate the interference of the Legislature with such a subject as that?—No, we do not; we seek it . . .

You say that what is technically called the Factory Question has been the main object of your combination for many years?—It has for more than 20 years, to my knowledge.

8n The implications of unionism

F. Engels, 'Labour Movements', *The Condition of the Working Class in England in 1844* (1892).

The history of these Unions is a long series of defeats of the working-men, interrupted by a few isolated victories . . .

If the employer had no concentrated, collective opposition to expect, he would in his own interest gradually reduce wages to a lower and lower point . . . [But] Every manufacturer knows that the consequence of a reduction not justified by conditions to which his competitors also are subject, would be a strike, which would most certainly injure him, because his capital would be idle so long as the strike lasted, and his machinery would be rusting, whereas it is very doubtful whether he could, in such a case, enforce his reduction. Then he has the certainty that if he should succeed, his competitors would follow him, reducing the price of the goods so produced, and thus depriving him of the benefit of his policy. Then, too, the Unions often bring about a more rapid increase of wages after a crisis than would otherwise follow. For the manufacturer's interest is to delay raising wages until forced by competition, but now the working-men demand an increased wage as soon as the market improves, and they can carry their point by reason of the smaller supply of workers at his command under such circumstances.

But, for resistance to more considerable forces which influence the labour market, the Unions are powerless. In such cases hunger gradually drives the strikers to resume work on any terms, and when once a few have begun, the force of the Union is broken, because these few knobsticks, with the reserve supplies of goods in the market, enable the bourgeoisie to overcome the worst effects of the interruption of business. The funds of the Union are soon exhausted by the great numbers requiring relief, the credit which the shopkeepers give at high interest is withdrawn after a time, and want compels the working-man to place himself once more under the yoke of the bourgeoisie. But strikes end disastrously for the workers mostly, because the manufacturers, in their own interest (which has, be it said, become their interest only through the resistance of the workers), are obliged to avoid all useless reductions, while the workers feel in every reduction imposed by the state of trade a deterioration of their condition, against which they must defend themselves as far as in them lies.

It will be asked, 'Why, then, do the workers strike in such cases, when the uselessness of such measures is so evident?' Simply because they *must* protest against every reduction, even if dictated by necessity; because they feel bound to proclaim that they, as human beings, shall not be made to bow to social circumstances, but social conditions ought to yield to them as human beings; because silence on their part would be a recognition of these social conditions, an admission of the right of the bourgeoisie to exploit the workers in good times and let them starve in bad ones . . . What gives these Unions and the strikes arising from them their real importance is this, that they are the first attempts of the workers to abolish competition. They imply the recognition of the fact that the supremacy of the bourgeoisie is based wholly upon the competition of the workers among themselves, *i.e.* upon their want of cohesion . . . And precisely because the Unions direct themselves against the vital nerve of the present social order, however one-sidedly, in however narrow a way, are they so dangerous to this social order. The working-men cannot attack the bourgeoisie, and with it the whole existing order of society, at any sorer point than this. If the competition of the workers among themselves is destroyed, if all determine not to be further exploited by the bourgeoisie, the rule of property is at an end. Wages depend upon the relation of demand to supply, upon the accidental state of the labour market, simply because the workers have hitherto been content to be treated as chattels, to be bought and sold. The moment the workers resolve to be bought and sold no longer, when, in the determination of the value of labour, they take the part of men possessed of a will as well as of working-power, at that moment the whole Political Economy of today is at an end.

9 The Short Time Movement: the question of hours

Child labour was essential to the economy of the cotton and woollen mills; two or three children were required for every adult male operative. But the only protection they had came from the inadequate act of 1819, which limited the hours of children in cotton mills to twelve hours a day.

The factory agitation came from two groups, from the philanthropists (doctors, clergy, Tory protectionists) who were horrified at the damage done to the bodies and souls of young children in factories; and from working men who saw that child labour cheapened adult labour (9a), but that if child labour were regulated, they could hope that the demand for and price of adult labour would rise.

The factory movement began when Richard Oastler (1789–1861) a Tory protectionist land-agent, wrote to the *Leeds Mercury* in 1830 that negro slaves were better off than Yorkshire children (9b), a theme that was echoed in the radical press (9c). Yorkshire radicals and protectionists together organized Short Time committees; Doherty brought over the Lancashire cotton workers from the old NAPL; Sadler (1780–1835), a Yorkshire M.P., and then Lord Ashley (1801–85) led the parliamentary campaign. A Select Committee and then a roving Royal Commission gathered evidence (9d), and in 1833 the Whigs passed the Factory Act, which forbade the employment of children under nine years, limited those under fourteen years to nine hours a day, and provided four inspectors. Cobbett mocked the indignation of political economists at this legislation.

The masters evaded the act; the men were bitterly disappointed because children could be worked in relays and would not therefore indirectly limit adult hours. John Fielden, (1784–1849), a Lancashire cotton master and MP for Oldham showed that child and adult labour were inseparable (9e). While Oastler continued to work for a ten-hour day, Doherty, Owen and Fielden now promoted the National Regeneration Society (9f) to campaign for an eight-hour day, and buttressed their case with under-consumptionist theories (see above, p. 59). The Society collapsed with the GNCTU in summer 1834. Meanwhile Andrew Ure suggested that child labour was charming, Cooke Taylor more soberly pointed out that child labour was a consequence of family poverty (9g). When Poulett Thompson on behalf of the masters sought to repeal the 1833 Act (9h), the Short Time Movement entered its most threatening stage. Oastler would teach children to ruin machinery (9i), and Joseph Rayner Stephens (1805–79), the fiery dissenting minister, brought curses down on the factory system and the new Poor Law indiscriminately. But in the name of free labour, free trade and foreign competition, the advocates of political economy fought back (9j); not until 1847 did working men obtain their ten-hour act for women and boys under eighteen (9k); not until 1874 did they obtain it for themselves.

Suggestions for further reading

See C. Driver, *Tory Radical* (1946); J. T. Ward, *The factory movement 1830–1855* (1963); N. Smelser, *Social Change in the Industrial Revolution* (1959).

9a Adults for children

A labourer, *Trades Newspaper*, 16 October 1825.

Wages can never sink below the sum necessary to rear up the number of labourers the capitalists want. The weaver, his wife and children, all labour to obtain this sum; the blacksmith and the carpenter obtain it by their single exertions . . .

The labouring *men* of this country, of all classes, should return to the good old plan, of subsisting their wives and children on the wages of their OWN labour, and they should demand wages high enough for this purpose . . . By doing this, the capitalists will be obliged to give the same wages to men alone, which they now give to men, women and children . . . I recommend my fellow labourers, in preference to every other means of limiting the number of those who work for wages, to prevent their wives and children from competing with them in the market, and beating down the price of labour.

9b Yorkshire slavery

R. Oastler, *Leeds Mercury*, 16 October 1830.

Let truth speak out . . . Thousands of our fellow-creatures and fellow-subjects both male and female . . . are this very moment existing in a state of slavery, *more horrid* than are the victims of that hellish system '*colonial slavery*'. These innocent creatures drawl out, unpitied, their short but miserable existence, in a place famed for its profession of religious zeal . . . The very streets which receive the droppings of an 'Anti-Slavery Society' are every morning wet by the tears of innocent victims at the accursed shrine of avarice, who are *compelled* (not by the cart-whip of the negro slave-driver) but by the dread of the equally appalling thong or strap of the over-looker, to hasten, half-dressed, *but not half-fed*, to those magazines of British infantile slavery—the *worsted mills in the town and neighbourhood of Bradford! ! !* . . .

Thousands of little children, both male and female, *but principally* female, from seven to fourteen years of age, are daily *compelled* to *labour* from six o'clock in the morning to seven in the evening, with only—Britons, blush while you read it!—*with only thirty minutes allowed for eating and recreation*. Poor infants! ye are indeed sacrified at the shrine of avarice, *without even the solace of the negro slave* . . . He knows it is his sordid, mercenary master's interest that he should *live*, be *strong* and *healthy*. Not so with you. Ye are doomed to labour from morning to night for one who cares not how soon your weak and tender frames are stretched to breaking! . . . When your joints can act no longer, your emaciated frames are cast aside, the boards on which you lately toiled and wasted life away, are instantly supplied with other victims, who in this boasted land of liberty are HIRED—not sold—as slaves and daily forced to hear that they are free.

9c The factory girl

Hetherington's *Destructive*, 13 April 1833.

'Twas on a winter's morning
The weather wet and wild
Three hours before the dawning
The father roused his child;
Her daily morsel bringing
The darksome room he paced,
And cried 'the bell is ringing,
My hapless darling, haste!'

'Father I'm up but weary
I scarce can reach the door,
And long the way and dreary,
O carry me once more.
To help us we've no mother
And you have no employ;
They killed my little brother
Like him I'll work and die'.

Her wasted form seemed nothing—
The load was at his heart;
The sufferer he kept soothing
Till at the mill they part.
The overlooker met her,
As to her frame she crept,
And with his thong he beat her,
AND CURSED her as she wept.

Alas what hours of horror
Made up her latest day
In toil and pain and sorrow
They slowly passed away;

It seemed as she grew weaker
The threads she oftener broke,
The rapid wheels ran quicker
And heavier fell the stroke.

The sun had long descended
But night brought no repose;
Her day began and ended
As cruel tyrants chose.
At length a little neighbour
Her halfpenny she paid
To take her last hour's labour
While by her frame she laid.

At last the engine ceasing,
The captive homeward rushed;
She thought her strength increasing
'Twas hope her spirits flushed.
She left but oft she tarried
She fell and rose no more,
Till by her comrades carried,
She reached her father's door.

All night with tortured feeling
He watched his sleepless child.
While close beside her kneeling,
She knew him not, nor smiled.
Again the factory's ringing,
Her last perceptions tried,
When from her straw bed springing,
'Tis time', she shrieked, and died.

That night a chariot passed her,
While on the ground she lay;
The daughters of her master
An evening visit pay;
Their tender hearts were sighing,
As negro wrongs were told,
While the white slave was dying,
Who gained their father's gold!

9d Committee, commission and legislation

The Herald of the Rights of Industry, 8 February 1834.

Most of our readers will remember, that application was made to Parliament, during the last session, at considerable expense and sacrifice, by the operatives of Lancashire and Yorkshire, for a law to limit the time of working in factories, for all persons under 18 years of age, to ten hours a day, and eight on the Saturday . . . Although committee after committee of both houses of parliament had sat, and elicited the most ample evidence, as to the destructive tendency of factory labour, and the deterioration of morals which it produced . . . 'honest Lord Althorp' resisted the application, until another enquiry should be gone into! . . . A Royal commission was appointed to gallop over the country, at the public expense, in search of evidence, to ascertain whether or not the children of the British artizans should be worked two or three hours a day longer than the convicted athletic felon, or the brawny black slave!

Well, the commissioners (for there were five of them) commenced their operations. They visited the masters, dined with them, praised their hospitality and wine; toasted the factory commissioners, and the Reformed House of Commons . . . and recommended the parliament to pass a measure, which there was not a tittle of evidence to support . . .

This measure is for eight hours a day for all children . . . who had not attained their thirteenth year! . . . 'relays' of *children* are to be got to work against the 'adults' of fourteen!

It was this scandalous treatment of the earnest prayers of the operatives, by the Reformed Parliament, and the apparent impossibility of enforcing the act . . . that led Mr. John Fielden, the honourable member for Oldham, to propose, that the operatives should legislate for themselves, and, taking the hint from the joint act of the whigs and mill-owners, cease their labours at the same time with the children, instead of working against two sets, as is now proposed by the act.

The backbone of England

William Cobbett, House of Commons, 18 July 1833.

I have only one observation to make, and I will not detain the House two minutes in doing so. We have, Sir, this night made one of the greatest discoveries ever made by a House of Commons, a discovery which will be hailed by the constituents of the Hon. Gentlemen behind me with singular pleasure. Hitherto, we have been told that our navy was the glory of the country, and that our maritime commerce and extensive manufactures were the mainstays of the realm. We have also been told that the land had its share in our greatness, and should justly be considered as the pride and glory of England. The Bank, also, has put in its claim to share in this praise, and has stated that public credit is due to it; but, now, a most surprising discovery has been made, namely, that all our greatness and prosperity, that our superiority over other nations, is owing to 300,000 little girls in Lancashire. We have made the notable discovery, that, if these little girls work two hours less in a day than they do now, it would occasion the ruin of the country; that it would enable other nations to compete with us; and thus make an end to our boasted wealth, and bring us to beggary!

9e Child and adult labour

John Fielden, *The Curse of the Factory System* (1836), pp. 34–5.

Any Factory Bill, to be effective, must restrict the labour, not only of children, but of those older hands with whom they worked; for that the work of both was so connected, that it could not be carried on by adult hands without the assistance of the younger. But this fact our adversaries always attempted to turn against us. Most of the masters are obliged to admit the excessive hours of labour imposed on children, and the Ministers have done it in the most solemn manner; but they cannot interfere with the labour, the 'free labour' of the adult, because that is against sound principle! According to their own showing, it is a choice of evils; but, contrary to reason, contrary to all acknowledged principle and to universal practice, they would choose the greater: they would overwork the child, though nature forbids it, rather than shorten the labour of the adult, who is also overworked. In short, their 'principle'; their true and scarcely disguised 'principle', is the principle of self against nature.

Here, then, is the 'curse' of our factory-system: as improvements in machinery have gone on, the 'avarice of the masters' has prompted many to exact more labour from their hands than they were fitted by nature to perform, and those who have wished for the hours of labour to be less for all ages than the legislature would even yet sanction, have had no alternative but to conform more or less to the prevailing practice, or abandon the trade altogether. This has been the case with regard to myself and my partners.

9f The National Regeneration Society

Herald of the Rights of Industry, 8 February 1834; 29 March 1834.

What is it we propose to do? Simply to reduce the time of daily labour from the present unreasonable number of hours to eight per day, and insist upon the same wages for these eight hours, as for the present twelve or fourteen. This must of course cause a proportionate advance in the price of the article produced. Now what will be the first effect of this measure, supposing it to be universally adopted? Clearly, this, according to all the principles of political economy, that the quantity of labour in the market will be reduced in the same proportion as the number of working hours are diminished. That will be about one third on the average. The result of this . . . is to increase the value of labour in the exact proportion of its diminished quantity . . . It is the quantity offered for sale, of any article, compared with the quantity wanted, that makes it dear or cheap . . . If to come to eleven hours a day would so reduce the quantity of goods produced, as to call in all the unemployed hands, to work the same number of hours, to make the difference . . . then, if we come down to eight hours, the difference between that and eleven hours is the amount of advantage gained by the workers. This would be actually reducing the quantity of labour in the market below the demand for it, and, of consequence, enhancing its value in the same proportion . . .

The great advantage of this measure consists in this, that it enhances the value of labour only, and must, therefore, proportionately diminish the profits or the value of idleness. Labour will be advanced indeed, and all who have that article to purchase, will then be compelled to give more for it than they now do, and the workmen themselves must do so too. When the shoemaker wants a hat, for instance, he must give, say, a third more for it than he now does, but he meets the advance upon the hat by a similar advance upon his shoes. Thus every workman meets the advance upon the price of his neighbour's labour by a similar advance upon his own, and the relative position of the workers is thus adjusted, and remains the same. But the advantage consists in this, that those who have not labour to set against labour, must give a larger amount of the savings of labour, wealth, than they now do. Thus we slowly but certainly get at the innumerable and immense masses of wealth which have been accumulated in the country, and gradually and imperceptibly scatter them again among the community.

. . . If the employers oppose, a struggle must ensue, and when the mass of the people, *of the workers*, are united, there can be no question as to who must give way. All the bad feelings and passions of victors and vanquished must then come into active operation, and all the consequences of such a state of things be felt throughout the whole range of society, and will be found embittering all the relations of social life. But this, by the way, we merely throw out the hint for the consideration of those who may feel disposed to push the matter to a struggle, but, more especially for those who affect such great and exclusive anxiety for preserving the 'most sweet harmony', which is said to exist between the various classes of British society.

9g The charms of child labour

A. Ure, *Philosophy of Manufactures* (1835), p. 301.

. . . I have visited many factories, both in Manchester and in the surrounding districts, during a period of several months, entering the spinning rooms, unexpectedly, and often alone, at different times of the day, and I never saw a single instance of corporal chastisement inflicted on a child, nor indeed did I ever see children in ill-humour. They seemed to be always cheerful and alert, taking pleasure in the light play of their muscles,—enjoying the mobility natural to their age. The scene of industry, so far from exciting sad emotions in my mind, was always exhilarating. It was delightful to observe the nimbleness with which they pieced the broken ends, as the mule-carriage began to recede from the fixed roller beam, and to see them at leisure, after a few seconds' exercise of their tiny fingers, to amuse themselves in any attitude they chose, till the stretch and winding-on were once more completed. The work of these lively elves seemed to resemble a sport, in which habit gave them a pleasing dexterity. Conscious of their skill, they were delighted to show it off to any stranger. As to exhaustion by the day's work, they evinced no trace of it on emerging from the mill in the evening; for they immediately began to skip about any neighbouring play-ground, and to commence their little amusements with the same alacrity as boys issuing from a school . . .

The necessity of child labour

W. Cooke Taylor, *Notes of a Tour* (1842), chapter 12.

Millowners have been whitewashed with small coal; . . . juvenile labour, as it should be called, in factories, is in fact a national blessing, and absolutely necessary for the support of the manifold blessings which have been placed upon the industry of this country. It is quite sufficient to say that the children of the operatives have mouths and must be fed; they have limbs and must be clothed; they have minds which ought to be instructed; and they have passions, which must be controlled. Now, if the parents are unable to provide these requisites—and their inability to do so is just as notorious as their existence—it becomes an absolute necessity that the children should aid in obtaining them for themselves. To abolish juvenile labour is plainly nothing else than to abolish juvenile means of support; and to confine it within very narrow limits is just to subtract a dinner or supper from the unhappy objects of mistaken benevolence . . . That legislative protection should be extended to the children nobody means to deny; but that protection is wanted, not against their employers, but against the extremes to which griping poverty in most instances, and grasping avarice in some, may drive their parents . . .

Juvenile labour is in fact a mere question of meat, drink and clothing: if the sentimental who have raised an outcry against it as a grievance, can show how the children are to be supported without their earnings in the factories, the operatives will gladly keep them home and thank them into the bargain; but if they have no better remedy to propose than sheer starvation, common sense will reject their interference as a mockery and an insult.

9h The evils of protection: labour and the Factories Regulation Bill

Hansard, third series, xxxiii, cols 739–40, 782, 9 May 1836.

The Bill was to repeal the clause of the 1833 Factory Act, limiting children of twelve to thirteen years to eight hours a day.

Mr. Poulett Thomson:

. . . He did not apprehend that sixty-nine hours work in the course of the week would be found injurious to them in any way . . . But there was another party who found fault with the measure on entirely different grounds . . . He alluded to those who were for extending the protection to adults as well as to children, and were for limiting the employment of all to at most ten hours per day . . . Both now and at all times, he protested against a course of that kind, since he believed that it would be to inflict the most grievous tyranny upon those who having only their labour to sell had a right to make the most of it. Great injury would thus be done to manufactures, but double injury to those employed in them. He had not, hitherto, looked at the subject with reference to the general interests of trade, but upon these he might fairly rest his opposition to a Ten Hours' Factory Bill. The Right Hon. Member for Tamworth, a few nights ago, had shown the great evil of only a very small tax 5/16 of a penny upon cotton, but how much would the evils of such a tax to the manufacturers be increased, if one-sixth of the labour now bestowed on the trade were deducted from it? That would be equivalent to a tax of *2d.* per lb. on raw cotton. Such a measure would be tyranny of the grossest kind to the operatives, and perfect destruction as regarded our manufactures. Capital and industry would then find their way into other countries, and England, which depended on foreign markets for the sale of two-thirds or three-fourths of our manufactures, would be undersold abroad . . . He believed that the operatives themselves were not anxious for the adoption of a Ten Hours' Bill, but they were led away by persons who were anxious to be appointed their delegates . . . These persons deluded the operatives into the belief that they would get twelve hours' pay for ten hours' labour. That, of course, was a proposition which could be treated only with ridicule by every person acquainted with the relation which existed between capital and profits . . .

9i Defending the law

Richard Oastler, *The Law or the Needle* (1836).

I stated that I was resolved, that, inconvenient as the Masters' own Law was, I was resolved to assist the Government and the inspectors to enforce it. I assured the meeting, that if the Factory Masters were more powerful than the Law and the King, I would *then* teach the Factory children, to defend themselves, to prevent themselves being murdered, contrary to Law;—and so I will. I will, in that event, print a little card about Needles, and Sand and Rusty-nails, with proper, and very explicit directions, which will make these Law-breakers look about them,—and repent that they were ever so mad, as to laugh at the Law and the King. These cards of mine, shall then, be the catechism of the Factory children,—I will take care to have every factory child well instructed in the art of self defence—and I will make the Factory-master, who, in that day, will have successfully defied the LAW, bow to the Banner of the 'Needle'.

9j Cheap humanity

Northern Star, 7 June 1845.

The Bill to extend to calico and other print-workers the provisions of the Factories Regulations Act enacted two session ago . . . [went to] the House of Lords. On that occasion

Lord Brougham said, he could not refrain from entering his protest against their insisting, year after year, on thus legislating in the wrong direction. Professing great concern for the working classes, they were doing all they could by their legislation to injure or oppress them, and were treating them with what he held to be more cruelty, under the false guise and garb of humanity. He had formerly entered his protest on the journals of the House in reference to this kind of legislation, and the objections which he had then urged appeared to him to apply . . . By stopping the children from working, the work of the men was stopped, as the children's labour was as necessary for the labour of the men as theirs was to the printing. His opinion was that it was not for lawgivers to protect children; it was for nature and divine providence which had provided the care of the parents. But the objection he had to the bill was one of principle, though he had a specific objection to that part of it which related to women being prevented from working with their own consent and that of their husbands. The Legislators had no right, with their fantastical opinions, to compel women to withhold their labour. Men were allowed to work all night and why not women? . . . He wished they would legislate against their own persons, if they legislated for humanity. In the name of common sense, and common justice, and common humanity towards the working classes themselves, he hoped they would not constantly be haunted with one of these measures after the other of cheap humanity, which cost nothing to the framers, but was at the cost of others . . .

'It is not for law-givers to protect children'! Then what, in heavens' name, are they *for*? Do they only exist to levy taxes, and absorb to themselves the fruits of industry? Is that the 'be-all and the end-all' of their existence? If so, would not society be *better* without them?

9k The politics of short time

Paul Hargreaves, chairman, Lancashire central short time committee, *Northern Star*, 31 January 1846.

The working men of Lancashire best knew what suited their interests, and the committee endeavoured, by all means in their power, to promote the passing of such measures as were likely to meet their views and administer to their wants. During the last eighteen years, in which he had been engaged in the advocacy of the question now under discussion, the agitation had assumed almost as many different shapes; at one time it was necessary to hold public meetings in order to draw public attention to the sufferings of the children, with a view of exciting sympathy with them; at another time it was necessary to petition parliament and make representation to the Government of the necessity of such a measure. This course was no longer necessary, the humanity part of the question had been conceded, but the opponents then began to discover that the trade would be ruined, and England's greatness for ever gone, unless the factory girls of Lancashire worked twelve hours a day. . . . To meet these objections the committee had applied the whole of their study; they had collected the best evidence on the commercial part of the subject which could be obtained, and had condensed the whole into a cheap pamphlet, and distributed it amongst the people and the members of Parliament, by which much good had been effected . . . They hoped to be able to send at least twelve delegates to London to support Lord Ashley in his endeavour to pass the bill this session . . . They would also be able to canvass the members at their own houses, and lay before them the wants and necessities of the factory operatives.

10 The new Poor Law, 1834

The old Poor Law provided outdoor relief; and this was expensive as judged by the rates and the morals of the labourer, for paupers had multiplied. So the new Poor Law sought to reduce the number of able-bodied unemployed (10a) by ending outdoor relief, by restricting relief to the workhouse and by making the workhouse sufficiently unattractive that only the desperate would come to it. Its diet was to be meagre, it was to separate husband from wife on the best Malthusian principles. Its basic assumption was that there was work for all if only labourers had sufficient incentive to seek it. However, in the arable south and east of England, there was little winter employment; and in the Midlands and north, unemployment came with slumps in the trade cycle. Both were beyond the power of the labourer to remedy.

When, in 1837, the Poor Law commissioners attempted to extend the system into Lancashire and Yorkshire, they met bitter and prolonged opposition from working men and some of their masters. The Short Time committees mobilized protest meetings, J. R. Stephens toured England using the language of blood and brimstone (10b). General Napier, commanding the government troops in the North, sympathized with him (10c). Oastler warned (10d) that the new Poor Law broke the social contract between property and the right of the poor to relief. As the *Northern Star* pointed out, the factory movement and the anti-Poor Law agitation were inseparable (10e); for if poor relief was always to be less 'eligible' or lower than the wage of a working man, then capitalists could reduce wages without restraint. The agitation was largely successful, for outdoor relief was never abandoned in the north.

Suggestions for further reading

See J. D. Marshall, *The Old Poor Law 1795–1834* (1968 pamphlet); S. Finer, *Life and Times of Sir Edwin Chadwick* (1952) (books 2 and 4); J. Poynter, *Society and Pauperism 1795–1834* (1969), focuses on attitudes to poor relief; M. Blaug, 'The Myth of the Old Poor Law' and 'The Poor Law Report re-examined' in *Journal of Economic History*, 1963–4; M. Rose, *The English Poor Law 1780–1930* (1971), for an edition of documents.

10a Paupers or labourers?

The Report of the Commissioners on the Poor Law (1834).

The most pressing of the evils which we have described are those connected with the relief of the Able-bodied . . .

In all extensive communities, circumstances will occur in which an individual, by the failure of his means of subsistence, will be exposed to the danger of perishing. To refuse relief, and at the same time to punish mendicity when it cannot be proved that the offender could have obtained subsistence by labour, is repugnant to the common sentiments of mankind . . .

In all extensive civilized communities, therefore, the occurrence of extreme necessity is prevented by almsgiving, by public institutions supported by endowments or voluntary contributions, or by a provision partly voluntary and partly compulsory, or by a provision entirely compulsory, which may exclude the pretext of mendicancy.

But in no part of Europe except England has it been thought fit that the provision, whether compulsory or voluntary, should be applied to more than the relief of *indigence*, the state of a person unable to labour, or unable to obtain, in return for his labour, the means of subsistence. It has never been deemed expedient that the provision should extend to the relief of *poverty*; that is the state of one who, in order to obtain a mere subsistance, is forced to have recourse to labour . . .

The first . . . principle . . . is that his situation on the whole shall not be made really or apparently as eligible as the situation of the independent labourer of the lowest class . . . In proportion as the condition of any pauper class is elevated above the condition of independent labourers, the condition of the independent class is depressed; their industry is impaired, their employment becomes unsteady, and its remuneration in wages is diminished. Such persons, therefore, are under the strongest inducements to quit the less eligible class of labourers, and enter the more eligible class of paupers. The converse is the case when the pauper class is placed in its proper position, below the condition of the independent labourer. Every penny bestowed, that tends to render the position of the pauper more eligible than that of the independent labourer, is a bounty on indolence and vice.

10b The demand for a repeal

Northern Star, 6 January 1838; 10 November 1838.

J. R. Stephens at Newcastle:
And if this damnable law, which violated all the laws of God, was continued, and all means of peaceably putting an end to it had been made in vain, then, in the words of their banner, 'For children and wife we'll war to the knife'. If the people who produce all wealth could not be allowed, according to God's word, to have the kindly fruits of the earth which they had, in obedience to God's Word, raised by the sweat of their brow, then war to the knife with their enemies, who were the enemies of God. If the musket and the pistol, the sword, and the pike were of no avail, let the women take the scissors, the child the pin or needle. If all failed, then the firebrand—aye, the firebrand—the firebrand, I repeat. The palace shall be in flames. I pause, my friends. If the cottage is not permitted to be the abode of man and wife, and if the smiling infant is to be dragged from a father's arms and a mother's bosom, it is because these hell-hounds of commissioners have set up the command of their master the devil, against our God.

at Norwich:
I put these things to the men of wealth and property in Norwich, in Manchester, and Birmingham and Leeds, and other manufacturing places, and I tell them, those great towns are not worth twelve months—twelve months did I say—not twenty-four hours' purchase. England stands on a mine—a volcano is beneath her; you may dance on it—you may pluck the flowers from its surface, but it only sleeps: the match is lighted, the train is laid, and unless the misery and distress of the poor be met by good feeling and speedy remedy, no man can tell what a day—what an hour may bring forth. (Hear, hear, and

cheers) . . . The day is come when no Government can exist—no Government *shall* exist, that will not repeal the Poor Law Amendment Act. (loud cheers) . . . I have a word for the rich—they know not what they are doing; I advise them to make their wills. The rich think to oppress the poor and to keep them down and trample on them by their power, but there is a great, a just, a more powerful God in Heaven, who takes care of the poor; they think to crush the widow and orphan, but there is one Being above all who has sworn to be the father of the fatherless, and the husband of the widow. The thunders and lightenings and brimstone from Heaven will come down on the oppressors of the poor, and a fate more dreadful than that which awaited Tyre and Sidon in the day of His wrath, will await the rich and powerful if they continue to trample on the rights of the people. If the poor have no right to the rates, then the rich man has no right to his rents; if the poor man has no right to maintenance from his labour, then the rich man has no right to the wealth which he possesses, and everyone has a right to do what seems good in his own eyes. . . .

J. R. Stephens, trial for seditious language, 15 August 1839
State Trials (new series), iii, col. 1224.

I have taught the people to fear God and honour the Queen; but I have taught them to hate everything that is unconstitutional and anti-Christian. I have told them to take the book of God in their right hand and the book of our laws in the left hand; to have the fear of God at their side, the love of God and their neighbour in their heart, and then to walk abroad upright, fearless of Attorney-Generals and all the awful roll of property-law prosecutors. Yes, gentlemen, there was a banner, 'For child and wife we will war to the knife'. Gentlemen, would not you, every man of you, adopt that banner? . . . I have told the people of England that by law their wives cannot, and their children cannot, be taken from them. I have told the people that by law they have a right to their own firesides; that they have a right to their earnings after their labour has been honestly and faithfully done; a right to their comforts, which their labour ought to procure for them in society, for their little ones, and for that partner to whom they have been bound, and whom they have sworn before God never to desert until death do them part. I have told the people of this country that anything which professes to overthrow the institution of Heaven is not a law according to our Constitution, and cannot be held to be a law in any Court of British jurisprudence, and cannot be expected to be obeyed by any party except the party holding power. Gentlemen, if it be better to obey man rather than God, judge ye.

R. Lowery, 'Passages', *Weekly Record*, 16 August 1856.

Few have understood Stephens; I never could until I came into personal contact with him. He cared nothing about the Charter or the Political Rights question. He and Richard Oastler simply went to the Chartist meetings to advocate a factory Act and a repeal of the New Poor Law. It was mostly in opposition to the latter that he uttered his wildest language, and I believe he so spoke with the hope and expectation that the Government would indict him for seditious opposition to that law . . . that its legality might be tried before the judges . . .

10c Misery and relief

Life of General Sir Charles Napier (1857) ii, pp. 111–15.

Misery is running riot through the greatest part of this district . . . The poor here have resolved to die rather than go into the union houses, and I have not the least doubt that numbers would have starved sooner than go there; certainly they would have resisted hunger until the feebler bodies of their children perished, or been so reduced as never to recover their health. Many who were willing were refused admittance. I know of an old man who being starving was told—Oh you can't have anything today, come again on Thursday. But I have gone two days without food, and shall be dead before Thursday. Oh, we can't help that, you must weather the storm as the others do. And he would have died if the mayor had not fed him . . .

If a starving wretch, irritated by the overseer's domineering insolence answers him, the unfortunate may die, for the overseer will not let him get assistance out of the house, or get admitted in. If he complains, the guardians say to the overseer—Well what are we to do in this case?

Oh! that's a terrible rascal, he is one of the discontented insolent villains that infest this town. 'My friend we can do nothing for you'. So Mr. Overseer is absolute despot . . .

Northern Star, 23 April 1842.

. . . Mr. Beesley then detailed the alarming destitution and misery which prevailed in North Lancashire. They were compelled to lie on shavings; they had no covering for the night save the rags which they wore during the day, and were compelled to have their shirts washed on a Saturday night to appear decent on Sunday; and were destitute of food during a considerable portion of the week. In some places the authorities had done all that laid in their power to put Chartism down; they had threatened to stop the relief of all who were Chartists; one individual who was in the receipt of 3*s.* 6*d.* per week from the authorities, was informed by them that they had heard he had subscribed to the Chartist fund; if he continued this they would give him no more relief; but he boldly told them that he would support the Charter until they had gained their rights as Englishmen, and if they stopped his relief, they should take him and wife and five children into the workhouse. This showed the determined spirit evinced by the men of North Lancashire.

10d The rights of the poor undermined

Richard Oastler, *Fleet Papers*, 1 May 1841.

The New Poor Law is a 'brat' of the Factory system, and like its Sire, it is unchristian, unnatural and unconstitutional. If it be enforced, the Altar, the Crown, and the title to property, will inevitably be destroyed. When the poor man's right to relief and liberty is questioned, the only bond which ties society together is loosened.

10e Wages and the Poor Law

Northern Star, 7 June 1845.

PENSIONER PARSON MALTHUS . . . *philosophized* . . . to inculcate the impious dogma that the poor have no right to live . . .

The abolition of the *legal* relief for the unemployed; the denial of all relief, except on terms that would deter everyone but the soul-destroyed starving slave from accepting it; the institution of the 'workhouse *test*' with its workhouse dress—its *brand* of poverty—its classification—its separation of man and wife and mother and child—its 'scientific' dietaries, of skilly, bread, 4 ozs. of bacon for a whole week, and a morsel of cheese—its dysentery, hurrying off its inmates as if stricken with the plague; all this was well calculated to make the labourer *offer his services* for almost any amount of wage, sooner than subject himself to the cruelties that awaited him if he applied for aid in his necessity to those facetiously called his '*guardians*'. And thus 'Philosophy' accomplished its aims. *It got at the wages of labour.* The Poor Law screw was well adapted to twine the labourer down to less and still less comfort. The less the 'share' of his productions kept for himself, the more there was for those who lived on his labour. Thus was the object of driving him to a 'coarser sort of diet' to be accomplished—and for the said purpose. Whatever, therefore, *interfered with*, or thwarted, this settled design, met with disfavour from '*Philosophy*'. The question of short hours of labour has been particularly opposed by it. The *reason* is sufficiently obvious. Short hours would have counteracted the designs of the 'Philosophers', as manifested in the law to reduce the labourers to live on 'a coarser sort of food'. Short hours would have caused a greater *demand* for labour. With increased demand comes increased prices. Increased wages would have given the labourers a *greater* SHARE of their own productions. This would not have answered the purposes of 'Philosophy'. . . .

11 Chartism

London radicals were from 1836 organized in the LWMA (see above, p. 138) and in May 1838 they drew up the Charter. The BPU had revived in 1837 with bad times, and drew up a petition containing the Six Points of the Charter. Together they provided the political platform for O'Connor's Great Northern Union which he had compounded from the Poor Law and factory struggles in the North. In August 1838 the Charter was nationally adopted; in February 1839 the Chartist convention met in London to prepare the petition for parliament. The petition was rejected in July. After discussing but rejecting a general strike, the convention dissolved in September 1839, and activity went underground, to erupt in the South Wales rising in November. It was quickly suppressed and chartist leaders imprisoned.

This marked the second stage of Chartism, from 1840 to around 1843, when O'Connor reorganized the movement into the National Charter Association, and in which the self-improvement dimensions of Chartism were embodied in the splinter movements of knowledge Chartism, temperance Chartism and Christian Chartism. The second petition was presented and rejected in 1842; tentative co-operation with middle-class radicals and dissenters was explored but collapsed in the Complete Suffrage Union.

The third stage came around 1844 when Chartism developed in two new ways; it became more closely associated with the trades, and O'Connor floated his land plan, estates of independent smallholders, self-sufficient and self-employed. Bad times occurred in 1847, and this third stage culminated with the presenting of the third petition in April 1848. Its rejection was followed by sporadic plotting, government mopped up the conspirators, and by September 1848 this stage of Chartism had ended. Only Ernest Jones, in prison, and the young Harney, remained to lead it into the 1850s.

The debate about the nature of Chartism is represented by 11a and 11b. The sympathetic saw it as a simple cry of distress, suspicious conservatives as a disguise for pillage, sophisticated conservatives as a socialist restructuring of society. Working men, too, hoped for prosperity, political rights and libertarian reforms from Chartism, a range of aspirations that was both old-style radical and new-style socialist. Instances of all of these were to be found in the National Petition of 1842 (11c) in which attacks on taxation and Old Corruption were as much in evidence as attacks on capitalism and a wage economy. Macauley's speech presented the classic conservative view of Chartism: it was an attack on property and thus on civilized society, so in the best interests both of the rulers and the ruled it must be firmly resisted.

Suggestions for further reading

For the national bearings of Chartism, see M. Hovell, *The Chartist Movement* (1918); F. Mather, *Chartism* (Historical Association pamphlet, 1965); G. D. H. Cole, *Chartist Portraits* (1941); A. Schoyen, *The Chartist Challenge* (1958), a biography of G. J. Harney; D. Thompson (ed.), *The Early Chartists* (1971).

For local studies, see A. Briggs (ed.), *Chartist Studies* (1959); A. Wilson, *The Chartist Movement in Scotland* (1970); A. J. Peacock, *Bradford Chartism* (1969); T. Tholfson, 'The Chartist crisis in Birmingham', *International Review of Social History*, 1958; J. Cannon, *The Chartists in Bristol* (1967); P. Searby, *Coventry Politics in the Age of the Chartists* (1965); G. Dalby, 'The Chartist Movement in Halifax and District', *Trans. Halifax Antiquarian Society* (1956); I. Prothero, 'Chartism in London', *Past and Present*, 1969; W. Maehl, 'Chartist Disturbances in North-eastern England in 1839', *International Review of Social History*, 1963; J. Edwards, 'Chartism in Norwich', *Yorkshire Bulletin of Economic and Social Research*, 1967; P. Wyncoll, *Nottingham Chartism* (1966); D. Williams, *John Frost* (1939).

11a Chartism: the middle-class interpretation

H. Martineau, *History of England during the Thirty Years Peace* (1849), ii, pp. 262–3.

And what were those stirrings? What was it all about? The difficulty of understanding and telling a story is from its comprehending so vast a variety of things and persons. Those who have not looked into Chartism think that it means one thing—a revolution. Some who talk as if they assumed to understand it, explain that Chartism is of two kinds—Physical Force Chartism, and Moral Force Chartism—as if these were not merely an intimation of two ways of pursuing an object not yet described! Those who look deeper—who go out upon the moors by torchlight, who talk with a suffering brother under the hedge, or beside the loom, who listen to the groups outside the Union workhouse, or in the public house among the Durham coal-pits, will feel long bewildered as to what Chartism is, and will conclude at last that it is another name for popular discontent—a comprehensive general term under which are included all protests against social suffering.

Archibald Alison, 'The Chartists and Universal Suffrage', *Blackwood's Edinburgh Magazine*, September 1839.

The working-classes have now proved themselves unworthy of that extension of the Suffrage for which they contend; and that, whatever doubts might formerly have existed on the subject in the minds of well-meaning and enthusiastic, but simple and ill-informed men, it is now established beyond all doubt, that Universal Suffrage in reality means nothing else but universal pillage . . . What the working-classes understand by political power, is just the means of putting their hands in their neighbours' pockets; and that it was the belief that the Reform

Bill would give them that power, which was the main cause of the enthusiasm in its favour, and the disgust of the failure of these hopes, the principal reason of the present clamour for an extension of the Suffrage.

Annual Register (1839), i, p. 304, quoted in M. Beer, *A History of British Socialism* (1940), p. 45.

Apart from the political demands of the Chartists, the movement is characterized by other noteworthy conceptions. The hostility of the Chartists is directed less against the privileged condition of society, which up to the present was the particular object of democratic indignation, than against capitalists in general. The movement is, in fact, an insurrection which is expressly directed against the middle classes. A violent change in the system of government is demanded by the Chartists not for the purpose of receiving more power and privileges, but—as far as their aim permits of any definition—for the purpose of producing a hitherto non-existent condition of society, in which wage labour and capital do not exist at all.

11b Chartism: the working-class view

Bronterre O'Brien, *Operative*, 17 March 1839.

Universal suffrage means meat and drink and clothing, good hours, and good beds, and good substantial furniture for every man and woman and child who will do a fair day's work. Universal Suffrage means a complete mastery, by all the people over all the laws and institutions in the country; and with that mastery the power of providing suitable employment for all, as well as of securing to all the full proceeds of their employment.

F. O'Connor, *Northern Star*, 1 August 1846.

That Chartism which has fustian jackets, blistered hands and unshorn chins as its emblems, has been denounced by those who would make it a thing of refinement and respectability, while we repeat the fact to our readers that Chartism means poverty—and poverty is a consequence of class legislation; the legitimate deduction from which is, that before poverty ceases class legislation must be destroyed.

B. Wilson, *The Struggles of an Old Chartist* (1887).

The Chartists were called ugly names, the swinish multitude, unwashed and levellers. I never knew levelling advocated amongst the Chartists, neither in public or private, for they did not believe in it, nor have I known a case of plunder in the town, though thousands have marched through its streets to meetings in various places. What they wanted was a voice in making the laws they were called upon to obey; they believed that taxation without representation was tyranny, and ought to be resisted; they took a leading part in agitating in favour of the ten hours question, the repeal of the taxes on knowledge, education, co-operation, civil and religious liberty and the land question, for they were the true pioneers in all the great movements of their time.

11c The 1842 petition

Hansard (third series), cols. 13–90, 3 May 1842.

TO THE HONOURABLE THE COMMONS OF GREAT BRITAIN AND IRELAND, IN PARLIAMENT ASSEMBLED.

The Petition of the undersigned people of the United Kingdom, Sheweth—That Government originated from, was designed to protect the freedom and promote the happiness of, and ought to be responsible to, the whole people,

That the only authority on which any body of men can make laws and govern society, is delegation from the people.

That as Government was designed for the benefit and protection of, and must be obeyed and supported by all, therefore all should be equally represented. . . .

That your honourable House, as at present constituted, has not been elected by, and acts irresponsibly of, the people; and hitherto has only represented parties, and benefited the few, regardless of the miseries, grievances, and petitions of the many. Your honourable House has enacted laws contrary to the expressed wishes of the people, and by unconstitutional means enforced obedience to them, thereby creating an unbearable despotism on the one hand, and degrading slavery on the other . . .

That your petitioners instance, in proof of their assertion, that your honourable House has not been elected by the people; that the population of Great Britain and Ireland is at the present time about twenty-six millions of persons; and that yet, out of this number, little more than nine hundred thousand have been permitted to vote in the recent election of representatives to make laws to govern the whole.

That the existing state of representation is not only extremely limited and unjust, but unequally divided, and gives preponderating influence to the landed and monied interests to the utter ruin of the small-trading and labouring classes.

That the borough of Guildford, with a population of 3,920 returns to Parliament as many members as the Tower Hamlets, with a population of 300,000; Evesham, with a population of 3,998, elects as many representatives as Manchester, with a population of 200,000; . . .

That bribery, intimidation, corruption, perjury, and riot, prevail at all parliamentary elections, to an extent best understood by the Members of your honourable House.

That your petitioners complain that they are enormously taxed to pay the interest of what is termed the national debt, a debt amounting at present to £800,000,000, being only a portion of the enormous amount expended in cruel and expensive wars for the suppression of all liberty, by men not authorised by the people, and who, consequently, had no right to tax posterity for the outrages committed by them upon mankind. And your petitioners loudly complain of the augmentation of that debt, after twenty-six years of almost uninterrupted peace, and whilst poverty and discontent rage over the land.

That taxation, both general and local, is at this time too enormous to be borne; and in the opinion of your petitioners is contrary to the spirit of the Bill of Rights, wherein it is clearly expressed that no subject shall be compelled to contribute to any tax, talliage, or aid, unless imposed by common consent in Parliament.

That in England, Ireland, Scotland, and Wales, thousands of people are dying from actual want; and your petitioners, whilst sensible that poverty is the great exciting cause of crime, view with mingled astonishment and alarm the ill provision made for the poor, the aged, and infirm; and likewise perceive, with feelings of indignation, the determination of your honourable House to continue the Poor-law Bill in operation, notwithstanding the many proofs which have been afforded by sad experience of the unconstitutional principle of that bill, of its unchristian character, and of the cruel and murderous effects produced upon the wages of working men, and the lives of the subjects of this realm.

That your petitioners conceive that bill to be contrary to all previous statutes, opposed to the spirit of the constitution, and an actual violation of the precepts of the Christian religion; and, therefore, your petitioners, look with apprehension to the results which may flow from its continuance.

That your petitioners would direct the attention of your honourable House to the great disparity existing between the wages of the producing millions, and the salaries of those whose comparative usefulness ought to be questioned, where riches and luxury prevail amongst the rulers, and poverty and starvation amongst the ruled.

That your petitioners, with all due respect and loyalty, would compare the daily income of the Sovereign Majesty with that of thousands of the working men of this nation; and whilst your petitioners have learned that her Majesty receives daily for her private use the sum of £164 17*s.* 10*d.* they have also ascertained that many thousands of the families of the labourers are only in the receipt of $3\frac{3}{4}$*d.* per head per day . . .

That notwithstanding the wretched and unparalleled condition of the people, your honourable House has manifested no disposition to curtail the expenses of the State, to diminish taxation, or promote general prosperity.

That unless immediate remedial measures be adopted, your petitioners fear the increasing distress of the people will lead to results fearful to contemplate; because your petitioners can produce evidence of the gradual decline of wages, at the same time that the constant increase of the national burdens must be apparent to all.

That your petitioners know that it is the undoubted constitutional right of the people, to meet freely, when, how and where they choose, in public places, peaceably, in the day, to discuss their grievances, and political or other subjects, or for the purpose of framing, discussing, or passing any vote, petition, or remonstrance upon any subject whatsoever.

That your petitioners complain that the right has unconstitutionally been infringed; and 500 well disposed persons have been arrested, excessive bail demanded, tried by packed juries, sentenced to imprisonment, and treated as felons of the worst description.

That an unconstitutional police force is distributed all over the country, at enormous cost, to prevent the due exercise of the people's rights. And your petitioners are of opinion that the Poor-law Bastiles and the police stations, being co-existent, have originated from the same curse, viz., the increased desire on the part of the irresponsible few to oppress and starve the many.

That a vast and unconstitutional army is upheld at the public expense, for the purpose of repressing public opinion in the three kingdoms, and likewise to intimidate the millions in the due exercise of those rights and privileges which ought to belong to them.

That your petitioners complain that the hours of labour, particularly of the factory workers, are protracted beyond the limits of human endurance, and that the wages earned, after unnatural application to toil in heated and unhealthy workshops, are inadequate to sustain the bodily strength, and supply those comforts which are so imperative after an excessive waste of physical energy.

That your petitioners also direct the attention of your honourable House to the starvation wages of the agricultural labourer, and view with horror and indignation the paltry income of those whose toil gives being to the staple food of this people.

That your petitioners deeply deplore the existence of any kind of monopoly in this nation, and whilst they unequivocally condemn the levying of any tax upon the necessaries of life, and upon those articles principally required by the labouring classes, they are also sensible that the abolition of any one monopoly will never unshackle labour from its misery until the people possess that power under which all monopoly and oppression must cease; and your petitioners respectfully mention the existing monopolies of the suffrage, of paper money, of machinery, of land, of the public press, of religious privileges, of the means of travelling and transit, and of a host of other evils too numerous to mention, all arising from class legislation, but which your honourable House has always consistently endeavoured to increase instead of diminish.

That your petitioners are sensible, from the numerous petitions presented to your honourable House, that your honourable House is fully acquainted with the grievances of the working men; and your petitioners pray that the rights and wrongs of labour may be considered, with a view to the protection of the one, and to the removal of the other; because your petitioners are of opinion that it is the worst species of legislation which leaves the grievances of society to be removed only by violence or revolution, both of which may be apprehended if complaints are unattended to and petitions despised.

That your petitioners complain that upwards of nine millions of pounds per annum are unjustly abstracted from them to maintain a church establishment, from which they principally dissent; . . . Your petitioners complain that it is unjust, and not in accordance with the Christian religion, to enforce compulsory support of religious creeds, and expensive church establishments, with which the people do not agree.

That your petitioners believe all men have a right to worship God as may appear best to their consciences, and that no legislative enactments should interfere between man and his Creator.

That your petitioners direct the attention of your honourable House to the enormous revenue annually swallowed up by the bishops and the clergy, and entreat you to contrast their deeds with the conduct of the founder of the Christian religion, who denounced worshippers of Mammon, and taught charity, meekness, and brotherly love. . . .

That your petitioners maintain that it is the inherent, indubitable, and constitutional right, founded upon the ancient practice of the realm of England, and supported by well approved statutes, of every male inhabitant of the United Kingdom, he being of age and of sound mind, non-convict of crime, and not confined under any judicial process, to exercise the elective franchise in the choice of Members to serve in the Commons House of Parliament.

That your petitioners can prove, that by the ancient customs and statutes of this realm, Parliament should be held once in each year.

That your petitioners maintain that Members elected to serve in Parliament ought to be the servants of the people, and should, at short and stated intervals, return to their constituencies, to ascertain if their conduct is approved of, and to give the people power to reject all who have not acted honestly and justly.

That your petitioners complain that possession of property is made the test of men's qualification to sit in Parliament.

That your petitioners can give proof that such qualification is irrational, unnecessary, and not in accordance with the ancient usages of England.

That your petitioners complain, that by influence, patronage, and intimidation, there is at present no purity of election; and your petitioners contend for the right of voting by ballot.

That your petitioners complain that seats in your honourable House are sought for at a most extravagant rate of expense; which proves an enormous degree of fraud and corruption.

That your petitioners, therefore, contend, that to put an end to secret political traffic, all representatives should be paid a limited amount for their services.

That your petitioners complain of the many grievances borne by the people of Ireland, and contend that they are fully entitled to a repeal of the legislative union.

That your petitioners have viewed with great indignation the partiality shown to the aristocracy in the courts of justice, and the cruelty of that system of law which deprived Frost, Williams, and Jones, of the benefit of their objections offered by Sir Frederick Pollock during the trial at Monmouth, and which was approved of by a large majority of the judges.

That your petitioners beg to assure your honourable House that they cannot, within the limits of this their petition, set forth even a tithe of the many grievances of which they may justly complain; but should your honourable House be pleased to grant your petitioners a hearing by representatives at the Bar of your honourable House, your petitioners will be enabled to unfold a tale of wrong and suffering—of intolerable injustice—which will create utter astonishment in the minds of all benevolent and good men, that the people of Great Britain and Ireland have so long quietly endured their wretched condition, brought upon them as it has been by unjust exclusion from political authority, and by the manifold corruption of class-legislation.

That your petitioners, therefore, exercising their just constitutional right, demand that your honourable House do remedy the many gross and manifest evils of which your petitioners complain, do immediately, without alteration, deduction, or addition, pass into a law the document entitled 'The People's Charter,' . . .

And that your petitioners, desiring to promote the peace of the United Kingdom, security of property, and prosperity of commerce, seriously and earnestly press this, their petition, on the attention of your honourable House.

And your petitioners, etc.

Chartism: the response of the House of Commons to the 1842 petition

Mr. T. Duncombe, 'Never were the people as determined as at the present moment by every constitutional means to obtain the franchise . . . When they see their interests disregarded, and their feelings insulted, and when they have no hope of better times or better treatment, unless they work out their own redress—when you offer them mere words, and endeavour to stop their cravings by the delusive promises of a Queen's speech—when you tell them that "you feel extremely for the distress of the manufacturing districts, which they have borne with exemplary patience and fortitude" but offer them no remedy beyond your compassion—what can you expect but that they should make their way to this house, and, as you will do nothing for them, endeavour to do something for themselves? . . .'

Mr. Fielden, '. . . By the bad legislation in that House, all the people had been made politicians, and they had got an impression on their minds that nothing but a Radical change in the constitution of that House would ever give the people what they had a right to.'

Sir John Easthope, '. . . The petition came from those who were suffering distress, and who displayed that discontent which was the natural concomitant of distress. . . . His sincere conviction was, that if they sought to aggravate the grievous distress which now existed, they could not be more successful than they would be if they obtained a grant of all the prayers in their petition.'

Mr. Macauley, '. . . I believe that universal suffrage would be fatal to all purposes for which government exists, and for which aristocracies and all other things exist, and that it is utterly incompatible with the very existence of civilization. I conceive that civilization rests on the security of property . . . If I understand this petition rightly, I believe it to contain a declaration, that the remedies for the evils of which it complains, and under which this country suffers, are to be found in a great and sweeping confiscation of property, and I am firmly convinced, that the effect of any such measure would be not merely to overturn those institutions which now exist, and to ruin those who are rich, but to make the poor poorer, and the amount of misery of the country even greater, than it is now represented to be. . . . I have no more unkind feelings towards these petitioners than I have towards the sick man, who calls for a draught of cold water, although he is satisfied that it would be death to him; nor than I have for the poor Indians, whom I have seen collected around the granaries in India at a time of scarcity, praying that the doors might be thrown open, and the grain distributed; but would not in the one case give the draught of water, nor would I in the other give the key of the granary; because I know that by doing so I shall only make a scarcity a famine, and by giving such relief, enormously increase the evil. No one can say that such a spoliation of property as these petitioners point at would be a relief to the evils of which they complain, and I believe that no one would deny, that it would be a great addition to the mischief which is proposed to be removed. But if such would be the result, why should such power be conferred upon the petitioners? That they should ask for it is not blameable; but on what principle is it that we, knowing their views are entirely delusive, should put into their hands the irresistable power of doing all this evil to us and to themselves? . . . Now is it possible that, according to the principles of human nature, if you give them this power, it would not be used to its fullest extent? There has been a constant and systematic attempt for years to represent the Government as being able to do, and as bound to attempt that which no Government ever attempted; and instead of the Government being represented, as is the truth, as being supported by the people, it has been treated as if the Government supported the people: it has been treated as if the Government possessed some mine of wealth—some extraordinary means of supplying the wants of the people; as if they could give them bread from the clouds—water from the rocks—to increase the bread and the fishes five thousand fold. Is it possible to believe that the moment you give them absolute, supreme, irresistible power, they will forget all this? You propose to give them supreme power; in every constituent body throughout the empire capital and accumulated property is to be placed absolutely at the foot of labour. How is it possible to doubt what the result will be? . . . Let us, if we can, picture to ourselves the consequences of such a spoliation as it is proposed should take place. Would it end with one spoliation? How could it? That distress which is the motive now for calling on this House to interfere would be only doubled and trebled by the act; the measure of distress would become greater after that spoliation, and the bulwarks by which fresh acts of the same character would have been removed. The Government would rest upon spoliation—all the property which any man possessed would be supported by it, and is it possible to suppose that a new state of things would exist wherein every thing that was done was right? What must be the effect of such a sweeping confiscation of property? No experience enables us to guess at it. All I can say is, that it seems to me to be something more horrid than can be imagined . . . Believing this, I will oppose with every faculty which I possess the proposition for universal suffrage . . .'

12 Protest Chartism

Chartism was seen above all as a protest against hunger and physical suffering (12a). Bad government was thought to be its cause, and universal suffrage as embodied in the Charter was to be its remedy. But what if the government ignored the demand for the vote? Most delegates to the Convention favoured a range of 'ulterior measures', such as exclusive dealing and even a general strike, to reinforce their demands (12b). Some, such as Harney and Dr John Taylor, were prepared to go further and advocate physical force as self-defence against starvation (12c), to the dismay of a Lovett or Hetherington who thought physical force simple folly. The line between physical and moral force was by no means clear cut, but it did distinguish between those who thought that the vote must be extracted from a hostile government and hostile middle class (on the model of Catholic Emancipation and 1832 itself), and those who thought it would come to a working class that was a proven and reliable member of the political community, an attitude that entailed an emphasis on self-improvement, moral reform and a willingness to collaborate with the middle class.

In the country there was widespread arming and the making of pikes (12d); and General Napier, the Northern Commander of troops, maintained a careful intelligence network (12e). The most popular and potentially powerful of 'ulterior measures' was the general strike (Benbow's National Holiday, see above, p. 167); but when delegates reported that few districts were fully prepared or had reserves of food, the Convention abandoned it in favour of a token demonstration. In Bolton, this was more than token, and Warden and Lloyd were charged with inciting to riot (12g). Warden's defence was an admirable statement of the Chartist case for the vote: the producers of wealth should become full members of the political public they sustained; Lloyd, for his part, made a moving statement of personal poverty and privation.

The Convention disbanded in September 1839, but arming went on, and a small secret committee met regularly in London with plans for a general rising in early November, centred on South Wales, the West Riding and possibly Newcastle. But bad communications and bad nerves meant that only South Wales rose (12h); its miners led by John Frost, a local Chartist magistrate, marched on Newport. Frost was threatened with execution, so a second round of conspiracy then began to save him; this broke out at Dewsbury and at Sheffield (12i) in middle January 1840, and in Bradford at the end of January. Frost was eventually transported, Holberry sentenced to four years' and Peddie to three years' imprisonment. By the summer, 500 leading Chartists were imprisoned, and the first stage of Chartism, primarily a 'protest chartism' that emphasized direct action, was over.

Suggestions for further reading

For the risings, see D. Williams, *John Frost* (1939); A. Peacock, *Bradford Chartism* (1969 pamphlet). On the government side, F. Mather, *Public Order in the Age of the Chartists* (1959).

12a Distress and desperation

R. Lowery, *Weekly Record*, 20 September 1856.

One delegate, a handloom weaver [Richard Marsden of Preston], described to me his privations for want of food, and how his starving wife, unable to supply nature's nutriment to her sucking babe, the infant had drawn blood from her breasts instead . . . There is something in the effects of hunger and of the sight of your family suffering from it which none can judge of but those who have felt it. The equilibrium of temper and judgement is deranged as your child looks up with piteous face and tearful eye, asking with suppressed voice for the bread it knows you have not. I have heard my own child so ask for the bread I had not to give, and my prayer is, God help the man so tried.

T. Cooper, *Life* (1872).

I saw lounging groups of ragged men in my time. I hope what I saw will never be seen again. And I heard words of misery and discontent from the poor that, I hope, are not heard now. I should not like to hear them again, for I know not what they might again impel me to say or do.

12b Ulterior measures

Charter, 19 May 1839.

From numerous communications we received we believe you expect us to collect the will and intentions of the country respecting the most efficient means for causing the People's Charter to become the law of the land. Anxious, therefore, clearly to ascertain the opinions and determinations of the people in the shortest possible time, and doubly anxious to secure their righteous objects bloodless and stainless, we respectfully submit the following propositions for your serious consideration:

That at all the simultaneous public meetings to be held for the purpose of petitioning the Queen to call good men to her councils, as well as at all subsequent meetings of your unions or associations up to the 1st of July, you submit the following questions to the people there assembled:—

1. Whether they will be prepared, at the request of the Convention, to withdraw all sums of money they may individually or collectively have placed in savings banks, private banks, or in the hands of any person hostile to their rights? Whether, at the same request, they will be prepared immediately to convert all their paper money into gold and silver? 2. Whether if the convention shall determine that a sacred month will be necessary to prepare the millions to secure the Charter

of their political salvation, they will firmly resolve to abstain from their labours during that period? 3. Whether they would refuse payment of rents, rates, and taxes? 4. Whether, according to their old constitutional right, they have prepared themselves with the arms of free men to defend the laws and constitutional privileges their ancestors bequeathed to them? 5. Whether they will provide themselves with Chartist candidates, so as to be prepared to propose them for their representatives at the next general election; and if returned by show of hands, such candidates to consider themselves veritable representatives of the people, to meet in London at a time hereafter to be determined on? 6. Whether they will resolve to deal exclusively with Chartists; and in all cases of persecution rally around and protect all those who may suffer in this righteous cause? 7. Whether, by all means in their power, they will perseveringly contend for the great objects of the People's Charter, and resolve that no counter-agitation for a less measure of justice shall divert them from this righteous object? 8. Whether they would abstain from purchasing newspapers which opposed them? 9. Whether the people will determine to obey all the just and constitutional requests of the majority of the Convention?

12c A meeting on ulterior measures

The Crown and Anchor, reported in *Northern Star*, 23 March 1839.

J. B. O'Brien . . . As the House of Commons was elected by only 700,000 out of 25,000,000 he did not consider that it existed by the consent of the nation. If he should see the petition signed by millions, he would consider that he had a right to try any measures from marbles to manslaughter for carrying out the petition . . . They would sign the petition, and be able to say with a correspondent of his from the North, who in a letter he received only the day before, said, 'There is not a labouring man here, from 16 to 60, who has not signed the petition, and there is a pike for every signature' (Loud cheers). Now he would not advise them to get pikes or guns, because the law did not allow him to—and that was his only reason (laughter). He was only an historian. All the men of Leeds and Lancashire had got pikes. He did not recommend those present to get them also—he only mentioned the fact . . .

G. J. Harney, Secretary of the Democratic Association, being loudly called for . . . would ask, should there be any more petitions (no, no,) unless signed with steel pens? (cheers). There should be no more Conventions. The 6th of May should be the last day for doubt or hesitation. The people should then set about asserting their rights in earnest, and should have before the close of this year Universal Suffrage or Death. (Loud cheers).

The Convention on ulterior measures

Northern Star, 27 April 1839.

Hetherington,

The manner in which physical force had been discussed by some of their members had been the cause of a great many persons not taking an active part in the proceedings, and the use of such language had been a handle to their enemies for imputing to them a doctrine which they had, as a body, done their utmost to repudiate. (Hear). In his late mission he found that the middle classes invariably raised objections against them in consequence of this constant recurrence to physical force . . . He would, when he found the people had tried the influence of moral force, and had found it insufficient to answer them, be found doing his duty as one of the foremost of the physical force men.

O'Connor,

There was no disposition on the part of the people to come into collision with the law; the people would not have recourse to that description of physical force which their enemies would wish . . . They would not be so foolish however as to bare their naked and unarmed breasts to the disciplined bodies of soldiers . . . the resistance of the people would consist in their abstinence from labour, and the men who derived their property from that labour, would find that they could not long maintain so unequal a contest (Hear, hear). The very argueing of the question of physical force, as it had hitherto been urged had given great strength to the Government . . . They might depend upon it, however, that the moment moral force failed physical force would slip in and, like an electrical shock, effect what the other had failed to accomplish.

12d Pikes and guns

Handbill of May 1839, quoted in General Sir Charles Napier, *op. cit.*, ii, p. 29.

Dear brothers! Now are the times to try men's souls! Are your arms ready? Have you plenty of powder and shot? Have you screwed up your courage to the sticking place? Do you intend to be freemen or slaves? Are you inclined to hope for a fair day's wages for a fair day's work? Ask yourselves these questions, and remember that your safety depends on the strength of your own right arms. How long are you going to allow your mothers, your wives, your children and your sweethearts, to be ever toiling for other people's benefit? Nothing can convince tyrants of their folly but gunpowder and steel: so put your trust in God my boys and keep your powder dry. Be patient a day or two, but be ready at a minute's warning; no man knows today what tomorrow may bring forth; be ready then to nourish the tree of liberty, WITH THE BLOOD OF TYRANTS.

You can get nothing by cowardice, or petitioning. France is in arms; Poland groans beneath the bloody Russian yoke; and Irishmen pant to enjoy the sweets of liberty. Aye dear brethren, the whole world depends on you for support; if you fail the working man's sun is set for ever! The operatives of Paris have again taken possession of the city. Can you remain passive when all the world is in arms? No my friends! Up with the cap of liberty, down with all oppression and enjoy the benefit of your toil. Now or never is the time: be sure you do not neglect your arms, but let the blood of all you suspect moisten the soil of your native land, that you may forever destroy even the remembrance of your poverty and shame.

Let England's sons then prime her guns
And save each good man's daughter,
In tyrants' blood baptize your sons
And every villain slaughter.
By pike and sword, your freedom strive to gain,
Or make one bloody Moscow of old England's plain.

Thomas Devyr, *The Odd Book of the Nineteenth Century* (1882), pp. 177–8.

I was present in some part of nearly every Saturday at the pike market, to take sharp note of the sales. The market was held in a long garret room, over John Blakey's shop in the Side. In rows were benches of boards, supported on tressels, along which the Winlanton and Swalwall chain and nail makers brought in their interregnum of pikes, each a dozen or two, rolled up in the smith's apron. The price for a finished and polished article was two shillings and sixpence . . . From that time [August to November 1839] . . . we counted sixty thousand shafted pikes.

12e Physical force

Life of General Sir Charles Napier (1857), ii.

The soldier's comment

March 1839

We have force to overthrow the Chartists. They have seemingly no organization, no leaders, and a strong tendency to turn rebellion into money, for pikes costing a shilling are sold for three and sixpence.

25 July 1839

The Chartists say they will keep the sacred month. Egregrious folly! they will do no such thing; the poor cannot do it, they must plunder and then they will be hanged by hundreds: they will split upon it, but if mad enough to attempt it, they are lost.

6 August 1839

The plot thickens. Meetings increase and are so violent, and arms so abound, I know not what to think. The Duke of Portland tells me there is no doubt of an intended general rising. Poor people! They will suffer. They have set all England against them and their physical force:—fools! We have the physical force, not they. They talk of their hundred thousands of men. Who is to move them when I am dancing round them with cavalry, and pelting them with cannonshot? What would their 100,000 men do with my 100 rockets wriggling their fiery tails among them, roaring, scorching, tearing, smashing all they came near? And when in desperation and despair they broke to fly, how would they bear five regiments of cavalry careering through them? Poor men! How little they know of physical force!

6 January 1840

The Chartists have what they call rockets, which they believe will, if thrust into a window, blow the roof off a house. Their arms are chiefly pistols and they have cast a vast quantity of balls. Their plan is to attack the middle classes and reduce them to the same state of poverty with themselves. They have no fear of the soldiers, because they mean to go about in small parties of fives and sixes according to their classes and sections, with their arms hidden and so as not to attract attention by their numbers . . . The moment any Chartist is convicted, whether it be Frost or any other, this warfare is to begin and all labour instantly to cease. . . .

12 January 1840

Patrolled all last night. Saw the Chartist sentinels in the streets; we knew they were armed with pistols, but I advised the magistrates not to meddle with them. Seizing these men could do no good; it would not stop Chartism if they were all hanged; and as they offered no violence, why starve their wretched families and worry them with a long imprisonment? I repeat it, Chartism cannot be stopped, God forbid that it should: what we want is to stop the letting loose a large body of armed cut-throats upon the public.

The Attorney General's comment.

Lancaster Trials, 1843, *State Trials* (new series), iv, col 1183.

. . . I am told about the words, 'peace, law and order'. Gentlemen, on this subject I think Mr O'Connor and the Chartists have made a great mistake in point of law—I may almost say in point of fact. They seem to think that, provided no bones are broken, peace, law and order are preserved. Their notion seems to be that if five thousand people march to a mill, and present their physical intimidation, bludgeons, etc., and with threats upon their brow, then provided the parties go out without being forced to, it seems to be the opinion of those defendants that there is no violation of the law. They fancy that physical intimidation is moral force. They say they do no mischief; but they go in such large numbers that no effectual resistance can be offered, and then they say, 'Don't break windows or heads' . . .

12f The general strike

R. Lowery, *Weekly Record*, 22 November 1856.

The 'National Holiday', or 'sacred month' of cessation from all labour, was an idea which had originated with the Birmingham men. Whatever might have been meant by it at first, it meant in the people's minds the chances of a physical contest; not an insurrection or assault on the authorities, but that by retiring from labour, like the Roman plebians of old to the Aventine-hills, they would so derange the whole country that the authorities would endeavour to coerce them back, and that they would resist the authorities unless their rights were conceded, and thus bring the struggle to an issue. Hence the *Northern Star* and the speakers had advised the people to arm.

F. O'Connor, *Northern Star*, 3 August 1839.

Of its supporters the delegates for Marylebone, Lambeth, Southwark, Bristol, Brighton, Bath and Hyde in Cheshire were seven of the thirteen who carried the vote, representing constituencies of which I may venture to assert, with the exception of Bristol and Hyde, not five hundred men would stop work. And are we thus to allow the votes of constituencies, by no means organized, to destroy the whole of the North, the Midland Counties, and Scotland? . . . Let the men of Marylebone, of Southwark, of Lambeth, and of Tower Hamlets, prove the theory of their Delegates by their practice. Let them commence the strike, and the post which carries the tidings, will operate with a magic influence upon every working man through out the length and breadth of the land . . .

Many men have threatened to abandon the Convention, or the cause, in the event of this or that measure not being carried. I never have, but I do now most emphatically warn you, that the attempt to stop work for a month would either have the effect of subjugating the working men more than ever to the will of their masters, or of terminating in a short and sanguinary sectional struggle, the result of which would be a licence for every rich man to shoot as many poor men as he thought proper.

I am aware that agitation is more the province of the poor, than the more comfortable labourer. I am aware that many who are starving say, 'we cannot wait, we will not wait,'—show me that the result would not lead to a longer 'wait', and it shall have my most hearty concurrence . . .

If I thought that you could test the value of labour by a month's holiday, I would say have it. If I thought you could live in peace any way, and not subject yourselves and your families to greater privations, I would say have it. But you know—you all know—that the baker will not bake; the butcher will not kill, and the brewer will not brew; and then, what becomes of the millions of starving human beings? . . . Make your necessary arrangements; have a three days' holiday, instead of a month's strike, and what you fail to effect by it, would have been equally lost by the month. For three days you can live in peace, while you exhibit your strength, and for three days the more fortunate would contribute to the sustenance and support of those who have been impoverished by the system; but, I never will, with a certainty of my own dinner, recommend a project which may cause millions to starve. No; I would rather go to battle. I would rather brave all than hear the cry of your hungry selves and your hungry children, and know that my folly had been the cause.

Charter, 11 August 1839.

That from the evidence which has reached this council from various parts of the country, we are unanimously of opinion, that the people are not prepared to carry out the sacred month, on the 12th of August. The same evidence, however, convinces us that the great body of the working people, including most of the trades, may be induced to cease work on the 12th instant, for one, two or three days, in order to devote the whole of that time to solemn processions and meetings, for deliberating on the present awful state of the country, and devising the best means of averting the hideous despotism, with which the industrious orders are menaced by the murderous majority of the upper and middle classes, who prey upon their labour . . .

12g The national holiday

John Warden and George Lloyd of Bolton, defendents at the Liverpool Assizes, reported in *Northern Star*, 11 April 1840. [Found not guilty.]

Attorney General, (Sergeant Atcherley,) in opening this case, said this was a prosecution of a serious character. The 12th of August last, it would be remembered was the day intended for the National Holiday . . . In the town of Bolton on that occasion mobs of people assembled of an alarming character, a stop was put to all public confidence and security, and public business was suspended; the military had to be called in; and the Riot Act had to be read. The indictment charged the two defendents [John Warden and George Lloyd] with being concerned in that riot . . .

Frederick M. Baker called—Witness said he was a police officer at

Bolton . . . A great number of people assembled during the day; and the effect was that the shopkeepers closed their shops, and business was almost entirely suspended . . . On the morning of the 12th, he saw Lloyd about six o'clock addressing the mob . . . He heard him say they were not to cause disturbance, but if interfered with, to act like men determined to have their rights. Let their tyrants see that they were not to be frightened into surrender of their birthright, but that they were determined to have it, and willing to die for the cause. They dispersed after that, and assembled again in the Marketplace . . . Lloyd then addressed them, and said he was not an advocate for rioting, but he would have them remember that the Reform Bill was gained by the riots at Bristol.—The mob continued to meet during the day. In the evening many thousands assembled again, and it was such a multitude that the civil force could not contend with . . . They then paraded the streets, some of them carrying bludgeons. There was great shouting, hooting the police, and creating great terror in the people. Even the shutters of private houses were closed. Witness, after the proceedings of the 12th received directions to apprehend the prisoners . . .

A police officer named Bradshaw was next called, and stated that the crowd on the 12th of August went about to a number of factories and induced the workmen to leave their work . . . The defendants were leaders of the crowd. Would give instances. They fell in rank when Lloyd told them, and *they insisted on rescueing him when he told them to be quiet*. (A laugh).

John Nicholson. Tea-dealer, Hotel-street, Bolton, was a special constable on the 12th August. At seven o'clock in the morning of that day, he saw a crowd there of 500 or more. He heard Lloyd say, the time is now arrived when the Charter must either become the law of the land, or we must remain passive slaves in the hands of our enemies. Be firm, be resolute, and the victory is yours. Peaceable if we can, but forcibly if we must. He then advised the crowd to take a walk round the town with him before breakfast. They did so . . .

John Warden,

My Lord and Gentlemen of the Jury . . .

Gentlemen, the principles of which I have been the feeble but fearless advocate and defender, are identical with those which in former days were promulgated by the Miltons, the Hampdens, and the Sydneys . . . They tend not in their effects, as you may have been led to suppose, to the production of bloodshed, of anarchy, and of strife; but they contribute on the contrary, to the conservation of the best interests of man—to the protection of property, to the preservation of social harmony, and to the defence of all that is time-hallowed and true in our institutions whether moral, political or religious . . . For if you once destroy the aspirations of the great mass of the people for political privileges, or debar them from the exercise or rights which they feel they ought to possess, you crush them into an abyss of slavery, and, having degraded them into slaves, you must expect from them nothing but the vices of slaves; immorality in all its multiplied form; social misery with social degradation; political hatred with political wrong. Once bestow upon the men who produce all your wealth—who build your houses—who fill your granaries—who make your table groan beneath the accumulated luxuries of every clime—who provide for your wants in peace, and who protect you in the hour of danger—who man your fleets, and who fight your battles;—once bestow upon these men the power of exercising those privileges which none have a right to deprive them of, and which all ought to possess, and you will put a stop to those political animosities which always disturb, and often destroy those social relations, without which no community can long exist, and without which no nation can be powerful and happy. We, the Chartists, have asked no more than this, and depend upon it, the great and growing wants of the people can never be satisfied with less.

Gentlemen, we live in new times—the labourer is no longer content to live as a mere passive serf, created only to minister to the wants of some feudal lord, or some rich commercial speculators. He has nobler aims and higher aspirations. He feels that he was not made for the purpose of conforming to institutions which he had not the power of modifying, according to his wants, and which, instead of multiplying his pleasures, tend in their general effects to extend the number of his miseries . . . he feels that the welfare of the people can only be promoted and secured when the laws, so potent in their influences over the happiness of the community, are made by all and for the interest of all . . .

What then, Gentlemen, do the Chartists require? They ask simply for a voice in the enactment of the laws which they are called upon to obey; a voice in the distribution of the taxes to which they are compelled to contribute. They demand the Ballot, in order that the vote which they give may be substantially their own; they require no Property Qualification for Members, in order that they may not be restricted in their choice; and they desire that those whom they elect may not have the power of remaining in office in opposition to the fairly expressed opinions and interests of the constituency. Do they ask too much? Do they ask anything incompatible with the dictates of common sense, or the principles of the Constitution? It may be said that the great mass of the people are too ignorant to exercise the elective franchise with interest to themselves individually, or to the community in the aggregate. Those, however, who profess this opinion forget that the great body of the people is *actually appealed to* on all questions of paramount public interest; and experience tells us that on most occasions the public mind has been far ahead of the Legislature or the Ministry. The repeal of the Corporation and Test Acts, Catholic Emancipation and the Reform bill . . . may be mentioned in illustration of this fact . . . And even now, is not the existence of the working classes, aye, of the working classes, invoked on all great questions? Do the rich manufacturers desire a repeal of the Corn Laws? They appeal to the people. Is a reform in the corporations considered desirable? The people are appealed to. Does one great party advocate church extension? Lecturers are sent out, and the people are appealed to. Does another party advocate the voluntary system? It appeals to the people. Does an armed body of insurgents appear at Newport or at Sheffield? The government, through the means of a royal speech, expresses its confidence in the good sense and the loyalty of the people. From the most insignificant local subject up to the most important national question, the working classes are appealed to by party interests, and yet with an inconsistency which is altogether unaccountable, we are told by the very same parties who make these appeals, that the people are too ignorant to perceive their own immediate and most palpable interests! . . .

It would not be difficult to prove . . . that the laws which restrict the number of electors are in opposition to the constitution as it existed in its pristine purity. To effect the restoration of that constitution has been the object of our labours . . . I have not sought to effect it by threats and violence. . . . but by calmly waiting for the time when our principles should be universally diffused, or by energetically assisting in their diffusion—by means of meetings—of discussion—of enquiry—which, and which alone, can lead to a concentration of public opinion . . .

. . . It was well observed by Mr. Gibbon Wakefield, during the agitation on the Reform Bill, that the making the possession of property the criterion of fitness for political right, would inevitably tend to the severance of the wealthy from the indigent, to the complete alienation of one class from another in sentiment, in feeling and in action. The present state of the public mind attests the truth of the observation. To reunite the classes whose real interests are identical, but who have been thus fatally severed, has been our only object . . .

Gentlemen, I have thought it necessary to trespass on your attention at some length, in order to dissipate the calumnies and the misrepresentations which have been so industriously circulated. I have thought it necessary you should be informed that we desire not to reduce the rich to poverty, but to raise the poor from indigence to comfort—I have thought it necessary you should know that we were not men who wished to destroy property, but that our only desire was to secure to the labourer his due reward—we desired not to destroy wealth, but to prevent wealth from destroying us—we desired to put an end to that state of things which made the possession of wealth the standard of intelligence, and gave to the possessors of bricks and motar the fit qualifications of an elector or a statesman . . .

George Lloyd,

My Lord and gentlemen of the jury,— . . .

I shall content myself with offering to you a very few observations in defence of the principles I entertain, and of my conduct in advocating those principles. It has been my fate, my Lord, perhaps to know various conditions of society. I have suffered, perhaps, as much poverty as any man in Britain; and I have known too what domestic comfort has been. And, my Lord, and Gentlemen of the Jury, knowing and feeling these things, I have made it my business in many of the manufacturing districts—feeling the rankling shaft of poverty in my own bosom—destroying my own peace as well as that of my family—I have made it my business to look at the condition of others, and I have found in following up my enquiries among the people, that in our boasted, our civilized England, such scenes of human misery and wretchedness exist as would disgrace the most barbarous land that spots the face of our globe. I have seen whole families, I have seen the widower, and his motherless children sitting down upon the cold floor, without a stool or a table, in wretchedness and rags which would scarcely cover the naked person from indecent exposure. I have seen such families sitting down to a boiled potato for their Sunday's meal; and when I tell you that such is the fact, I feel convinced that you, as men, as Englishmen, as a Jury, in whose hands rests my liberty and my future prospects will hardly wonder that the conviction has been forced upon me even against my will, that something was rotten in our system of Government, or in the administration of our laws, for had it not been so, such scenes as these which I have thus faintly described, could never have existed . . .

My Lord and Gentlemen of the Jury, it has been frequently asserted by those who have opposed the cause which I and others have espoused, that those who have taken a leading part in it, have had their own purposes and their own interests to serve; but I will ask your Lordship whether, after the facts which I am about to state, this agitation has served any interest of mine, or placed me in a position at all superior to that which I might have enjoyed, had I not felt for the wrongs of others, and sought on their behalf to obtain redress. I have to state, my Lord, that in my case the part has been the very reverse—that simply for holding principles which did not accord with the principles of those from whom I had previously to obtain my bread, I have to state, that for the sake of holding those principles for the last seventeen or eighteen months, I have been prevented from following my usual employment. I have been forced, my Lord, unwillingly forced, in consequence of having seen the unparalled amount of wretchedness which exists in this country: I have been forced to adopt those principles. I find that I want protection; I find that my family want protection: and I also find that in connection with this cause, I have suffered much, more than I really deserve to suffer, even, supposing that it had been clearly proved that I was guilty of the serious crime laid to my charge.

My Lord, what have I suffered? I was arrested early on the morning of the day after 12 August—a day on which there had been no disturbance—no riot—no breach of the peace; I was hurried away after my examination before the magistrates, who committed me without anything like evidence, and who have instituted this prosecution rather to screen themselves from their own negligence and imprudence than to punish me for any supposed crime—I was carried away and denied the constitutional privilege of bail—I was hurried away from my home and from my family, guarded by two troops of dragoons, one on each side of the carriage which brought me to prison, as though I had been guilty of some enormous offence—I was hurried away to Kirkdale, there to remain without the privilege of putting in bail, which could have procured bail of sufficient responsibility, I was hurried along to the prison, where I remained for six weeks, and had afterwards to sit in a dark cell, under this Court, during the whole of the proceedings of the last Assizes; and all this I had to suffer, simply for asserting the rights of my fellow-creatures. And my Lord and Gentlemen of the

Jury, when I tell you that I have suffered this much, and that while I was in this confinement news was brought to me that my wife and two children had died in consequence of the illegal and sudden arrest made upon my person, then I say, my Lord and the Gentlemen of the Jury, knowing that you are not without the feelings of men, and of Englishmen, will admit that I have suffered more than enough, even supposing the worst charges in that indictment should be fully proved against me. I will not, however, deceive your Lordships and the Jury. The report to which I have just alluded, although calculated to induce, in the mind of any man, the most painful sensations, and to render under such circumstances an illegal imprisonment more dreadful than death in its worst forms, did not turn out to be true. My wife did not die in consequence of my imprisonment, although she had had a premature confinement brought on by it. When I came out of prison, the first thing I had to do was to endeavour to tranquillize a dear and affectionate child, who, in consequence of the arrest of her father, had been deprived of reason. I succoured that child, but in vain—she died in my arms; and when dead, my circumstances were such, that I had to beg the price of materials to make her a coffin, and even had with my own hands to make that coffin, before her remains could be committed to the dust . . .

These things, my Lord, and Gentlemen of the Jury I have suffered simply for asserting the rights of my fellow creatures—(Here Mr. Lloyd himself seemed to be much affected, and overpowered for a moment, but with a nerve that few men have been known to possess, he resumed his address in a tone of manly dignity, and proceeded:)—My Lord, and Gentlemen of the Jury, afflicting as those circumstances are to me—afflicting as they must have been to any man placed in my situation, I am prepared for the sake of those principles, to part with everything which is dear to me—with everything which can be called sacred in the enjoyment of domestic society and domestic peace, and to suffer ten times more than I have suffered, or more than I can imagine myself capable of suffering, rather than give up that which I am persuaded it is the right of every Englishman to enjoy. My Lord, and Gentlemen of the Jury, I will not trouble you with any further observations. I leave my case in your hands with confidence, knowing that I shall receive justice. My Lord, justice is all I ask; mercy I do not need.

12h The Newport rising

'Reformator', *Charter*, 17 November 1839.

. . . At least eight thousand men, mostly miners employed in the neighbourhood (which is very densely populated) were engaged in the attack upon the town of Newport and that many of them were armed. Their design seems to have been to wreak their vengeance upon the Newport magistrates, for the prosecution of Vincent and others, now lying in Monmouth gaol, and after securing the town, to advance to Monmouth, and liberate these prisoners. The ultimate design of the leaders does not appear; but it probably was to rear the standard of rebellion throughout Wales, in hopes of being able to hold the royal forces at bay, in that mountainous district, until the people of England, assured by successes, should rise, *en masse*, for the same objects. According to the evidence now before the world, Mr. Frost, the late member of the Convention, led the rioters, and he, with others, has been committed for high treason. On entering Newport, the people marched straight to the Westgate Hotel, where the magistrates, with about 40 soldiers were assembled, being fully apprised of the intended outbreak. The Riot Act was read, and the soldiers fired down, with ease and security, upon the people who had first broken and fired into the windows. The people in a few minutes found their position untenable, and retired to the outside of the town, to concert a different plan of attack, but ultimately returned home, without attempting anything more. The soldiers did not leave their place of shelter to follow them. About thirty of the people are known to have been killed, and several to have been wounded . . . It is fortunate that the people did not think of setting fire to the buildings adjoining the Westgate Hotel, which would have compelled the soldiers to quit their stronghold, and surrender themselves prisoners . . . but it is far better for the sacred cause of liberty that this foolish rising was so ill-conducted as to be checked at the outset. The rioters did not disgrace themselves by any wanton destruction of property nor by plunder. The Chartists, as a body, are too well-informed to offer any

countenance or encouragement to any such resorts to violence, for the attainment of their just rights.

Charter, 17 November 1839.

Some time since I enrolled myself as a Chartist at Newport, and attended their public meetings . . . I saw Jenkin Morgan at Newport; he is a cowman and lives at Pillgwelly. I have met him at the Chartist lodges, and know him to be a Chartist. He asked me, 'How do the Chartists get on upon the hills?' . . . I said things were very uneasy upon the hills, and for God's sake to tell me how it was going on. He told me it was no use for me to go to the hills, for there would be no work done on the hills. On Sunday night, the 3rd of November, at about 11 o'clock, I saw him again. He came to my house and said he was captain of ten men, and that I was appointed his man; he also said that Frost was on the hills, and was coming down with thousands of men to attack the soldiers. He said he was coming down that night at 2 o'clock, and that the Charter would be the law of the town of Newport on Monday morning, and that it would be the law of the land before daylight. He told me that I should be in danger if I did not join them, but that if I joined them I should be in no danger, because Frost's men would attack the soldiers. Upon that I went with him and several other men to the outskirts of the town. He told me there was powder at Crossfield's warehouse, and I said it used to be kept at Pill, but we found no powder. He also told me that there was to be a rising through the whole kingdom on the same night, and the same hour, and that the Charter would be the law of the land . . .

12i Plans for a general rising

Northern Star, 21 March 1840.
Sheffield, trial of Samuel Holberry, etc.

Thomas Rayner, police supt.

On Saturday evening, at twelve o'clock, I and Wilde and several police officers went to Holberry's house in Ayre-lane . . . we went upstairs, and found Holberry in bed with his clothes on. He got upon one elbow, and then Wilde caught hold of a dagger from a side pocket in his coat, which was in a red leather case, and like the one produced. Wilde then asked him if he was one of the people called Chartists, and he said 'Yes'.

He then asked him whether he was a moral-force Chartist or a physical-force Chartist?—He replied 'a physical-force Chartist'. I said that is a deadly weapon, pointing to the dagger,—you surely would not take life with it?—He replied 'Yes; but I would, in defence of the Charter and to obtain liberty;' but he added, 'mind, I am no thief' . . .

We went into the garret, and the first thing I saw was a pistol, which Wilde took up and which was found to be loaded. After that I found the basket on the table, with twelve hand-grenades, the cases for which were stone bottles stuffed with blasting powder, pebbles and pitch, with a fuse and touchpaper. I also found a number of fire-balls there, some tin cases for hand-grenades, three torches, about forty ball cartridges, about three dozen iron bullets, and an iron pot . . .

Thomas Booker was brought in about four or five o'clock. He was asked where he lived, and he said No. 2, in Bencroft-Lane. We went there with a detachment of infantry. When we got into the house, we found over the chimney-piece two guns, and I saw Mr. Wilde take a loaded pistol from the drawer. Upstairs we found the two bomb-shells produced. They are made the same way, I apprehend, as the hand-grenades. We found also 390 rounds of ball cartridge, a long pole pointed as for a pike, and four daggers . . .

Samuel Thompson . . . I belonged to a Chartist Association, of which I became a member on the Sunday after the disturbance in Wales . . .

There was a room in Fig Tree Lane where the Chartists met. There were two sorts of meetings, one a public meeting, to whom any person was admitted; and a private meeting, which was a secret meeting, to which none but members were admitted. I was admitted . . . I recollect the Sunday before this disturbance, and I saw Holberry there on that day, and two or three men whom I have seen at the Chartist meetings there . . . Holberry said he had been to Dewsbury, and he was happy to say that the day, and the hour, and the moment were near, a unanimous rise should take place. But only two people in each town were to know the time. He said he had pledged his word at that meeting that no place of worship, church or chapel, should be destroyed; nor any provision stores . . . He said he had another journey to go and he should want some money. He was to go to Nottingham for one place . . . [On the following Saturday, at a meeting in a public house Holberry announced plans for the rising.] He said we must all be at the Town Hall and the Tontine [Hotel] by two o'clock, as they must be the places to be first taken. The classes were to come up to take these places, one man first from every class, and then two, and the whole body. Exactly as the clock struck two they were to rush into the Town Hall and Tontine, and take possession of them. Boardman said he could bring about fifty, and I said I could bring about fifty . . . If they got the Tontine, they were to shut the gates, and barricade them with the coaches inside. When they got into the Town Hall, one party were to occupy the floor, and the others were to go above. We then began to talk about the 'cats', the instruments to lame the horses, and it was proposed to throw them in Snig Hill, leading from the barracks, and they were to be thrown at the corner of the Town Hall and the Albion. Holberry said that he and eighty-three picked men were to go after the soldiers when they were called out and fire the straw chamber. One of them was to do it by climbing the spout and throwing a fire-ball in it. That, it was said, would set fire to the Riding School. The ones and twos who came up were to assassinate all the soldiers and watchmen they met . . . Holberry said in the event of their being baffled, they must 'Moscow' the town . . .

Plans for general rising—Bradford

Trial of Robert Peddie and others.

Attorney General: . . .

They were in Bradford on the night between Saturday night and

Sunday morning; they were on that night to take possession of the town, then they were to proceed to the neighbourhood and take possession of certain iron works, . . . [where there] were some cannons, and they expected to get some pieces of artillery, which would assist them in their proposed schemes—then they were to go to Dewsbury,—and after they were to proceed to the Metropolis and take possession of the Government . . .

John Smith, greengrocer . . .

Holloway came about nine o'clock and said there was going to be a rising that night for the Charter. I told him, 'I'se not going to rise, and I would advise all here present to do the same'. Holloway then began cursing and swearing, and called me a d——d fool. 'If everybody were like me', he said, 'there never would be any rise'. Peddie came there about ten o'clock . . . and said, 'Now men, you know what you are about'. I said 'I think they hardly do, or they would go to bed'. Peddie said they must not go to bed, for there was going to be a general rise in the West Riding of Yorkshire. I said, 'I think there are not many physical force men at Leeds'. He said there were, and that there were four tons of gunpowder in the magazine, which they were going to blow up, and he had seen the train. He also said that the Leeds Chartists would be in Bradford that morning, at five o'clock. The Dewsbury men were to come in the afternoon. He said one hundred would come from Leeds, and that they would have all the money in the banks before four o'clock the next morning. Peddie said he would send 100 men to the Low Moor, for two mortars and some shells, to face the military with. I said I thought they would have something to do to get the money. They said they would get it very easily. Peddie said when he got the money in the banks, he would get a chaise and four and ride into the North, and whenever it was known that there was a rise in the West Riding, Dr. Taylor would come at the head of 5000 men. He said there were one hundred soldiers in Halifax, and as soon as they knew there was a rising in Bradford, and him at the head of it, they would be at Bradford in five minutes, and fight up to their knees in blood for him. Peddie took out a pistol and loaded it with two balls. I said there has been a great deal of talk about Frost lately, and you are very near his situation. He replied, 'No, I am not like Frost; if any man attempt to take me, I'll blow his brains out' . . .

13 Self-help Chartism

The rejection of the first petition, the collapse of conspiracy and the mass arrest of Chartists together devalued protest Chartism and direct pressure on government. The newly formed National Charter Association, dominated by O'Connor (13a), specifically employed only peaceful methods, and in particular favoured the incursion into popular politics to display the dignity of working men and the righteousness of their cause. O'Brien showed how Chartists could stand as parliamentary candidates (13b) and at the 1841 general election several Chartists played the hustings to maximum publicity. In Leeds, other Chartists contested muncipal elections (13c), in the tradition of the parish radicals (see above, p. 150), though only a handful were ever successful. Where Chartists did not have the vote, they could exercise pressure by 'exclusive dealing' on those who did (13d). The *Nonconformist*, Miall's liberal dissenting paper that was to urge complete suffrage, found the hustings moving and politically compelling (13e).

The Scottish Chartists, on the one hand, and the London Chartists of the old LWMA on the other, were less susceptible to O'Connorism, and from 1840 developed styles of self-help and moral rearmament which spoke to the self-taught weaver or west country tailor whose exposure to Chartism was to its newspapers, its coffee houses and its reading rooms. Together they sought to elevate and emancipate working men from political, intellectual and social darkness. (See the addresses of the LWMA, pp. 138–41 above.) Christian chartism (13f) overcame the identification of established religion with establishment politics by offering working men a pure and practical Christianity in chapels of their own that spanned the workshop and the meeting place. Teetotal chartism was its natural corollary (13g), dignifying working men and undermining government finance; Vincent and Lowery both passed from Chartism into the temperance movement as professional lecturers. William Lovett offered another New Move, an educational plan (13h and i) of schools and libraries, repeating what the Unstamped had taught a decade before that without rational knowledge there was no authentic union, and without union no power. But O'Connor insisted that all such moves betrayed Chartism in a double sense (13j): ideologically, because they implied that working men must meet moral, religious or educational standards before they could have the vote; and tactically, because such moves were inevitably sectarian, schismatic and would shatter Chartism. Samuel Bamford, a veteran of Peterloo, writing in apocalyptic language but pessimistic vein in the same year, re-stated the rationalist stand—self control must precede social control, personal reform must precede political reform (13k). Otherwise, all was dust and disillusion.

Suggestions for further reading

See B. Harrison and P. Hollis, 'Chartism, Liberalism and the life of Robert Lowery', *English Historical Review*, 1967; and A. Briggs's introduction to Lovett's *Chartism* (1970), for self-help. For Christian Chartism, H. Faulkner, *Chartism and the Churches* (1916).

13a The National Charter Association, 1840

Northern Star, 1 August 1840.

After the Newport rising, local Chartist societies were organized into the NCA, based on Manchester. Members joined small classes which were grouped into wards, wards into town councils, town councils into county councils, and from county councils candidates were nominated for the National Executive Committee. This was found to be illegal so in March 1841 the NCA abandoned its ward and branch structure, for nation-wide elections to the General Convention. The rules had again to be remodelled in April 1844.

Designation of the association

1. That the Chartists of Great Britain be incorporated in one Society, to be called 'The National Charter Association of Great Britain'.

Objects

2. The object of this association is to obtain a 'Radical Reform' of the House of Commons, in other words, a full and faithful representation of the entire people of the United Kingdom.

Principles

3. The principles requisite to secure such a representation of the people are:—The right of voting for members of Parliament, by every male of twenty-one years of age, and of sound mind; Annual Elections; Vote by Ballot; no Property Qualification for Members of Parliament; Payment of Members; and a division of the Kingdom into Electoral Districts; giving to each district a proportionate number of representatives according to the number of electors.

Means

4. To accomplish the foregoing objects, none but peacable and constitutional means shall be employed, such as public meetings to discuss grievances arising from the existing system; to show the utility of the proposed change, and to petition Parliament to adopt the same . . .

Some means for the attainment of the great end

1. The people shall, wherever convenient and practicable, put into operation Mr. O'Brien's plan of bringing forward Chartist candidates at every election that may hereafter take place, and especially select where possible those as candidates who are legally qualified to sit in Parliament.

2. The members of this ASSOCIATION shall also attend all Public Political Meetings, and there, either by moving amendments or by other means, enforce a discussion of our rights and claims, so that none may remain in ignorance of what we want . . .

13b The move into popular politics

John Fraser, *True Scotsman*, 13 February 1841, quoted in A. Wilson, *The Chartist Movement in Scotland* (1970).

During the last two years the Chartists have been sowing the seeds of great principles, and not in vain for they have taken deep root in the public mind, and cannot now be eradicated . . . We can hardly open a newspaper without finding a record of Chartist proceedings, or criticisms on its character and tendencies . . . How are we to reap the harvest? Teaching the doctrine of political equality will not secure it. Three cheers for the charter at every meeting will not make it the law of the land. Many run to and fro and give a knowledge of its nature . . . Societies may be organized, meetings held weekly, and monies collected to pay their expenses; but all these things make no conquest to us of the Charter. We may preach peace, charity and goodwill to the middle and upper classes, but the goodly work will not secure for us the prize we want. Violence has failed to win it, and so even will mere peacefulness of conduct . . . Public opinion may sanction the Charter; but that does not make it law. It can only be made law by a revolutionary declaration of the majority of the people in its favour, or by the decision of a majority of the members of Parliament to the same purpose. The former step is now but little contemplated by the people; we have therefore no alternative left but to promote the last . . . We call on the Chartists, then, to direct their attention to elections, and make their power felt on all these occasions.

Popular politics—plain and simple rules for conducting an election

Northern Star, 26 June 1841.

Every Chartist in the neighbourhood of an election should consider it his duty to attend the hustings where a Chartist candidate is to be proposed, whether he intends to go to the poll or not . . .

The body, when assembled, should then go towards the hustings, as large a number as is prudent getting in front, with a good reserve in the rear, and well-flanked. They should not wear any colours, and for this reason, they will be just as well known by the want of them; and should a row take place, every bird that is plucked of his plumage will, of necessity, be compelled to fall into the Chartist ranks, and fight against his feathered brethren in selfdefence . . .

The Chartist candidate or candidates should have a short stick with a flag, and a man with some distinguishing mark, such as a hankerchief around his head, should stand behind the candidate or candidates; and when the Chartists see their candidate and fuglemen hold up their flags, then they should hold up BOTH HANDS: mind, both hands, and then you cannot be outjockied, for the others will hold up both . . . All hands be kept up till the candidate and fugleman shall lower their flags; that done, clap all hands three times, then set up a groan, dismal, loud and long for the Whigs, and a funny derisive laugh for the Tories, and three rousing cheers for the members; for mind, they are members for all that day, and the next, till the close of the poll. Then give nine cheers for the Charter, and as many more for Frost, Williams and Jones . . . This done, get your men and chair them all over the town . . . In the evening get up cheap tea parties and dancing, and be jolly, and go to bed happy in the thought you have done your duty . . .

On the day of election, . . . they should have two committees, one working the electors, the other the non-electors. The non-electors' committe should never stir from the spot where they shall be posted, after they have assisted in forming the procession to escort the candidates to the hustings.

If any row is got up by the factions, the non-electors' committee should instantly go for their candidate, and placing him at their head, rally round him, and when excitement is once got up, never try to allay it. . . .

Popular politics and Chartist candidates

R. Lowery, 'Passages in the Life of a Temperance Lecturer', *Weekly Record*, 18 April, 9 May, 23 May 1857.

A general election being now announced [1841] it was determined by the working men to bring forward candidates to advocate our principles wherever possible. Two objects were to be gained by this—first, an opportunity to address the influential classes and electors on the question, which he could not accomplished at any other time or place as well; secondly, if we succeeded in the show of hands it would be a victory showing the candidates returned by the demand of a poll did not represent the people . . . [Lowery stood first at Edinburgh against Macauley, where he won the show of hands as his supporters put up both hands; and then at Aberdeen, against a Whig and a Tory.]

On it coming to my turn to address the people, after dwelling for a short time on the sacred duty they had met to perform, and the principles of civil and religious liberty taught in the Scriptures, and their responsibility as Christian men to try to remove falsehood and wrong wherever met with, I pointed down to the electors in the enclosure, and turned to the authorities, and then again to the mass, and asked them, had that mighty mass of the citizens to elect a representative to serve them in Parliament, or only the small group within the railings? Was there any gentleman who would dare to affirm that that small group—the electors—however good individually, contained a tithe of the intelligence and virtue, industry and wealth, that the mighty crowd around them possessed? The anomaly was so obvious, and I appealed to them so solemnly, that those in the enclosure hung their heads, while the mass beyond them made the air ring with their applause. From this basis I reasoned against the class privileges and other monopolies. The enthusiasm was such, that when the Sheriff took the show of hands, not only the whole mass held up their hands for me, but also the electors within the rails. The other gentlemen demanded a poll, which was fixed to take place on the ensuing Monday, it then being Friday. In the evening the enthusiasm of the Chartist Association was high. The working men felt as if for the moment they stood on an equality of public respect with the other political parties. It was urged that they should go to the polls, for, although they could not then succeed, it would prove to the Whigs their earnestness, and that at the next election, if they did not advance, they would lose the seat. It was finally agreed that it would confirm the impression that had been made if some were to poll, care being taken not to let in the Tory. The meeting adjourned until next evening. During the interval the shops were to be visted, to solicit funds for the electioneering expenses, and to enlist volunteer clerks for the polling. On meeting on the Saturday night it was stated that the necessary funds had been subscribed,—above £30—and that a full staff of polling clerks had volunteered.

. . . Although only some thirty odd votes were polled, some of them were men of influence and property, and as a whole they represented an average of society. Many had ridiculed the idea of the non-electors having candidates nominated, that they might get their claims brought before the electors, but the results in almost every instance were highly favourable to the extension of liberal views.

13c Municipal Chartism

Northern Star, 29 October 1842.

We have often endeavoured to press upon the Chartists of the kingdom the imperative necessity there exists, if they would make themselves '*respectable*', FELT and FEARED, to obtain possession of these outposts to general government,—the local offices. . . . *Local Power* is the key to general power. Local 'authorities' have the administration of general laws . . . Whenever the Chartists have obtained possession of these outposts of general Government, from that moment may date the success of their general endeavours to establish RIGHT . . . The Chartists can *acquire this Local Power*. It rests with them to put forth their hand, and clutch it . . . Whenever it has been enforced, good, *great good*, has followed. It has brought out principles before the money-making sordid section of the community in a striking and novel manner. It has stirred up the cess-pool of local corruption, and put the local birds and beasts of prey into fearful commotion . . . It has taught those who have hitherto treated us with supercilious scorn, and lorded it over us all the airs of *established* authority; it has taught these that *we are somebody*; that we have a power within ourselves; and that we can deprive *them* of the plumes which they so proudly toss and flaunt. It has produced a wonderful *change of tone* towards the Chartists wherever it has been put in operation! . . .

In this gathering together of power with which to battle the general enemy, we are happy to say that LEEDS has taken the lead . . . They elected the last Board of Improvement Commissioners . . . They elected also a Chartist lot of Churchwardens. They are by their conduct in office, heaping honour upon the cause of Chartism, which seated them at the vestry board.

13d Popular politics and exclusive dealing

B. Wilson, *The Struggles of an Old Chartist* (1887).

The general election of 1846 in Halifax.

Meetings were held nightly, excitement was very great, and party feeling ran very high. Exclusive dealing became very common, and was never known to be so extensively carried out as at this election. Mr. Boddy, a grocer in Northgate and a supporter of Messrs. Jones and Miall, became very popular; I have seen his shop many times crowded with customers, and considerable numbers of people in the street opposite; he did a large amount of business for many years and then retired. He erected the fine block of buildings in Northgate known as 'Boddy's Buildings', and it is said that he saved the bulk of his money out of profits of that agitation. . . . The bulk of the publicans voted in favour of Wood and Edwards, but those who voted for Jones and Miall did a roaring business. The Queen Inn became one of the most noted and popular public houses in the town—John Bancroft was the landlord; I have seen every room in his house crowded on a Saturday night, principally with carpet weavers, and for many years it was well patronized.

13e Let us join the oppressed

Nonconformist, 6 October 1841.

Yet Chartism spreads, and the principles of the charter spread still more. The show they have made at the hustings, the returns they have received upon the show of hands in some cases, and the forests of hands held up in all populous places where the destitution exists, and serfdom and ignorance do not, will not be lost . . . these men will go home strengthened in their convictions of personal injustice because those hands were counted as nothing, not because their owners did not possess human souls, but because they did not possess acres of land or the requisite number of bricks . . . The hustings' movements cannot but present to the mind of the thoughtful and just politician the conviction that hungry men, who take these pains to enforce their claims to political emancipation upon others, are not to be evaded much longer by hustings' professions, after-dinner clap-trap, or parliamentary roundabouts . . .

13f Christian Chartism

Chartist Circular, 28 March 1840.

A sprinkling of small Chartist churches, teaching practical and simple Christianity, flourished in Birmingham under Arthur O'Neill and John Collins, in Vincent's west country, and in Scotland.

In every district there ought to be a Chartist Church planted for the benefit of Chartist families. It may be a private house, a school, or a public hall, tended by an association, for public meetings, education, and religious worship; and every Sabbath day a gospel should be preached in it by a religious, honest missionary, chosen by the Chartists . . . It is also necessary that baptism and marriage should be regularly dispensed by Chartist missionaries, and likewise the ordinance of the Lord's Supper, otherwise the parish and voluntary clergymen will keep a tenacious hold of Chartist families . . .

Northern Star, 20 November 1841.

The great practical duties of mankind, personal, social, civil and political, should form the Alpha and Omega of Chartist preaching. About these there can be no mistake. The object of Chartist churches, if we understand them at all, is two fold: first, to provide temples wherein the Chartist may find those principles of government and society which he believes to be the principles of truth and of the Bible acknowledged by his priest; and where, therefore, his understanding shall not be insulted, nor his degradation mocked, in a manner which is too common amongst both 'established' and 'dissenting' ministers; and secondly to form a practical exhibition, as far as our means go, of that system of 'exclusive dealing' which is not less potent when applied to the pews of the parson than when applied to the till of the shopkeeper. All Chartists who are Christians agree that the principles of Chartism are those of Christianity—that they form the practical exhibition and development of the grand law of love on which the Lord has declared the whole law and the prophets to hang . . .

It seems to us therefore, that the only 'articles of faith' which can with the slightest degree of propriety or consistency be acknowledged as generally binding on the members of a Christian Chartist church should be the divinity of the Lord and of the Holy Scriptures, and the principles of Chartism as taught in those Scriptures. On every other matter, every member should be at perfect liberty to hold his own doctrines and opinions, whether Methodist, Calvinist, Quaker, Ranter, Jumper or Roller . . . The Christian Chartist feels it to be his duty to worship God—a duty which he neither can nor dare omit; there is no church in which he can do so with comfort and without liability to insult, or injustice or both; hence he requires and needs a Chartist Church.

R. Lowery, *Weekly Record*, 13 December 1856.

. . . I remember well one intelligent working man, with a large family, relating to me how he had been imposed on by his employer, who was a member of the same church with him. 'I wish we could establish a chapel for ourselves' said he; 'I strive all I can to banish ill-feeling from my mind towards him, but often when I have seen him in the church, and have sat down at the "Lord's Table" with him whom I knew to be defrauding me and other labourers of our hire, I could not help feeling bitterly. I would be better away at such a time'. . . .

13g Teetotal Chartism

Chartist Circular, 7 March 1840.

There are almost a thousand ways of attacking, disarming and overcoming the oppressors of the industrious classes, without resorting to the dangerous, distressing and unscriptural mode of redress—an appeal to arms . . . Young and old could abstain for a short time from the most heavily taxed exciseable commodities . . . alarm would be generated in the minds of the fundholders, national confidence destroyed, and a national bankruptcy ensured. This course of conduct would call for a great deal of self-denial on the part of the people, but it would be self-denial calculated to increase their present comfort, and extend their political influence . . . A drunken Radical is a disgrace. Reform should begin at home. Let all such amend their own errors, ere they begin to tinker the state. Such a course of abstinence . . . would shut the mouths of objectors—elevate the individual in the scale of society—save him the time spent in tippling—exempt him from unnecessary and avoidable expense—permit him either to apply the time and money thus saved, to increase his domestic comforts, or promote the cause of liberty.

An address to working men of Great Britain

H. Vincent, Rev. Hill, J. Cleave, C. Neesom, H. Hetherington, *Northern Star*, 28 November 1840.

Impressed with a sincere desire to promote the political freedom and social happiness of our country, and to witness the extirpation of all systems and vices which impede our progress, and believing that the ignorance and the vices of the people are the chief impediments in the way of all political and social improvement, and being convinced that no revolution can be permanently successful unless achieved by the mind of a nation, we are led to address ourselves to you, in order to point out what we conceive to be the mainstay of oppression, and the weakness of the oppressed . . .

Have we not oppression enough, without adding to it by our vices? Are not thousands starving for want of sufficient wages to purchase food? Have not class legislation, heavy taxes, monopolies and national debts sunk us sufficiently low, without sinking ourselves still lower . . . The love of intoxicating drinks is the mainstay of the aristocracy, tending as it does, to debase and still further pauperize a politically oppressed and pauperized people . . .

We especially appeal to all leaders of the Chartists to adopt the teetotal pledge, and set the people a proper example. We appeal to the Chartists as a body—we call upon them to give the teetotal question their deepest consideration; and we trust they will so far overcome all prejudice as to abstain for a time, and give the principle a fair trial. And in the event of their finding—as we are assured they will—that they are better without intoxicating drinks than with them; and on their further perceiving the other advantages resulting from the sobriety, to form themselves into Chartist teetotal societies in every city, town and village. By adopting this course, the habits of the people will be at once changed . . .

13h Chartist schools

Chartist Circular, 14 March 1840.

The first thing to be done when you employ your own teachers, is to get a Chartist catechism prepared and published for the use of families and schools . . . Children should commit a portion of it to memory every day at school, until they have mastered it . . . Particular attention should also be devoted in Chartist schools to female education . . . Females ought to be taught as much knowledge as men, and in some cases more, for they are the great primary instructors of the rising race . . . Experimental philosophy, history, ethics, politics, and religion, should be soundly instilled into all young minds; and parents should assist the schoolmaster by making their children rehearse and practise these lessons at home . . .

If a universal system of national education, based on the principle of the Charter, with philosophy and ethics, were honestly established by the people . . . in a few years mankind would think and reason together and act in harmony. One rational opinion and wish would prevail, namely, the speedy accomplishment of civil and religious freedom, and honest justice to all mankind . . . All men will be reasonable, free, equal, and happy, and simultaneously practise benevolence and honesty . . . The impressions that are made on the mind and brain by education, in infancy, childhood and youth, remain in more or less activity till we die . . . It is therefore of vital importance to mankind, that Chartist schools be immediately established in every district, one for every one hundred and fifty children; and that honest and intelligent teachers be employed. By this method, a race of men and women will spring up in the land, who will not remain passively like their fathers in slavery . . . It is the greatest and best blessing we can bequeath to posterity . . .

13i Knowledge Chartism and the new move

Address of the National Association, October 1841, printed in William Lovett, *Life and Struggles* (1876), pp. 209–14 in the 1967 edn.

William Lovett and John Collins, a Birmingham toolmaker, were imprisoned in August 1840 for twelve months, and while in Warwick Gaol they wrote *Chartism: A New Organization of the People*, proposing a National Association to promote a network of schools, libraries and lecturers which would emancipate the people from political darkness. On his release, Lovett became director of a National Hall in Holborn.

. . . We felt anxious *to redeem by reason what had been lost by madness and folly*.

We accordingly, about five months ago, put forth a proposal for forming a National Association, as set forth in a pamphlet, written in Warwick Gaol, entitled *Chartism*—a plan embracing such objects as, in our opinion, were best calculated to unite the elements of Chartism, and secure the cooperation of benevolent minds who were desirous of benefiting the great mass of the people politically and socially.

In publishing that plan, we explicitly stated that *we had no wish to interfere with the societies then in existence*; our object being to form a general association for certain explicit purposes. These purposes being, first and foremost, to create and extend an *enlightened public opinion* in favour of the People's Charter, among persons of all creeds, classes, and opinions, by the means of missionaries, lecturers, circulating libraries, tracts, etc. And in order to secure proper places of meeting for those purposes, we proposed a systematic and practical plan for the erecting of *Public Halls for the People* in every district of the kingdom; by which means our working-class brethren might be taken out of the contaminating influences of public-houses and beer-shops—places where many of their meetings are still held, in which their passions are inflamed, their reason drowned, their families pauperized, and themselves degraded and politically enslaved.

Seeing, also, that vast numbers of our infant population are the neglected victims of ignorance and vice, creating on the one hand the evils we are seeking to remove, on the other—seeing that the selfish, the bigoted, and the fanatic, are intent on moulding to their several purposes the infant mind of our country; and that the different parties in the state have for several years past been devising such national schemes of instruction as shall cause our population to become the blind devotees and tools of despotism—we urged on our brethren the necessity of remedying and averting those evils, by adopting *a wise and General System of Education* in connection with these Public Halls . . .

This proposal, while it was warmly greeted by the press, and received the commendations of a great number of intelligent minds among all parties, was met with falsehood, intolerance and bitterest rancour, by the most prominent organ of Chartism, the *Northern Star*. Its proprietor and editor jointly denounced it as a production of Messrs. O'Connell, Hume and Roebuck! as a plan intended to destroy Feargus O'Connor's political supremacy and subvert one which he had previously concocted. *Education* was ridiculed, *Knowledge* was sneered at, *Facts* were perverted, *Truth* suppressed, and the lowest passions and prejudices of the multitude were appealed to, to obtain a clamorous verdict against us . . .

Our calumniators have falsely asserted that we are for delaying the franchise on the grounds of ignorance. So far from this being true, we have reiterated and published in various forms the contrary of this doctrine . . . But while as *a right* we thus insist on our just share of political power, we are desirous of seeing the most *effective steps taken to gain it*, and of seeing our brethren *preparing to use that power wisely when they shall have obtained it*; and not to be half a century exercising the franchise, and at the end of it still find themselves the sport of cunning schemers and wily politicians.

First, then, as regards the best means of obtaining our Charter.—We are of those who are opposed to everything in the shape of a physical or violent revolution, believing that a victory would be a defeat to the just principles of democracy; as the military chieftains would become—as all past history affirms—the political despots . . . We think that all that is necessary for the carrying of that measure is, soberly and rationally, to convince all classes of our population how far it is *their interest to unite with us*, in order that we may peaceably obtain it; for a combined people have always numerous means for the attainment of their object without violence.

But it is not the *mere possession of the franchise* that is to benefit our country; that is only *the means to a just end*—the election of the best and wisest of men to solve a question which has never yet been propounded in any legislative body—namely, *how shall all the resources of our country be made to advance the intellectual and social happiness of every individual*? It is not merely the *removing of evils*, but *the establishing of remedies* that can benefit the millions; and in order to check the natural selfishness and ambition of rulers, and induce them to enact just and salutary laws, *those who possess the power to elect must have knowledge, judgment, and moral principles to direct them*, before anything worthy of the name of just government or true liberty can be established . . .

The Northern Star *on the National Association*

Northern Star, 24 April 1841.

In fact, it is nothing more or less than a new mode of canvassing for support for Mechanics Institutes, and the Brougham system of making one portion of the working class disgusted with all below them; and thus effect, for another while, by an aristocracy of labourers, by galling contrast, what has hitherto been effected by taxation and the cannon.

However, people who work sixteen hours a day from the age of nine to about thirty-five, when they are thrown into a bastille as unfit for use, have very little relish for a protracted course of 'education' though it were certain in one hundred and twenty years to gain the Charter *for them.*

13j The verdict on all these new moves

Feargus O'Connor, *Northern Star*, 3 April 1841.

My fustianed, blistered, unshorn friends—

When a principle is once agreed upon, the safe, the sure, and the speedy means of its accomplishment should be the one great and never abandoned object of its advocates; and, therefore, the labour which I have undertaken becomes narrowed to the simple consideration of the fact, whether Church Chartism, Teetotal Chartism, Knowledge Chartism, or Household Chartism, are, each or all, or any of them, likely to be a safe, a sure, and a speedy means towards the achievement of the Charter.

I contend for it, that unless the four sections form of themselves, in the first instance, a quadruple alliance, that their four distinct and different means to an end, though that end be identical and the same, constitute a *prima facie* case against them, and is calculated to lead to sectional and party dispute, and, ultimately, to class distinction . . .

Chartism is, although an extensive, yet a well-defined political designation of a political party. Christian Chartism, though apparently all-embracing in the meaning, carries with it exclusion of all other sects from whom we expect political aid . . .

I object to Teetotal Chartism, because all who do not join in it, and I fear they are many, will be considered as unworthy their civil rights.

I object to Knowledge Chartism, because it impliedly acknowledges a standard of some sort of learning, education, or information, as a necessary qualification to entitle man to his political rights. In fact, the Whigs think opposition to Whiggery, and the Tories think opposition to Toryism, a perfectly good and valid ground, whereon to establish popular ignorance, and a consequent political disqualification.

I object to Household Suffrage Chartism, because it is not Chartism at all.

In fact, I look for the Charter to promote Christianity, to insure temperance, to inculcate knowledge, and to give the House and *something more*, while the use of those several qualifications, as a means to an end, will but place the Charter, year after year, further from our reach. The Christians will say, 'you haven't your Chartist catechism'. The Teetotallers will say, 'you're drunk'. The teachers will say, 'you're ignorant' and the Householders will say 'you're houseless'. So that you need *not one* qualification, but *four* qualifications . . .

Believe me, if you allow these four sections to mix up each their peculiar tenets with your cause, you will have raised unto yourselves four powerful enemies . . .

I am anxious to see every Chartist a good Christian, a good neighbour, and a good friend. I am desirous of seeing every Chartist sober, industrious, and honest, full of knowledge and filling houses . . . But once make non-conformity ground for exclusion, and you establish sects and sections, instead of one universal corps of regenerators.

My friends, get your Charter, and I will answer for the religion, sobriety, knowledge, and house, and a bit of land into the bargain.

Ernest Jones, *People's Paper*, 8 May 1852.

Parallel movements are hostile movements, under another name. It is only by a united and concerted action that the people can conquer. Let them be split into a dozen parties, all advocating a similar thing, but advocating it in a different way, and there would be an end to all their hopes . . . Union is the only guarantee of success.

13k Self-control and social control—a plea

S. Bamford, *Passages in the Life of a Radical* (1841), chapter 50.

In our progress now retrospectively scanned, how great was the portion, as we perceive, of folly which accompanied our good intentions? Groping in a mental and political twilight, we stumbled from error to error, the dim-eyed calling on the blind to follow; we fell as a natural consequence, and a happy circumstance would it have been, had our fall served in later times as a warning to others, but it did not.

'For a nation to be free, it is sufficient that she wills it', and we may add, a nation cannot be free unless she does will it. We thought the will to be free already existed—foolish thought—we looked for fruit ere the bloom was come forth; we expected will when there was no mind to produce it, to sustain it; for rational will is the result of mind, not of passion; and that mind did not then exist, nor does it now.

The agitators of the present day, Radicals I may not call them, have suffered greater humiliations than we did. With the example of our disasters before them, they have not avoided one evil which we encountered, nor produced one additional good. On both occasions, there was too much of the 'sounding brass and tinkling cymbal', but latterly it was varied by dark counsels and criminal instigations from their own authorized ones. Then followed delegations, and the silly egotism of pictures, and mock-solemn conventions, and formal self-displaying orations, and words and phrases bandied beyond all human entertainment. Next came multitudes deserted of leaders—who stood at a safe distance—and they drove before them a cloud and a whirlwind of terror and confusion, through which were seen flashes, and conflagrations, and bloodstreaks; and when it had passed, all was vanished, and there remained dungeons, beside whose open gates were weeping wives and children, and prisoners, some victims to their own folly, and some to the wickedness of others, were marching in, chained by scores.

Oh no! the still small voice of reason has not been listened to now, more than it was formerly. It speaks a language too pure, too unassuming, too disinterested, for any human crowds that have yet appeared. It requires great sacrifices for the obtainment of great results—a stripping of all vanity—an abandonment of all self—and a cleansing from all lucre. Its appeal could be understood by rare minds only, and they have not been found . . .

Mildly and persuasively as a mother entreating, would reason lead us to self-examination, self-control, and self-amendment, as the basis for all public reform. Canst thou not control thyself and wouldst thou govern a household? Canst thou not govern a household, and yet wouldst thou direct a nation? Come to thine own bosom and home, and there commence a reform, and let it be immediate and effectual. One evening spent there in the acquirement of useful knowledge—

in rational conversation—in the promotion of kindly feelings—in the restraints of sobriety—in the comforting of families—in the blessings of children, and the improvement of their hearts and understandings—in the devisement of cheerful economy and industry—in the feeling of mercy towards all God's creatures, and of love of all goodness, for his sake; one evening so spent, were to thyself and thy country, worth more than all thou hast seen, heard or done at Radical or Chartist meetings, since sun-light or torch-light first illumined them.

14 Chartism and the middle-class alliance

Co-operation with the middle class was something of a tactical and intellectual tightrope. In its favour, Lovett and some of the 'self-help' Chartists argued that it would bring them respectability and a parliamentary hearing, and that it would vindicate Chartism's claim to be a national and not just a class movement (14a). Both, after all, shared a common hostility to Old Corruption and a common commitment to radical and libertarian causes. But O'Brien and O'Connor thought this utopian amnesia; 1832, the new Poor Law and the middle-class hostility to the ten hours campaign, all showed that the middle-class alliance would be bought only by sacrificing certain working-class concerns and turning working men into fodder for middle-class causes (14b). Only *unconditional* middle-class support for the Charter was welcome.

On the middle-class side, three groups of radicals and dissenters, loosely cemented in the Anti-Corn Law League, wanted a *rapprochement* with the working class—first were those men of Christian good will, Joseph Sturge (1793–1859) and later Charles Kingsley, who for social and religious reasons were appalled at the deterioration of class relations. Their call was for 'class reconciliation'. Secondly, parliamentary radicals around Place and Hume wanted a further instalment of parliamentary reform for its own sake, household suffrage certainly, universal suffrage eventually, and the ballot immediately. Finally, the radicals of the Manchester Cobdenite school who dominated the League, wanted 'leverage' in the battle against aristocracy, landlordism and protection.

Two main opportunities presented themselves, the Complete Suffrage Union and the League. The Rev. Miall (1809–81) put the liberal case for manhood suffrage in a series of influential articles in the *Nonconformist* (14c). And in 1842, middle-class radicals led by Sturge, and Chartists of the moral force and self-help school came together to define a common platform (14d). But though manhood suffrage was acceptable, the full implications of the Charter were not, and the Union broke up. An alliance around the League was even less plausible (14e), for it invoked competing notions of political economy as well as political strategy. Engels saw this more clearly than perhaps his evidence would justify (14f). But just as O'Brien came to realize that middle-class support was not only desirable but crucial (14g), so too did O'Connor, then Harney and finally Ernest Jones.

14a The propriety of a middle-class alliance

Collins and O'Neill, letter to the *Northern Star*, 20 February 1841.

The dignity of labour bids fair to secure its legitimate place in society, and without opposing wealth, to demand that it shall be placed with it upon a political equality. We are more and more persuaded, that the most efficient way to prepare a people for the enlightened use of their rights, is to engage them in an agitation to obtain them . . . They were no longer as they used to be, assenting inferiors, or mere pressure-from-without machinery; they asked not of the middle classes leadership but alliance; not superiority but cooperation; their motto was a bold and independent one—with you if we may, without you if we must.

. . . We therefore say receive all men who admire the principles of your Charter, without distinction of sect or class; nay more, we say invite all. The man who gains a single penny to the funds, or a single name to the list of Chartism, has inscribed his name honourably on the the pages of Liberty's book of Life, no matter from whatever class they come. . . .

W. Lovett, letter to the *Northern Star*, 1 May 1841.

Believing that the principles of Chartism are purely democratical, calculated to benefit all classes, and not the working classes exclusively, I cannot agree with the general denunciation against all kinds of union with the middle classes, nor do I approve of the abuse, calumny, and despotic conduct which have reeently been put forward against all these who think a union of all classes desirable.

14b The middle-class union

Bronterre O'Brien, *Northern Star*, 24 April 1841.

We have a perfect right to hold them responsible for those evils—seeing they will neither remove them themselves, nor suffer us to do so—and that as no sane person would think of uniting for any purpose with known enemies, our proper business as Chartists, is to combine together as one man, not *with* the middle class, but *against* them, in order to put an end to their usurpations.

But, it is said, some of them are friendly to us, would you exclude them? Certainly not; if they be really friendly, they will unite with us to get *the Charter*—if they be not, they will exclude themselves. We cannot reject any man, of any class, who *bona fide* admits our principles; nor have we ever spurned the cooperation of middle class Chartists. On the contrary we have always received them with open arms, and will do so again . . . The People's Charter excludes no one from the rights of citizenship; neither will the Chartists exclude anyone from their 'Unions', who not exclude the Charter. But we can form no alliance—we can enter into no compact with men who require from us, as the conditions of their joining us, that we renounce the Charter. To renounce the Charter would be either to renounce our own rights—which would be madness—or to barter away the rights of others, which would be wickedness . . . It is asking us either to degrade ourselves, or betray one another . . . Once admit the infamous policy of setting off 'cheap bread' against invaluable principles, of placing men in the same category as bricks and mortar, and sacrificing each other's rights to the guilty fears and cupidity of our enemies—once, I say, admit that infamous policy, and away goes everything which now helps to bind us together in the strength of unity, power, character, self respect, mutual confidence, the consciousness of growing power, the terror we have struck into the enemy, the certainty of ultimate success—in short, we become morally and politically defunct.

If the middle classes choose to establish a Household Suffrage system, they can do so without our assistance—indeed, as well without as with us—for we have no votes to give. The only aid we can give any party is the 'pressure from without'. That aid we will give to any party that goes for Universal Suffrage. We cannot be expected to do so for any party that goes against it (for that would be going against ourselves) nor that goes for anything else—for anything that can be got without Universal Suffrage is not worth getting. Household suffrage is not worth 'a pressure from without'—repeal of the Corn Laws is not worth it—nothing that the middle classes have hitherto offered or promised is worth it—nothing that they ever will offer will be worth it—Universal Suffrage alone is worth it.

'But without the aid of the middle classes, how is Universal Suffrage to be got?' This means—'How are the unrepresented people to get the franchise without the consent of the middle classes, expressed by their representatives in Parliament?' I answer the question by putting another—'How did the middle classes get the franchise?'

If you answer this question honestly, your answer will be—'Why, by taking it to be sure'. Or, which amounts to the same thing, 'by letting the Government see that they would take it, if not freely and promptly conceded'. This is the only way that any people have ever got enfranchised; and whenever the working people shall be united and resolute as were the middle classes in 1831, they will get enfranchised in the same way . . .

Away, then, in God's name, with all talk about uniting with the middle-classes. Last year, and the year before, a pack of knaves and fools brought ridicule upon us by everlastingly arguing on the comparative merits of moral and physical force. One set declared themselves for *moral*, the other for *physical*—and they seemed quite ready to employ the latter force against one another, to decide which of the two forces they should employ against the common enemy. It never occured to the belligerents to enquire whether we were really in possession of either description of force, much less did they reflect that they were taking the most effectual course to leave us destitute of both. This year they seem disposed to play a similar game . . .

That the middle classes will not unite with us for the Charter is manifest. 'Tis equally clear that nothing short of Universal Suffrage or the Charter will accomplish the changes we require; why waste breath, then, arguing, 'whether we ought or ought not to unite with the middle classes?'

14c The suffrage question

Nonconformist, 13 October, 27 October, 10 November, 17 November 1841.

If ever the two classes are happily brought to shake hands with cordiality, it will be on the question of the suffrage. Minor differences may easily be reconciled when once we have succeeded in effecting union in this matter . . .

We venture to remind the middle classes that that which we withhold from the unrepresented, is not our own. We are not in the position of men who deny a favour which it may be inexpedient to grant—but of those who refuse a right to which there exists an equitable title . . . We can give no reasons for our enjoyment of the freedom which is not equally forcible in their mouths . . . If representation is necessary for the protection of our interests, fully as necessary is it for the protection of their's . . . It may be urged in reply that we do them no wrong—that it is clearly inexpedient to allow them their claim, however equitable—and that, in point of fact, their interests are better in our hands, than they would be if placed under their own management. To this reasoning, several replies are obvious.

1. Who made us judges of what is, or what is not, for the interest of the labouring classes? Turn the tables, and imagine the aristocracy acting towards ourselves on the same maxim . . .

2. When we urged that the extension of the franchise to the labouring poor is inexpedient, we are bound to show for who it would be so. We can hardly pretend that it would be inexpedient for them—for they cannot be much worse off than they are. We mean it would not be expedient for us. . . . We deny our fellow-men their rights, because we deem the extension of them would prove inconvenient and incompatible, with our own interests . . . Nor what more than this do the landowners practically affirm, for affirming which we overwhelm them with execrations.

3. If we hold the franchise exclusively in our hands, we must hold

it in trust for them as well as for ourselves. We are bound therefore to afford them protection to the same extent as they might justly take in case the franchise was theirs. But how stands the fact? They are most wholly unprotected. They are taxed more heavily than any other class. Law, accessible to others, is of small avail to them, for justice is expensive, and they have no means to purchase it. The fruits of their toil are wrested from them, and industry and skill, their own property, taken from them to augment the boundless wealth of the landlords. To the poor, then, we do not answer the end, for which we say we are invested with the franchise. Their welfare, notoriously, suffers incalculably in consequence of the present arrangement. Now either we can or we cannot prevent the wrong inflicted upon them. If we can, and do not, there is an end to the pretence that their interests are better in our hands than in their own. If we try, but cannot, why then we are not justified in undertaking for them what we cannot perform, and in preventing them from undertaking for themselves what, if we did not stand in their way, they could manage with ease . . .

They [the middle classes] are besieging the aristocracy with a view to wrest from them their rights long withheld. They have made a lodgement within the citadel. They are unable to effect their purpose. The labouring classes without the walls ask to be let in—for they also have been robbed—and they will render the additional aid necessary to compel the surrender of the common foe . . .

Treat men as slaves, and they will soon betake themselves to the vices of slavery—would you fit them for freedom, you must make them free . . . Tell any class of men that they are a worthless *caste*, not to be trusted with their own rights, incapable of understanding their own wants—but a scant degree above the level of brutes—treat them with suspicion, call them the unwashed rabble, harass them with trespass and game laws, set before them the ultimate prospect of union-house fare and union-house confinement, and if you do not make them reckless and dissolute, careless of others' rights, negligent of education, and negligent of religion, it is no fault of yours. You have done your best.

. . . On the whole, we have no manner of doubt that the moral effects to be anticipated from complete suffrage would be even more valuable than those which are purely political. The bonds by which society is held together would be drawn more closely—party conflicts would soon cease—reason and right would have fair play—education would be coveted—morals would improve—and religion itself would appeal with much greater probability of success to the myriads who now suspect it to be an instrument of oppression. . . .

We do believe, whatever we [the middle classes] allege to the contrary, that the industrious classes are competent to take rational views of leading political matters. Whenever we wish to carry a question, we address ourselves to them. We argue, we appeal, we illustrate, we supply information without any notion that they are incapable of discerning truth. We organize them into societies. We make demonstrations of their unanimity. We encourage them to display their mind, with a view to influence the mind of the senate. Now since we practically appeal to their suffrage, it is too late to urge, when they claim to be allowed to embody it in a vote, that they are not sufficiently intelligent . . .

14d The Complete Suffrage Union

Northern Star, 19 February 1842.

Joseph Sturge, the Quaker corn-merchant, persuaded the Anti-Corn Law League to support manhood suffrage, and in April 1842 he called the first complete suffrage conference at Birmingham. Many of the 'self-help' Chartist leaders attended, and with some hesitation on the middle-class side, the individual points of the Charter but not the Charter itself, were endorsed by the conference. In December the conference met again; O'Connor, who had bitterly attacked it in April, had now in the aftermath of the strikes and riots of the summer, come to support it. But when the middle-class members of the conference again refused to endorse the Charter as whole, Lovett led the working-class attack, and the conference collapsed amid regrets and recriminations.

Corn Laws and suffrage

A meeting of the Anti-Corn Law delegates and others favourable to the extension of the suffrage, London, 11 February 1842.

Rev. E. Miall, editor of the *Noncomformist*,

'Some persons had urged the necessity of superseding the Corn Law movement by the suffrage movement, and others had argued for superseding the Suffrage movement by the Corn Law movement. Let them look at the House of Commons as it had been recently elected, through intimidation and bribery he would allow,—but elected by the middle classes—(cheers)—why, it was one which would establish every principle of monopoly to its fullest extent. Now, the only way of remedying this state of things was by giving a prominent place to the Suffrage movement (Hear). At the same time he would not desist from agitating the Corn Law question. The Corn Law League by their agitation, did good to the Suffrage movement. They opened the eyes of the people, and he believed verily that the agitation had done more to forward the Suffrage movement among the middle classes than anything else. That agitation had now been going on for three years; they had had their meetings, their conferences, their bazaars, and what effect had they produced upon the aristocracy! Before they did that they must have a broader base to rest upon. They required some stronger lever to move the aristocracy than any they had yet worked, and they could only find that lever by extending the suffrage . . . Neither the middle nor the working classes were sufficiently powerful to carry their point, but by uniting they would break the yoke beneath which they now groaned . . .'

W. Lovett,

'He should like to see a cordial union among the people; he should like to see the middle and the working classes combined; they would never see, or be able to bring about, any change worth mentioning but by this means . . .'

Joseph Sturge, *The Address of the National Complete Suffrage Union to Political Reformers* (1842).

We are also desirous that a conference shall be held as the means of effecting a better understanding and closer union between the middle and working classes, than has hitherto existed; feeling convinced, that so long as the enemies of the people can keep them divided, so long will both classes be victimized to a corrupt and liberty hating aristocracy. We call, therefore, upon the middle classes to send their representatives to confer with *those* of the working classes, to see how far they can remove the causes of animosity, apprehension, and disunion; how far arrangements may be made to secure our *mutual objects speedily and peaceably*, and thus free ourselves from the grasping insolence of faction, guard against the storm of anarchy, be secure against military despotism, and unitedly raising up the intelligence and virtues of the democracy on the basis of free institutions, hasten the consummation of that happy period, when 'our swords shall be beaten into ploughshares and our spears into pruning hooks,' and when every man shall sit down in peace and security to enjoy the fruits of honest industry.

. . . Our paramount object is to effect a *union between the middle and working classes, to secure the just and equal representation of the whole people* . . .

Complete Suffrage Union of December 1842: the background

Thomas Cooper, *Life written by Himself*(1872), pp. 220–7.

Our Chartist delegates were the most numerous party in the Birmingham Conference; but my expectation rose when I saw so many persons present belonging to the middle class. I thought that if such persons would assemble with us to confer about presenting a petition to Parliament for making a law whereby all mature men should have the franchise, it showed we were really advancing. If the strike for the Charter had ended almost as soon as it begun,—and had ended disastrously,—if neither we nor the Anti-Corn-Law League had succeeded in paralysing the government,—it looked as if there were a party in the country who were determined yet to let the Government understand that there was real cause for discontent, and it was time the wrong should be righted.

The truly illustrious Joseph Sturge was elected chairman of the Conference by acclamation—for not a single working-man delegate wished for any other chairman. And now, if Mr. Sturge himself, or Edward Miall, or the Rev. Thomas Spencer, or the Rev. Patrick Brewster of Paisley, or Mr. Lawrence Heyworth of Liverpool, or any other leading member of the Complete Suffrage party present, had risen in that assembly, and spoken words of real kindness and hearty conciliation, I am persuaded that not even O'Connor himself, if he had desired it, could have prevented the great body of working-men delegates from uttering shouts of joy.

But there was no attempt to bring about a union—no effort for conciliation—no generous offer of the right hand of friendship. We soon found that it was determined to keep poor Chartists 'at arm's length'. We were not to come between the wind and *their* nobility. Thomas Beggs of Nottingham, a mere secondary member of the Complete Suffrage party, was put up to propose their first resolution, to the effect,—That the 'People's Bill of Rights' form the basis from which the petition should be drawn that this Conference would present to Parliament.

But what was the 'People's Bill of Rights?' A document which had been drawn up by a barrister, it was said, at the request of the Complete Suffrage party, in which the six points of our Charter were embodied, and some definite propositions were made for distributing the country into equal electoral districts. But Chartists knew nothing of all this. And it was preposterous to ask us to vote for what we knew nothing of. Copies of the new bill were laid on the table. But who could be expected to read and digest a mass of print amounting to many pages, in the lapse of a few hours, or while listening to exciting speeches, and then give a judgment on it? Murmers of discontent, and soon of indignation, began to arise—when up rose William Lovett, throwing his tall form to its full height, and, with a glance of haughty defiance toward the Complete Suffrage leaders, to our utter amazement he led the attack on them! . . .

Lovett's conduct won the hearts of all who were O'Connor Chartists, and, apparently, of O'Connor himself . . . We had looked on Lovett and his friends as a doubtful party when the Conference was opened. All thought of that was now gone; and the debate soon began to be very stormy . . . The Revd. Patrick Brewster of Paisley distinguished himself by the length of his speech; and Mr. Lawrence Heyworth by his offensiveness.

'We will espouse your principles, but we will not have your leaders', he cried; and when the outcry against him grew strong, he grew still more offensive—'I say again,' he shouted, 'we'll not have you—you tyrants!' . . .

When the decisive vote was taken, we were apparently as three to one, and Joseph Sturge, after a little hesitation, rose and told us that he and his friends had come to the determination to leave us: they would withdraw and hold a Conference by themselves . . . What a wretched look did the face of good Joseph Sturge wear as he uttered his last words to us, and stepped down from the chair!

'Cooper', said O'Connor to me, 'that man is not happy. He does not want to leave us'. And I thought so too . . .

Complete Suffrage: the debate

Northern Star, 31 December 1842.

Resolution of the Complete Suffrage Conference, December, 1842: 'That this conference . . . having for its paramount object the consideration of the necessary details of a bill embodying the principles . . . extension of the suffrage to all male adults . . . vote by ballot, equal electoral districts, abolition of a property qualification for M.P's. payment of members . . . and annual Parliaments, do now declare its adoption of these principles; pledges itself to employ such means . . . as are of a strictly just, peaceful, legal and constitutional character . . .'
W. Lovett, 'But he maintained that the Charter had the prior claim. In the first place it had born the brunt of the present agitation for five years, and in order to secure its enactment, vast numbers of their fellow countrymen had suffered imprisonment and transportation . . . He was one, as the Conference might probably be aware, who had differed materially with the great body of Chartists as to the mode of carrying that Charter into law. He had condemned the conduct of many of them. He thought they had inflicted considerable mischief, and had greatly retarded the cause; and he also thought that it was owing to this cause that a considerable degree of prejudice had been created in the minds of the middle classes against the Charter (hear hear). But after all, it was prejudice, and should they yield principle to prejudice? (No no). They might be told that the Bill preferred by the Council of the Complete Suffrage movement embraced all the principles of the Charter. If it were so, then it was a reason why the bill should not be introduced, seeing that the Charter embraced all that the people desired to obtain (Hear hear). Why should the Association introduce a measure of that description which could only serve to make wider the line of demarcation which at present unhappily existed between the various classes of society . . .'
Dr. A. Wade, 'In his opinion it was not the name of the Charter to which the middle classes whom the Complete Suffrage party wished to conciliate, objected but the principles it contained. (Hear hear). He believed that if the advocates of the Charter consented to change the name of the document, that the very next day the members of the Association would contrive some other loophole out of which to escape (Hear hear).'

Amendment moved by W. Lovett, seconded by F. O'Connor: 'That the document entitled the People's Charter . . . having been before the public for the last five years has, in the opinion of this meeting, a prior claim over all other documents professing to embrace the principles of just representation . . .'

For the Complete Suffrage Bill: 94

For Lovett's Amendment: 193

14e Chartism and the Anti-Corn Law League

R. Lowery, *Weekly Record*, 24 January 1857.

The Anti-Corn Law League was founded in 1839 and focused the attacks of middle-class radicals on landlords, aristocracy and protectionists. The Chartists responded in two ways; many of the 'self-help' Chartists thought that free trade was desirable but that universal suffrage which could bring about that and other reforms should have precedence; other Chartists, led by O'Brien, favoured protection because it meant that domestic wages were not beaten down in the name of foreign competition. Chartists of all creeds deplored the distracting activities of the League. The Corn Laws were repealed in 1846.

The debate

Much animadversion was cast on the Chartists for their refusal to join the Anti-Corn Law League and for interrupting their meetings; but the origin and nature of these differences were not understood by those who had not mixed with the working classes . . .

At first they [the League] were chiefly composed of Whigs, mostly of the shopkeepers, whom the working men had aided to get the franchise, but who would not now with their votes aid them to get theirs. They felt they could not succeed without the people, and urged them to join them. Seeing this the answer to the Anti-Corn

Law men was, 'No, you should join us. Ours include yours, and without an extended franchise you have little chance of success. We expose the evils of the Corn Laws and sign petitions against them, but we have no vote to help you to repeal them. We are organizing to procure the vote that we may repeal them and all other unjust taxes.' Hence a discussion of policy was general. This widened into attacks on the position of many of the capitalist employers, who were charged with being ever ready to beat down labour to the lowest point, even when profits would enable them to give better wages. . . .

The Corn Laws and protection

Northern Star, 28 March 1840.

We have no doubt that the effect of a repeal would be a great reduction in the value of agricultural produce . . . Corn being unmarketable, would not be grown; land would be let out of cultivation, and laid down to grass; labourers would be thus unprovided with employment, and an already over-stocked labour-market would be still further over-stocked. Such labourers therefore as would be still needed to tend the flocks etc. would be hired on perfectly starvation terms, while the rest would flock into the manufacturing districts to bid for labour against the artisans, to the manifest deterioration of their wages. Meanwhile, improvements in machinery are going on; producing more and more goods, with fewer and fewer hands, and thus continually adding to the redundant population, by the numbers which each successive 'improvement' throws upon society as an unneeded 'surplus'. Thus would wages be brought down to the lowest pitch at which the 'cheap bread' could possibly be had. The labourers would then be actually worse off than they are now; with the chance of an entire famine in the land whenever a general continental war might cause our ports to be blocked, or whenever a failure of crops abroad might cause exporting nations to keep their corn at home, or whenever the glutting of foreign markets with our manufactured goods should cause a temporary cessation in the demand for them.

Besides, who is so blind as not to see that the abolition of the protective duty upon corn, would be instantly followed, and justly too, by a demand from the agriculturists, for the abolution of all other protective duties . . . Those goods then must be reduced in price here, by reducing the workmen employed in their productions to such a rate of wages as will enable the manufacturers of them to outsell the foreigner; or, failing this, they must, like our corn, be imported; and thus a new 'surplus' of the labouring population will be again thrown into the market to compete with their half-famished fellows for a small portion of the 'cheap bread'.

All this time, never let it be forgotten that all money-men and profit-mongers would be getting rich out of the general spoil of labour and of the landlords. Every fundlord, every officer in the army and navy, every functionary employed under Government, every parson or lay impropriętor of tithes, every man who lives upon a fixed income from whatever source derived, would be enriched by the repeal of the Corn Laws; because the inevitable tendency of that repeal must be to make money dear and everything else cheaper. Eventually, if the system were permitted to go on, which it never would be, the whole country, land, and wealth, and Government and all, would be grasped by a small knot of overgrown capitalists. The people, as they became less and less needful to this heartless crew of Molochs, would be starved, hung, transported, or driven away by thousands, . . .

Let the people, then, reserve their energies . . . for a more worthy struggle; a struggle which, when made successfully, shall give them the power of providing food and raiment and employment and comfort for all, without injustice to any, and without depending upon any but ourselves.

Class harmony and the League

W. Cooke Taylor, *Notes of a Tour* (1842), pp. 212, 282–4 in the 1968 edn.

The operatives know well that their condition was never so prosperous as when machinery was most fully in work, and they are not, thank God, likely to be duped by the implied suggestion of the orators who use these unreasonings: in South Lancashire and North Cheshire they will not be induced to destroy mills and print-works . . . I am as persuaded as I am of my own existence, that the Anti-Corn Law League at this moment alone preserves the public peace in the north of England. Were its members to suspend their operations, or to dissolve their body, declaring, 'We have done all that we could do, and we now must abandon our efforts in sheer despair', there would instantly be a break-up of the body politic; society would resolve itself into its original elements, and no man could predict the consequences . . .

The interests of the employers and the employed are identical, and that perfect confidence must necessarily spring up when this identity is clearly perceived . . . [But manufacturers had] virtually abandoned their position, and thus threw all existing relations into confusion. The operatives, thus abandoned by their natural guides, were left free to follow any leaders that offered,—Unionists, Chartists, and political adventurers of every grade and description. Up to the commencement of the anti-corn-law agitation, there was a dangerous and increasing chasm between the employers and the employed. The League has bridged it over; by getting the masters to recognize and hold firm to their own order and position, it has brought the men to get a clear view of the relations which connected them with that position. The previous disruption was perilous, and might have been fatal, but it would be grossly unjust to throw all the blame of the breach upon the operatives.

The beneficial influence of the League, in thus reconciling the capitalists with those by whom capital is and must be worked, has not escaped the notice of the apostles of mischief and sedition; there are no more bitter impugners of anti-corn-law agitation than the advocates of physical force; they are perfectly furious against the League on account of its success in wresting the elements of insurrection out of their hands.

14f Chartism and the bourgeoisie

F. Engels, *The Condition of the Working Class in England in 1844* (1892), pp. 229–35 in the 1952 edn.

Chartism was from the beginning in 1835 chiefly a movement among the working-men, though not yet sharply separated from the bourgeoisie. The Radicalism of the workers went hand in hand with the Radicalism of the bourgeoisie; the Charter was the shibboleth of both. They held their National Convention every year in common, seeming to be one party . . .

The fruit of the uprising [the Plug Plots] was the decisive separation of the proletariat from the bourgeoisie . . . This was one point of dissension, even though this was removed later by the assertion of the Chartists . . . that they, too, refrained from appealing to physical force. The second point of dissension and the main one, which brought Chartism to light in its purity, was the repeal of the Corn Laws. In this the bourgeoisie was directly interested, the proletariat not. The Chartists therefore divided into two parties whose political programmes agreed literally, but who were nevertheless thoroughly different and incapable of union. At the Birmingham National Convention, in January, 1843, Sturge, the representative of the Radical bourgeoisie, proposed that the name of the Charter be omitted from the rules of the Chartist Association . . . The working-men laughed at him and quietly went their way.

From this moment Chartism was a purely working-man's cause freed from all bourgeois elements . . . The Radical bourgeoisie joined hands with the Liberals against the working-men in every collison, and in general made the Corn-Law question, which for the English is the Free Trade question, their main business . . .

The Chartist working-men, on the contrary, espoused with a redoubled zeal all the struggles of the proletariat against the bourgeoisie. Free competition has caused the workers suffering enough to be hated by them; its apostles, the bourgeoisie, are their declared enemies. The working-man has only disadvantages to await him from the complete freedom of competition. The demands hitherto made by him, the Ten Hours' Bill, protection of the workers against the capitalist, good wages, a guaranteed position, repeal of the new Poor Law, all of the things which belong to Chartism quite as essentially as the 'Six Points', are directly opposed to free competition and Free Trade. No wonder, then, that the working-men will not hear of Free Trade and the repeal of the Corn Laws (a fact incomprehensible to the whole English bourgeoisie), and while at least wholly indifferent to the Corn Law question, are most deeply embittered against its advocates. This question is precisely the point at which the proletariat separates from the bourgeoisie, Chartism from Radicalism; and the bourgeois understanding cannot comprehend this, because it cannot comprehend the proletariat.

Therein lies the difference between Chartist democracy and all previous political bourgeois democracy. Chartism is of an essentially social nature, a class movement. The 'Six Points' which for the Radical bourgeois are the beginning and end of the matter, which are meant, at the utmost, to call forth certain further ends. 'Political power our means, social happiness our end', is now the clearly formulated war-cry of the Chartists. The 'Knife and fork question' of the preacher Stephens was a truth for a part of the Chartists only, in 1838, it is a truth for all of them in 1845. . .

14g The middle-class alliance

Bronterre O'Brien, *British Statesman*, 9 July 1842, quoted in M. Beer, *op. cit.*, p. 127.

. . . Many of you looking back to our language in the *Poor Man's Guardian* and other publications of ours are apt to suspect that we have to some extent deserted your interests, because we do not come out in the *Statesman* with the same withering denunciations of the middle classes which formerly characterized our writing. Do not, good friends, judge us after this fashion. . . . In 1834 the middle classes treated us with scorn; now vast numbers of them not only recognize us as an integral part of the body politic, but they have actually paid court to us. Never mind the motives of this. Never mind whether they act thus from policy or principle. Our business is to deal with them as we find them—to accept their advance and proffered aid in a frank and friendly spirit, to reciprocate such acts by every means at our disposal that involve no compromise of principle, and above all not to commit the suicidal folly of confounding the honest portion of them, who would give us our rights, with the selfish knaves who would not—by involving the whole class in one indiscriminate cloud of abuse. Working men! We appeal to your reason whether this be not an honest as well as a sound policy, and whether we are not justified in using a different language towards the middle classes now from what we used five, or even one year ago, when they were in open arms against us?

15 Chartism and trade unionism

General Unionism collapsed in 1834, and only a few individual trades were able to fight the wage cuts that came with the bad times of 1837. In 1842, Chartism and trades unionism revived simultaneously. Those artisans who were most vulnerable to sweating—carpenters, shoemakers and tailors—had always been prominent in London and urban Chartism; now delegates to the 1842 annual Chartist conference reported that these trades were adhering to Chartism in their collective capaity (15a). London Chartism was enormously strengthened.

In the summer of 1842 a strike of factory workers against wage cutting spread like wildfire across Lancashire, the Plug Plots (15b); and local Chartists among the trades persuaded the trades conference at Manchester to declare for the Charter. The NCA, also meeting in Manchester, gave the general strike its hesitant support, suspecting the hand of the Anti-Corn Law League behind the unrest (15c).

Some fifty-nine men, including O'Connor and the National Executive of the NCA, were charged with seditious conspiracy. At the preliminary hearing in Chester, Lord Abinger outraged moderate opinion when he instructed the grand jury that the Plug Plots were instigated by the Chartists, that the Six Points could only mean the end of property, law and order, and that their very advocacy could not be tolerated by civil society (15d). The defendants traversed to the Spring Assizes at Lancaster, and there Richard Pilling, one of the 'fathers' of the factory movement, defended himself by describing the persecution and the privations he had suffered in its name (15e). He brought even the judge to tears. The trial was immaculately fair; many of the defendants were found not guilty, others were subsequently acquitted on a technicality, and the rest were never called to judgment.

Simultaneously, the miners came out on strike in South Staffordshire (15f); again the Chartists moved in to stiffen the leadership, and again the strikers were starved into submission.

In 1845 a style of federated unionism developed, the National Association of United Trades for the Protection of Labour, welcomed by the *Northern Star* (15g), which looked forward to the amalgamated unionism of the 1850s in its distaste for strikes, but back to the 1830s in its proposals for local boards of trade to regulate wages, co-operative self-employment, and the placing of surplus labour on the land (15h). Their patron was the radical MP for Finsbury, T. S. Duncombe (1796–1861). The NAUT survived into the 1860s.

15a The involvement in politics

The West London Boot and Shoemakers Charter Association to the Trades of London, *Charter*, 28 April 1842.

Fellow-workmen,

Most of us have hitherto, like too many of our class, regarded *politics* as something foreign to our interests . . . We have been content . . . to regard our trade affairs as a paramount interest, and to consider those only our enemies who sought to reduce our wages or infringe on our prices; without extending our inquiries to ascertain how far our trade, our wages, and the very feeling of our employers towards us, were dependent on, and subject to, superior influences—those of our *political institutions* . . . We firmly believe brethren that our wages have been greatly supported by union, and that without our unions we should ere now be ground down to the lowest point of subsistence; but we have recently perceived that even the very *existence of our unions* is dependent on the mere caprice or despotic of an *irresponsible government*, which at any moment has the power to enact the most rigorous laws for our annihilation . Why, let us ask, has this system of injustice been permitted so long? Simply, fellow workmen, because the *working classes conceived they had nothing to do with politics* . . . A political movement is now making throughout the length and breadth of the land to give the working men an equality of political rights, a right in making the laws they are compelled to obey. We would therefore call on you earnestly to join, as we have done, in this struggle for freedom, to form as we have formed, a Chartist Association in connection with your own trade . . . [sic]

Chartist Annual Conference, reported in *Northern Star*, 23 April 1842.

Dr. M'Douall was one of the delegates for the Metropolitan Counties . . . it was in a better position now than at the last Convention, and much better than at the first Convention . . . All bid fair if a plan of central agitation could come out. With regard to the trades, five or six trades had come out, as trades, in favour of the Charter . . . Bodies of the shoemakers, the tailors, the basketmakers, the hatters, and a body of carpenters were now actively working in support of the Charter . . . With regard to the middle classes in London, he was fearful, they could not look to them for much support; they had many electors who were Chartists, but the great body of the liberal shopkeepers were in favour of Sturge's plan; another large body in favour of Lovett's plan; but taking them as a whole, a vast number entertained Chartist principles. They had in connection with the National Charter Association, a good body of electors, more especially in Southwark and Marylebone . . . They had a large body of the trades, and they had the great majority of the working classes . . . The Metropolis was in a better state that it had ever yet been, and in a few months time he had no doubt but London would contain quite as many active intelligent Chartists as any other district of the same number of population in the kingdom.

15b The Plug Plots, 1842

Thomas Cooper, *Life written by Himself* (1872), chapters 18–20.

I was lodging at the George and Dragon, an inn [at Hanley] to which a large room was attached in which Chartist meetings were usually held. When I reached my inn, the members of the Chartist committee told me the reason why they had urged me to announce the meeting for nine o'clock the next morning. They had received instructions from the Chartist Committee in Manchester to bring out the people from labour, and to persuade them to work no more till the Charter became law—for that *that* resolution had been passed in public meetings in Manchester and Stockport, and Staleybridge, and Ashton-under-Lyne, and Oldham, and Rochdale, and Bacup, and Burnley, and Blackburn, and Preston, and other Lancashire towns, and they meant to spread the resolution all over England.

'The Plug Plot', of 1842, as it is still called in Lancashire, began in reduction of wages by the Anti-Corn-Law manufacturers, who did not conceal their purpose of driving the people to desperation, in order to paralyse the Government. The people advanced, at last, to a wild general strike, and pulled up the plugs so as to stop the works at the mills, and thus render labour impossible. . . . [Cooper decided to flee from Hanley] . . .

My friends had purposely conducted me through dark streets, and led me out of Hanley in such a way that I saw neither spark, smoke, or flame. Yet the rioters were burning the houses of the Rev. Mr. Aitken and Mr. Parker, local magistrates, and the house of Mr. Forester, agent of Lord Granville (principal owner of the collieries in the Potteries) during that night . . .

Nor did the outbreak end with that night. Next morning thousands were again in the streets of Hanley, and crowds began to pour into the town from the surrounding districts. A troop of cavalry, under the command of Major Beresford, entered the town, and the daring colliers strove to unhorse the soldiers. Their commander reluctantly gave the order to fire; one man was killed, and the mob dispersed. But public quiet was not restored until the day after this had been done, and scores had been apprehended and taken to prison . . .

When I entered the railway carriage at Crewe, some who were going to the Convention recognized me—and, among the rest, Campbell, secretary of the 'National Charter Association'. He had left London on purpose to join the Conference; and, like myself, was anxious to know the *real* state of Manchester. So soon as the City of Long Chimneys came in sight, and every chimney was beheld smokeless, Campbell's face changed, and with an oath he said, 'Not a single mill at work! something must come out of this, and something serious too!'

In Manchester, I soon found McDouall, Leach, and Bairstow, who, together with Campbell, formed what was called the 'Executive Council of the National Charter Association' . . . In the streets, there were unmistakeable signs of alarm on the part of the authorities. Troops of cavalry were going up and down the principal thoroughfares, accompanied by pieces of artillery, drawn by horses . . . We met . . . the next morning, Wednesday, the 17th of August, when James Arthur of Carlisle was elected President. There were nearly sixty delegates present; and as they rose, in quick succession, to describe the state of their districts, it was evident they were, each and all, filled with the desire of keeping the people from returning to their labour. They believed the time had come for trying, successfully, to paralyse the Government. I caught their spirit—for the working of my mind had prepared me for it. . . . When the executive, and a few others, had spoken, all in favour of the universal strike, I told the Conference I should vote for the resolution because it meant fighting, and I saw it must come to that. The spread of the strike would and must be followed by a general outbreak. The authorities of the land would try to quell it; but we must resist them. There was nothing now but a physical force struggle to be looked for. We must get the people out to fight; and they must be irresistable, if they were united.

15c The declarations

State Trials (new series), iv, cols. 945, 948–50, 1035.

A resolution of the trades conference, Manchester, 12 August 1842:
That we, the delegates representing the various trades of Manchester and its vicinities, with delegates from various parts of Lancashire and Yorkshire, do most emphatically declare, that it is our solemn and conscientious conviction that all the evils that afflict society, and which have prostrated the energies of the great body of the producing classes, arise solely from class legislation; and that the only remedy for the present alarming distress and widespread destitution is the immediate and unmutilated adoption, and carrying into law, of the document known as the People's Charter—'That this meeting recommend the people of all trades and callings forthwith to cease work, until the above document becomes the law of the land'.

The address of the Executive Committee of the NCA, adopted by delegates to the NCA conference, Manchester 17 August 1842.

Brother Chartists,—The great political truths which have been agitated during the last half-century have at length aroused the degraded and insulted white slaves of England to a sense of their duty to themselves, their children, and their country. Tens of thousands have flung down their implements of labour. Your taskmasters tremble at your energy, and expecting masses eagerly watch this great crisis of our cause. Labour must no longer be the common prey of masters and rulers . . .

We do now universally resolve never to resume labour, until labour's grievances are destroyed, and protection secured to ourselves, our suffering wives, and helpless children, by the enactment of the People's charter. Englishmen! the blood of your brethren reddens the streets of Preston and Blackburn and the murderers thirst for more. Be firm, be courageous, be men! Peace, law and order have prevailed on our side—let them be revered until your brethren in Scotland, Wales and Ireland are informed of your resolution; and when a universal holiday prevails, which will be the case in eight days, then of what use will bayonets be against public opinion? . . . The trades, a noble, patriotic band, have taken the lead in declaring for the Charter, and drawing their gold from the keeping of tyrants. Follow their example. Lend no whip to rulers therewith to scourge you.

Intelligence has reached us of the widespreading of the strike; and now, within fifty miles of Manchester, every engine is at rest, and all is still, save the miller's useful wheels and friendly sickle in the fields . . .

Our machinery is all arranged, and your cause will, in three days, be impelled onward by all the intellect we can summon to its aid: therefore, whilst you are peaceful, be firm; whilst you are orderly, make all be so likewise; and whilst you look to the law, remember that you had no voice in making it, and are therefore the slaves to the will, the law, and the price of your masters. All officers of the association are called upon to aid and assist in the peaceful extension of the movement, and to forward all moneys for the use of delegates who may be expressed over the country. Strengthen our hands at this crisis. Support your leaders. Rally round our sacred cause, and leave the decision to the God of justice and of battle.

Mr O'Connor, at the Manchester conference of the NCA:

He stated that it was the duty of the Chartists to take advantage of passing events. Not that he anticipated so much from the present strike, but after we had expended so much money and time in inducing the trades to join us, we could never get them to join again unless we passed some such resolution.

15d Chartism: a conspiracy

Northern Star, 15 October 1842.

The Chester special commission, investigating the Plug Plots. Lord Abinger is speaking to the grand jury.

A due regard for the public safety makes it essential that all tumultuous and unlawful assemblies of the people should be put down by force if necessary, and punished with the utmost rigour of the law . . . I need hardly tell you that it is one of the evils incident to a nation of great manufacturing and commercial prosperity, that the country which was flourishing from that prosperity should occasionally be subject to great reverses. It is the nature and habit of industry and enterprise to keep full the channels of supply, sometimes to overflowing, and whenever a check to the demand occurs there must follow for a while a suspension of employment, a diminution in the price of manufactured produce and the wages of labour, and very often, unhappily, distress and misery of the manufacturing classes . . . We cannot view without emotions of compassion the situation of the industrious classes, who, not having a competent knowledge to form a judgement of their own as to the principles or the rights of property, or upon the questions on which their own prosperity is involved, imagine that they can by force and violence dictate terms to their masters, and thereby rescue themselves from a degree of privation and discomfort, against which no Government, however it might be formed, and no law, whatever its intentions, could effectually secure them. Nevertheless you will find many, in that situation of life to which I have just alluded, and with that infirmity of judgement easily inflamed, when subjects are touched on relating to their own means of existence and state of discomfort, induced by crafty persons, who excite and mislead them, to imagine that they are the fittest persons to govern themselves and that they ought to have an equal share, if not a superior share, in the conduct of the Government and the making of the laws. I am afraid that the manufacturing classes have of late been the dupes of this sort of persuasion; and you will find in the occurrences which have called you together sundry examples of this delusion. You will find that there is a society of persons who go by the name of Chartists, and who, if they have not excited or fomented these outrages which will be brought under your notice, have, nevertheless, taken advantage of them for their own purposes, have endeavoured to prevent the unfortunate people from returning to their work, and sought so to direct them that they might be conducive to the attainment of political objects. And what is the object of the Charter which these men are seeking? What are the points of the Charter? Annual Parliaments, Universal Suffrage, and Vote by Ballot. Yet, Gentlemen, you will find by the evidence which will be produced before you, that it has been inculcated upon many misguided persons, that the sovereign remedy for all abuses, and the only means of putting themselves in possession of such a share of power as would enable them to vindicate their own rights and secure themselves against oppression, is by the enactment of what they call the People's Charter. In what a strange situation this country would be placed if those who have no property were to possess a preponderating voice in the making of the laws! These unhappy men do not consider that the first object of civilized society is the establishment and preservation of property and the security of person. What, then, would be the state of any country if multitudes were to make the laws for regulating property, or were permitted to employ physical force to restrain individuals from employing their own labour according to their own judgement, or preventing their subsistence? The foundation of civilized society may be considered to consist in the protection of property and the security of person; and if these two objects were removed, society must be dissolved . . .

15e Richard Pilling's defence, 1843

State Trials (new series), iv, cols 1097–108.

My Lord, and gentlemen of the jury, I am come quite unprepared with any defence; neither do I intend to take up much of your time. I have took no notes of what the witnesses have sworn against me; but they have sworn hard—some of them. I can prove, to demonstration, that Mr. Gregory, the prosecutor's attorney, has sent home some of the first witnesses and paid them off, because they would not swear more against us than they did. Gentlemen of the jury, it is stated by one of the witnesses, that I was the father of this great movement—the father of this outbreak; if so, then punish me, and let all the rest go free. But I say it is not me that is the father of this movement; but the House. Our addresses have been paid before that House, and they have not redressed our grievances; and from there, and there alone, the cause comes . . . Gentlemen, I am somewhere about forty-three years of age. I was asked last night if I were not sixty. But if I had as good usage as others, instead of looking like a man of sixty, I should look something like a man of thirty-six. I have gone to be a hand-loom weaver, when I was about ten years of age—in 1810. The first week I ever worked in my life, I earned sixteen shillings a-week by the hand-loom. I followed that occupation till 1840. Then I was the father of a family—a wife and three children. In 1840 I could only earn—indeed the last week I worked, and I worked hard, I could only earn six and sixpence; but I should do that or become a pauper. I should go to the factory, which I detested to the bottom of my heart, and work for six and sixpence a-week, or become a pauper. But although I detested the factory system, yet, sooner than become a pauper on the parish I submitted. I was not long in the factory until I saw the evil workings of the accursed system—it is a system, which, above all systems, will bring this country to ruin if it is not altered. I have read some of the speeches by the late Mr. Sadler, and I have read many letters of that noble king of Yorkshire—Richard Oastler—I have read many of his letters, and very shortly I became an advocate of the Ten Hours' Bill.

I continued to advocate the Ten Hours' Bill up to the present day, and as long as I have a day to live, so long will I advocate the Ten Hours' Bill.

After working in the factory seven years, a reduction began to creep in, one way or the other. I was a resident at Stockport . . . There were some masters always who wanted to give less wages than others. Seeing this to be an evil, and knowing it to be injurious to the master, the owner of cottage-property, and the publican,—knowing that all depended on the wages of the working man, I became an opponent to the reduction of wages to the bottom of my soul; and as long as I live I shall continue to keep up the wages of labour, to the utmost of my power. For taking that part in Stockport, and being the means of preventing many reductions, the masters combined all as one man against me, and neither me nor my children could get a day's employment. In 1840, there was a great turn-out in Stockport, in which turn-out I took a conspicuous part. We were out eight weeks. We were up every morning from five to six o'clock. Upwards of 6000 power loom weavers were engaged in that turn-out. We had our processions. We went to Ashton, Hyde, and Duckinfield in procession. We had our processions in Manchester, and all over the country, and we were not interfered with. No one meddled with us—no one insulted us. We were never told, at this time, that we were doing that which was wrong. Considering, from the act of parliament that was passed when the combination laws were repealed in 1825, that I had a right to do so; I did believe, as an Englishman, and factory operative that, in consequence of that act, I had a right to do all that ever lay in my power to keep up wages. In 1840 the master manufacturers, to the number of about forty, had a meeting, and they conspired together—if there is conspiracy on the one side there is conspiracy on the other—and they gave us notice for a reduction of one penny a cut. Some people think a penny is a small reduction, but it amounts to five weeks' wages in the course of the year. It is 2*s.* 6*d.* a week. Thus by that reduction they were robbing every operative of five weeks' wages . . . Hyde, Ashton, Staleybridge, Bolton, Wigan, Warrington, Preston, Blackburn reduced. In another year all the towns in the manufacturing districts reduced again. Not content with that reduction, about twelve months after they took off another penny a cut, besides taking two shillings off the Throstle spinners who had only eight shillings a week and eighteenpence off the card spinners, who had only eight shillings a week and so on. When they took the other penny a cut off, I pulled all the hands out, and we went round again to all the manufacturing districts, and brought things to a level again. The manufacturers of Stockport met again and said—'We cannot compete with Blackburn and Preston, and we must reduce again,'—and this is the way they will go on until at length they reduce so low that we shall all become paupers.

Gentlemen, I went to Ashton. Myself and my two sons were then working at the mills for twelve-pence half-penny a cut. Our work was thirty cuts a week—which makes £1. 11*s*. 3*d*. When Stockport reduced, my employer took off a penny a cut; then he took off a halfpenny a cut—I am not blaming him; he was only following others. If one master reduced, the others must reduce also. They all have to meet in one market, and if one man at a certain price has a penny profit, and the other only a farthing, he who has only the farthing will break. I was in very poor circumstances then, having a wife and seven children to support, and only three of us earning wages, as I told you . . . I had to pay three shillings for rent, one shilling and sixpence for fire, sixpence for soap, and two shillings for clothing, leaving, after reckoning all up, about one pound a week for provisions. When he took this penny off it caused a reduction in my wages of two shillings and sixpence. Shortly after he took off a halfpenny a cut, which was a reduction of one shilling and threepence a week more. Fifteen months since they took another penny off; then they took a farthing a cut off, and at the mill we worked at we turned out against the farthing. Three men who were out on that strike were turned off when the hands returned to their work. I am not ashamed to state that I did all I could along with other individuals to prevent the reduction. We accomplished that . . . and if I am found guilty of doing my best to promote the interests of those whom I love, I shall still rejoice in considering that my exertions have prevented a reduction which would have been injurious to so many. Peace, Law, and Order was our motto, and we acted up to that motto. In Ashton-under-Lyne one pennyworth of damage was not done to property, although we were out for six weeks.

My Lord and gentlemen of the jury, it was then a hard case for me to support myself and family. My eldest son but one, who was sixteen years of age, had fallen into a consumption last Easter and left his work. We were then reduced to 9¾*d*. a cut, which brought our earnings down to something like sixteen shillings a week. That is all I had to live on, with my nine in family, three shillings a week going out of that for rent, and a sick son lying helpless before me. If I have gone home and seen that son—(here Pilling was moved to tears, and unable to proceed for some time)—I have seen that son lying on a sick bed and dying pillow, and having nothing to eat but potatoes and salt . . . with neither medical aid, nor any of the common necessaries of life. Yea, I recollect some one going to a gentleman's house in Ashton, to ask for a bottle of wine for him; and it was said, 'Oh, he is a Chartist, he must have none.' (Great sensation in court). Oh, such usage from the rich will never convince the chartists that they are wrong. Gentlemen, my son died before the commencement of the strike; and such was the feeling of the people of Ashton towards my family, that they collected £4 towards his burial. Gentlemen of the jury, it was under these circumstances that I happened to call at Stockport—excited I will admit by the loss of my son, together with a reduction of 25%; for I will acknowledge and confess before you, gentlemen of the jury, that before I would have lived to submit to another reduction of 25%, I would have terminated my own existence. That was my intention.

Let us now come to the facts of the case. I will tell you what was the origin of the strike . . . Mr. Rayner of Ashton had given notice, within a day or two of that time, that he would reduce 25%. So indignant were the feelings of the people of Ashton and the surrounding district, not only the chartists, but all sorts assembled; a room that would hold a thousand people was crammed to suffocation, and the whole voice of the meeting was, that it was of no use trying to get up a subscription for others, but to give up. And that was just the way the strike began; it rose in a minute from one end of the room to the other; whigs, tories, chartists, sham radicals, and all sorts. Then it was thought proper that a committee should be appointed, and that committee issued the placard headed 'The day of reckoning draweth nigh' . . . That placard stated, that if another reduction was offered we would cease working till we had a fair day's wages for a fair day's work, but the Charter was never mentioned . . . Another resolution was, that the reduction of wages was injurious to all classes of the community. This was done at a meeting where there were 15,000 present, and the entire population is only 25,000. Nearly all Ashton was there; shopkeepers, publicans, spinners, lawyers (no, not lawyers, they live on the wages of others, and they had no business there), all were at the meeting . . . Well, we had a turn-out to prevent a reduction; and when Rayner saw the spirit of the meeting he withdrew his reduction. A meeting was then called at Staleybridge, and everyone withdrew the reduction except Bayley. Now, if there is one man who ought to stand here as a defendant that is the man. If he had withdrawn the reduction there would have been no strike; the people would have settled down and enjoyed a glorious triumph in preventing the reduction. A meeting was also held at Hyde; and the people of Hyde declared that if the masters attempted to make another reduction they (the working people) would give over. At Droylesden the same. This is the history of the turnout. I would say to the jury and the people assembled here, that if it had not been for the late struggle, I firmly believe thousands would have been starved to death . . . After these public meetings placards were issued by the committees, of which I will read one . . . that we considered strictly legal:—

> The voice of the People is the Voice of God.
> To the masters and tradesmen of Ashton-under-Lyne, and its vicinities—We, the operatives of Ashton-under Lyne, in public meeting assembled, feel it our duty to tell you thus publicly, that such are our sufferings in consequence of low wages, and numerous other things, that we can no longer tamely submit to it. We, therefore, wish you to give us the same prices that we received in the year 1840 . . . We want a uniform price for the whole of the manufacturing districts; and it is the interests of masters to have it, in order that one man cannot undersell another in the market. Much is said about over-production, and about the market being glutted. In order to obviate the past, let us all work ten hours per day, and we are sure it will lessen the amount of goods in the market. The home consumption will also be considerably increased by increasing the wages of the labourer . . .

I was stating, that on the 20th August, we had a delegate meeting from all trades in the manufacturing districts, for the purpose of drawing up a list of prices to submit to the masters. We endeavoured to find out the secretary of the Manchester manufacturers to ascertain from him if they would consent to reduce the hours of labour to ten hours a-day, and give the wages of 1840 . . . Then follows the resolution, in which the workmen declared their intention not to resume work till they got the prices they left off at—that is, the prices of 1840. Gentlemen, if there is any illegality in that, I acknowledge I am guilty . . .

Suppose, gentlemen of the jury, you were obliged to subsist on the paltry pittance given to us in the shape of wages, and had a wife and six helpless children, five of them under thirteen years of age to support, how would you feel? Though you were to confine me to a dungeon I should not submit to it. I have a nervous wife—a good wife—a dear wife—a wife that I love and cherish, and I have done everything that I could in the way of resisting reductions in wages, that I might keep her and my children from the workhouse, for I detest parish relief. It is wages I want. I want to be independent of every man and that is the principle of every honest Englishman; and I hope it is the principle of every man in this court . . . I was twenty years among the handloom weavers, and ten years in a factory, and I unhesitatingly say, that during the whole course of that time I worked twelve hours a day with the exception of twelve months that the masters of Stockport would not employ me; and the longer and harder I have worked the poorer and poorer I have become every year, until, at last, I am nearly exhausted. If the masters had taken off another 25%, I would put an end to my existence sooner than kill myself working twelve hours a day in a cotton factory, and eating potatoes and salt. Gentlemen of the jury, I now leave my case in your hands. Whatever it may have been with others it has been a wage question with me. And I do say that if Mr. O'Connor has made it a chartist question, he has done wonders to make it extend through England, Ireland, and Scotland. But it was always a wage question, and ten hours bill with me. I have advocated the keeping up of wages for a long time, and I shall do so till the end of my days. And, if confined within the walls of a dungeon, knowing that as an individual I have done my duty; knowing that I have been one of the great spokes in the wheel by which that last reduction of wages was prevented—knowing that by means of that turn-out thousands and ten of thousands have eaten the bread which they would not have eaten if the turn-out had not taken place, I am satisfied, whatever may be the result . . . And, now, Gentlemen of the jury, you have the case before you; the masters conspired to kill me, and I combined to keep myself alive.

15f Miners and magistrates

Appendix to *First Report of the Midland Mining Commission* (1843).

The Staffordshire miners, encouraged by Chartists like Arthur O'Neill, attempted to resist wage cuts and remove their grievances, by going on strike in the summer of 1842. But it crumbled when blackleg labour was imported.

Shelton, a collier.—I have constantly advised the men to keep the peace, to wait upon their masters and state their grievances, and let them know what they suffered from the butty colliers.
Lord Dartmouth.—That was good advice, and very just.
Collier.—But our masters will not meet us, because we are poor labouring men. Instead of meeting us, they walk about the ground where we meet, and talk to their butties. They cannot know the state of the case unless they converse with those men who have suffered . . .
Hughes—a collier.—The oppression, my lord, upon the colliers is very great. We are 12 hours in the bowels of the earth, and that is too much; we are kept in complete darkness, and our children will be the same; we have no means of learning or obtaining grace or light for ourselves; we hardly see daylight for the best part of the year.
Shelton then stated the grievances under which they laboured. The masters employ butties to get the coal; these butties employ the men, and pay them as they please; they make them work half a day for a quarter's wages; the ale they give them to drink is not fit for swine, though the masters allow them 3d. a quart for it; the butties are tyrants and ill use the men; if a man spoke to or offended one of them he told another butty, and the poor man was sure to be turned away; they keep beer shops, where they make the men spend their money; worst of all, they have the truck system in many places, so that a man could never count upon his wages. Now he thought the masters must be ignorant of all that, and that was what they wanted to state and get removed. It could not be a benefit to the masters to keep such a system,

because the butties had all been able to make a great deal of money out of the pits. The masters had to pay the same price for getting up the coal, although the men did not get the wages . . .
Mr. Willett.—Well, can't you get masters who will not truck?
Collier.—My lord, we are too numerous, and they don't want us all, and we can't get masters that won't truck, even when they want plenty of work.
Shelton.—I was turned off my work for asking for my wages.
Hughes.—Now, my lord, what advice would you give us poor men? We are not idlers. I myself have always worked hard, and no man could ever say a word against me. I have been a consistent Methodist for many years, strived to live well, and all the harm I have ever done to the butties was to tell them that their deeds would not stand on the day of judgment; yet for this I know they say I shall not have work.

15g Chartism and the trades

Northern Star, 1 February 1845.

The trades have selected a period of comparative 'prosperity' as the time for holding a Conference, wherein the several matters interesting to their body can be discussed, have at least purged their proceedings of all suspicion that *hunger alone* can move the Working Classes. True, when the people were poor and hungered, Chartism was described as the 'howl of the hungry.' We never denied the assertion; but, on the contrary, admitted that social suffering and inequality always led to political discussion. . . . Satisfied then as we were, even with a bad state of things that induced thought and discussion which led to the almost universal adoption of a great principle, we are much better satisfied with the prospect of forthcoming events, which are not shadowed forth in squalid wretchedness and misery.

The 'howl of the hungry' for food is a dangerous assailant; but may be met by the crushing force of organized authority, to the total subversion of the 'ordinary' law. When what is called a 'mob' clamours for food, and assumes a threatening aspect, the 'necessity' for instant suppression binds every faction in the State together: and under their combined influence, *striking examples* and prompt barbarity are represented as the perfection of humanity. The inevitable tendency of such a reverse is to dispirit, weaken, convulse and ultimately destroy the Movement party. On the other hand, men who leave their homes in obedience to the summons of their fellows in times of comparative 'prosperity', with the view of maturely considering how, without recourse to violence or even declamation, they may present a sufficient amount of combined knowledge and power to ensure their fair share of the growing 'prosperity' of the country, must be regarded by all parties in the State as the representative power of the republic of Labour, met to devise means for carrying into effect what the legislature itself has characterized as just, but what its ignorance of all the ramifications of industry cannot reduce to practise . . .

It is not a chartist move, further than the impossibility of separating the principles of justice from the rights of Labour . . . The colliers' strike was not a Chartist movement; nor did any speaker on the platform ever attempt to mix up the two questions; but the several delegates who assembled in London and elsewhere, were proud to bear honourable testimony to the valuable support they received from the Chartist body. The recent strike in the Building Trades in Manchester was not a Chartist movement; and yet the Chartists were foremost in the battle of right against might! . . . The Trades will find Chartism as all others seeking their rights have found it,—a zealous co-operator, a steady friend and uncompromising advocate.

15h The theory and tactics of unionism

Northern Star, 29 March 1845.

The report of the committee to the National Conference of the Association of United Trades.

The primary object of all Trades Unions is to secure to the Operative a fair and just participation in the wealth he assists to produce. For some years past an opinion has been gradually gaining ground among these bodies, that their organization and the application of their funds heretofore, have neither been the best nor the most effective that might have been adopted. Repeated failure has induced scepticism as to the efficiency of STRIKES ALONE to protect the labourer from the aggression of CAPITAL, and to arrest that downward tendency which is the most prominent feature of his condition . . . The great cause of the continuous decline of the wages of Labour . . . is a redundance of workers, compared with the demand for their labour . . . Experience has proved that *Strikes* alone are not sufficient for this purpose, and some other modes must be devised whereby the 'surplus labour' shall be absorbed, or kept out of the market, and an equality be maintained between the work to be done and the number of those required to do it.

Strikes, limitation of apprentices, and the support of tramps, were no doubt well-adapted for the objects had in view when they were originally adopted, and to a period when manual labour was *aided* instead of *mastered*, by machinery: but the enormous increase of the latter productive power must be met by the adoption of additional measures on the part of the operatives, suited to the new circumstances it has created. While CAPITAL possesses the unlimited power of creating automaton workers, it is utterly impossible for manual labour, in its present position, to maintain a successful struggle against its aggressions . . . The working classes must expend their funds—locally or generally—in the erection of machines that will work for them and not against them; and instead of investing funds with bankers, to be used by large capitalists, in a way which inevitably lowers the condition of the contributor, they must apply them to the production of real worth and profitable results for themselves.

The time may not yet have arrived when practical measures for this purpose can be commenced . . . The *immediate measures* which it appears to your Committee, this Conference may usefully take into consideration are the following:

1. A society, to be called the Association of United Trades for the Protection of Industry.

2. A Central Committee to carry out the objects of the said Association, and the formation of a fund to defray the necessary expense.

3. The leading objects of the Association may be divisible into two departments—the first external, having reference to the influence of the legislature on the condition of the industrious classes; the second internal, or to efforts made by the Trades to improve their own condition.

With respect to the first of these divisions, your Committee suggest that the Central Committee should be empowered and instructed to take every opportunity, by means of petitions to Parliament, deputations to Government and members of both Houses of the Legislature, cheap publications, public meetings, and other legal, reasonable, and peaceable measures to enforce the adoption of shorter hours of labour wherever practicable . . .

4. Another measure to which serious considerations should be directed is, the establishment of Local Boards of Trade, similar to those which have so long existed in France and Belgium, composed of masters and operatives, to whom all matters affecting the regulation of wages, duration of labour, disputes etc. shall be referred, and their decisions have the authority of law.

(It is conceived that these two measures would very materially improve the condition of the labouring classes. Short time would keep production and consumption more upon a level with each other; equalize the condition of the workers, who would thus all be enabled to share in whatever work there might be in the market; and by giving time for mental and moral improvement, raise the character of the whole population. On the other hand, the proposed Boards of Trade, being equally composed of employers and employed, would have a tendency to prevent strikes and turn-outs by all differences being first submitted to an impartial tribunal, and authoritatively settled by it.)

Under this general division of the business of the Association, would also fall the promotion of all public movements having reference to improved sanitory conditions for the labouring population; and generally of all such measures as would conduce to the promotion of health, intelligence and morality.

5. The second division of the Association should be the collection and diffusion of information, as to the means by which the capital and skill and labour of the Trades can be applied for their own benefit, and especially to enable them to abstract from the labour market, and set to profitable employment, the redundant hands, who, if suffered to remain in it, would reduce the wages of the whole trade to which they belong.

Statements of the delegates

Mr. Prior, Tailor said . . . He thought the working men, when they had a proper understanding, could do more for themselves than any Act of Parliament. What could the workmen expect from men who declared that they would rather walk the streets in their shirt sleeves, than that the Tailors should obtain their just rights? . . . He could not come to the conclusion that Local Boards of Trade would work well (hear, hear). . . .

Mr. Webster, Hull, asked whether the present mode of adjusting disputes (even when the labourer had justice on his side) was at all satisfactory? Were his grievances rightly adjusted? No, certainly not. All the power was at present on the side of the capitalists. He came from a maritime town, where disputes were referred to the magistrates, whose decisions not infrequently caused the greatest disgust. The proposed Local Boards would be composed equally of employers and employed, and would thus give the employed *half the* power on the settlement of disputes. They would consequently be calculated to allay prejudice, and create a better feeling between the masters and workmen . . .

Mr. J. S. Sherrard, Hand-loom weaver, Spitalfields, said he believed he was warranted in saying that the whole body of Weavers in the united kingdom was in favour of local boards. They believed it to be one of the best means that existed to better their condition. It was the only means of making dishonourable capitalists act justly. It would benefit their whole body, who with their families and their dependents, numbered not less than 800,000 . . .

Mr. Sykes, File-smith . . . There were few working men but who felt great diffidence in the presence of their employers, and consequently in such a position would not act up to principle. It was fallacious to talk of their interest being identical. Therefore, he had no great faith in acting with the capitalist . . .

Mr. Blackhurst, Sheffield, would ask, would Local Boards of Trade place more wealth in the hands of the workmen? We did not wish merely to walk, talk, dance or gamble with the employers; the working men wanted the power of dining with them. Local Boards might equalize wages in some districts, but they would not increase them. He objected to Local Boards, because they would give other men the power of selling his labour, instead of learning him to sell it himself. The masters had always acted treacherously towards them, and hence they could not trust them as arbiters. It was said the Boards would not be eternal—no; the Poor Law was not to be eternal; but they were still cursed with it . . .

Mr. Prior, Tailor . . . The Tailors, the body represented, had formed a joint stock company, and with a fund raised, had employed their unemployed hands exchanging their labour with the unemployed of other Trades. They had executed a contract by this means to the amount of £150. If they had possessed Land at the same time, and been enabled to obtain the first necessary of life on their own account, he had no doubt their success would have been ample . . .

Mr. G. White, Woolcomber, then moved—That this Conference recommend to all Trades the propriety of becoming the possessors of their own labour, and that we recommend the various Trades to establish manufactories and stores to supply themselves with provisions, the profits arising therefrom to be devoted to the purchase of land on which to employ surplus labour . . .

Mr. William Evans, Potter . . . believed the Trades of Sheffield had been benefited by lessening the number of apprentices, as well as by shortening the hours of labour. He thought it behoved delegates to take means to employ the surplus hands. It had been said that Land and Labour were the source of all wealth; this was true. They (the Potters) had acted upon this truism; they had found that in America they could get 12,000 acres of land for £3,000 on which they thought of forming a township, the true means, he believed, of employing their surplus hands. But there was another place where good land could be had for nothing, in the Republic of Venezeula, and where they could have also the privilege of electing their own governors; in fact, they could have the 'Charter' in full force. He thought they might combine emigration, home colonization, and stores in one proposition . . .

16 The Land Plan

A regular remedy suggested for surplus labour in the early nineteenth century, was 'home colonization', the intensive farming of often marginal land. It was dignified by Owen into agrarian communities, politicized by the League in its attack on the aristocracy, and was available to unions attempting to maintain wages in an overstocked trade. Its most popular form was O'Connor's Land Plan of 1845, which commanded enormous Chartist support all over England. Capital was raised by shares to purchase an estate, which was then to be mortgaged to raise the capital for another estate. Shareholders would be selected by lot to become self-sufficient smallholders renting plots and cottages from the estate. Some four estates were settled this way (Herringsgate, near Watford, renamed O'Connorville; Lowbands, near Gloucester, and close by, Snigs End; and Charterville at Minster Lovell, near Oxford); but by 1848 its finances were so precarious that it was investigated by a House of Commons committee, and the scheme was wound up.

Suggestions for further reading

See J. MacAskill, 'The Chartist Land Plan', in A. Briggs (ed.), *Chartist Studies* (1959); A. M. Hadfield, *The Chartist Land Company* (1970).

16a The Land Plan as presented to the Chartist annual conference of April 1845

Northern Star, 26 April 1845.

We know that we have a large number of surplus hands, not only not applied to the production of anything, but still further, maintained in idleness by a crushing tax raised upon the industry of those who are yet allowed to labour. Every writer upon agriculture admits the facility with which the agricultural produce of these countries might be increased two-fold . . . There is no earthly reason why every cultiveable acre in England may not be brought to the same state of perfection as a market garden. My calculations of the value of labour applied to land is as follows:—An industrious person, of very moderate strength, will be enabled to support himself, a wife and three children, upon an average of six hours' labour of each day throughout the year upon four acres of land, and will have a surplus in each year of £100, after the best of living and the payment of all expenses. The great value that I attach to the system of small agricultural divisions is this—it creates a certainty. It enables the labourer to live upon his own resources, and enjoy the entire sweets of his own industry; it makes him more jealous of any inroads upon the condition, the privileges, or the rights of his class.

I now proceed to show . . . how by application of labour rendered surplus by machinery, a standard of wages may be established for all descriptions of labourers, no matter of what craft or calling . . . If the employment of a pauper-reserve would have the effect of increasing wages by destroying competition, how much greater would be the effect if the working classes generally would agree upon some plan by which they could so adjust the number working at each trade to the amount of produce required from each as to insure a healthy settlement of demand and supply . . . I propose my land project firstly for the purpose of establishing the value of free labour, in order thereby that the working classes, when offering their labour for sale, may have some scale by which to judge of its value; and because under the present system, the land is the only raw material to which individual labour can be applied to test its value without the possibility of being created by a competitive labour surplus.

I contend that there is no other neutral ground save the land, upon which the surplus of all trades and crafts can meet without jealousy, or without the notion that in any arrangement to carry it out partiality or injustice has been manifested. Individuals brought up in one trade, cannot, when that trade becomes slack, apply their unrequired labour profitably to any other calling . . .

Northern Star, 26 July 1845.

Suppose that 50 occupants have been located at a cost of £4,125, and that they pay £250 per year, and that there is left in the Society's possession a surplus of £875. Instead of selling the estate so let, and so certain to rise in value from the application of so much labour, I, if it was mine . . . would mortgage it for £4000, instead of selling it for £5,000, or at twenty years purchase. I would then add £125 of the surplus of £875, to the £4000 borrowed on mortgage, and locate fifty more . . .

Let me now presume that eight drafts, at fifty each draft, have been located in two years. That is, that the society has bought 800 acres, built 400 cottages, and given £15 to each of 400 occupants; that £28,000 has been borrowed on mortgage at four per cent., the interest on which would be £1120 a-year. The rent of 400 holding at £5 each, would be £2000 a-year, leaving an annual profit in favour of the society of £880 per annum . . . Our object should be to enable the occupants of each division to become purchasers for ever of their respective allotments; and this I pledge myself each can do out of his savings in less than five years . . .

16b Free trade and the Land Plan

Evidence of Feargus O'Connor, *Select Committee on the National Land Company* (1848), qus 2439–40.

Feargus O'Connor,

The cause of my first establishing this society was the conviction impressed upon my own mind . . . of the effect which free trade, when completed and carried out, would have upon the working classes of this country . . . I found I could make the land produce three times as much by spade husbandry as I could by ploughed husbandry. Then, in 1845, I determined to establish this company, and I established it at a conference of working men, called from different parts of the country . . . As soon as they had raised £4,000 it was determined to carry the plan into instant operation. I purchased the estate at Herringsgate . . . I then found that I could sell or mortgage the land . . . I would have it observed, that I am advocating the co-operative system, not the principle of communism. My plan is entirely opposed to the principle of communism for I repudiate communism and socialism. My plan is based upon the principle of individuality of possession and co-operation of labour . . .

Chairman,

It appears that the object of your scheme is to buy estates in the whole, and to sell them in retail, and thereby cause a certain amount of improvement?—Yes.

17 1848

Bad times and the example of the February revolution in France again made Chartism a mass movement. A Chartist petition was organized and a Chartist Convention was called to discuss 'ulterior measures' if the petition was rejected. On 10 April the petition was presented and rejected; a National Assembly was elected but then adjourned, and activity went underground, but by September mass arrests had brought it to an end.

17a Ulterior measures

John Street Institution, *Proceedings of the National Convention* (1848).

1st.—That in the event of the National Petition being rejected by the House of Commons, this Convention prepare a National Memorial to the Queen to dissolve the present Parliament, and call to her council such ministers only as will make the People's Charter a cabinet measure.

2nd.—That this Convention agree to the convocation of a National Assembly, to consist of delegates appointed at public meetings, to present the National Memorial to the Queen, and to continue permanently sitting until the Charter is the law of the land.

3rd.—That this Convention call upon the country to hold simultaneous meetings on Good Friday, April 21st, for the purpose of adopting the National Memorial, and electing delegates to the National Assembly.

4th.—That the National Assembly meet in London on April 24th.

5th.—That the present Convention shall continue its sittings until the meeting of the National Assembly.

17b Military preparations

R. Gammage, *History of the Chartist Movement, 1837–1854* (1894), pp. 312–13.

The ever memorable 10th of April arrived, and vast preparations were made by the Government. Besides the regular troops quartered in the metropolis, others poured in from Windsor, Hounslow, Chichester, Chatham, Winchester and Dover. The marines and sailors of the Royal Navy at Sheerness, Chatham, Birkenhead, Spithead, and other government towns, as well as the dockyard men, were kept under arms. The Thames police kept watch upon the mercantile marines, lest they should show any leaning towards the Chartists. Heavy gun-batteries were brought from Woolwich, and placed at various points. Many of the troops were disposed of secretly, to be ready in case of necessity. The mounted police were armed with broad swords and pistols. All the public buildings were put in a state of defence. Two thousand stand-of-arms were supplied to the general post office, for the use of the clerks and officers of that department, who were all sworn in as special constables; and the officials at other public places were equally well provided. All the steam vessels were ordered to be ready for any emergency, in order to convey troops. At the Tower the guns were examined, the battlements strengthened by barricades, and the troops held in readiness to march at a minute's notice. The labourers at the docks were sworn in as specials. The city prisons were guarded by military, and the churches were converted into barracks. The public vehicles were generally withdrawn from the streets. In the city seventy thousand persons were sworn in as special constables, and military officers commanded them. The royal carriages and horses, and other valuables, were removed from the palace. The military force amounted to nine thousand men. It being believed that the procession would go from Kennington Common, over Blackfriars Bridge, to the House of Commons, great preparations were made in that quarter. At Stepney Green, Finsbury-square, and Russell-square, bodies of the Chartists met with bands and banners, and paraded the streets on their way to Kennington Common, where six thousand police, and eight thousand specials were in attendance. Before eleven o'clock Trafalgar-square was filled with police . . . Every commodious place in this vicinity was filled with military, police or specials. The artillery was also present . . .

17c A foreigner's comment

David Cairns (trans. and ed.), *The Memoirs of Hector Berlioz* (1969), p. 44.

Today, the 10th April, the two hundred thousand English Chartists are to hold their demonstration. In a few hours, maybe, England will be engulfed like the rest of Europe and this refuge too will have failed me. I shall go out and see how the issue is decided.

(8 p.m.) Your Chartist is a very decent sort of revolutionary. Everything went very satisfactorily. The cannon, those eloquent orators and formidable logicians whose arguments appeal so powerfully to the masses, were in the chair. They were not required to utter a word, their presence being enough to persuade everybody of the inexpediency of revolution, and the Chartists dispersed in perfect order.

My poor friends, you know as much about starting a riot as the Italians about writing a symphony. The Irish are doubtless the same, to judge from O'Connell's injunction, 'Agitate, agitate, but never act'.

18 Co-operation and trading

After 1834 Owenism was less and less an integral part of working-class radicalism, and Owen himself no longer a leader of working-class protest. Significantly, the GNCTU, a trades union, became the Association of All Classes of All Nations. Subsequent Owenite activity focused on communitarianism and education. In the late 1830s, communities were established at Manea Fen in Cambridgeshire and Queenwood in Hampshire, and after their collapse, 'redemption societies' attempted to build up funds for further experiments. Social missionaries and Halls of Science furthered the second strand of Owenism, particularly in Manchester and London, but their brand of rational religion and education seldom lasted long.

Co-operative storekeeping had been an important part of Owenite methodology in the 1830s and now again became popular, when the Rochdale Pioneers in 1844 introduced the 'dividend' by which profits were no longer retained by the society for community building but were distributed to members in proportion to their purchases. But it did retain many of the older aspirations of co-operation (18a). Fifteen years later, *Meliora*, the journal of Victorian scientific philanthropy, surveyed a story of financial and moral self-help (18b), undiluted by Owenite utopianism.

18a Rochdale Pioneers

G. J. Holyoake, *History of the Rochdale Equitable Pioneers* (1857), p. 11.

These Pioneers, in 1844, declared the views of their Association thus:—

'The objects and plans of this Society are to form arrangements for the pecuniary benefit and the improvement of the social and domestic condition of its members, by raising a sufficient amount of capital in shares of one pound each, to bring into operation the following plans and arrangements:—

The establishment of a Store for the sale of provisions, clothing, etc.

The building, purchasing, or erecting a number of houses, in which those members, desiring to assist each other in improving their domestic and social conditions, may reside.

To commence the manufacture of such articles as the society may determine on, for the employment of such members as may be without employment, or who may be suffering in consequence of repeated reductions in their wages.

As a further benefit and security to the members of this Society, the society shall purchase or rent an estate or estates of land, which shall be cultivated by the members who may be out of employment, or whose labour may be badly remunerated.'

Then follows a project which no nation has ever attempted, and no enthusiasts yet carried out:—

'That, as soon as practicable, this society shall proceed to arrange the powers of production, distribution, education, and government; or, in other words, to establish a self-supporting home colony of united interests, or assist other societies in establishing such colonies.

That, for the promotion of sobriety, a Temperance Hotel be opened in one of the Society's houses as soon as convenient.'

18b Co-operative societies in 1860

'Cooperative Societies', *Meliora*, iv, 1860.

The cooperative stores have had their share of rough usage; have struggled through failure, through contempt, through interested opposition, into success and respect; and with careful management they promise well for the future . . .

Here is an account of a store which seems to have worked its way from small things without much trouble except the want of capital. The Rawtenstall Industrial Society was commenced in 1850 by six working men. They managed to save a few shillings each, and bought one load of meal or flour. They then rented a cottage as a store at 1.3*d.* per week, and met every evening to dispose of their goods. At the end of the first quarter they divided 1. 6*d.* in the pound on purchases, after paying 5 per cent. on capital. They were soon obliged to take larger premises. They now own the building used as a store, and have a paid up capital of 3,000., and number 387 members; their business amounts to about 310 weekly, and they generally divide about 2*s.* in the pound quarterly on purchases. A purchaser who is too poor to pay for a share is allowed to rank for profits on his purchases until the price of a share is realized . . .

There are now in existence at least two hundred cooperative stores, and they are rapidly increasing in every direction . . . Some of them hold inflexibly, like the Rochdale model, to cash payments, whilst others give credit to members to the extent of one-half, two-thirds, or three-fourths of the paid-up capital of the debtor. They vary also in the amount which constitutes a share, and in the number of shares required or allowed to be held by each member. Some share their profits with non-members who desire to become members, whilst others require a payment on account of shares prior to any participation. In all, candidates for membership have to submit to their chance of election, and in all, the thorough democratic principle of one vote to each member obtains, no matter what the amount of his investment . . . In every case of division of profits, capital takes the first five per cent. after allowing for depreciation of stock; then in some cases a proportion is set aside to increase capital, and the remainder is divided according to purchases, whilst in others the whole is divided after the shares are once paid up, and the members are left to increase their shares within the prescribed limit or not as they please . . .

The practical result of these establishments appears, therefore, to be to enable the members to secure unadulterated food at the prices generally charged for the adulterated, and to give also from 7½ to 10 per cent discount; in other words, they put the poorest man upon a par with the richest, so far as their purchases of food and clothing are concerned: they do for the articles of the workman's daily consumption what Freehold Land and Building Societies have done for land and houses—they sell by retail at wholesale prices; but they also do more than this, by offering 5 per cent. increase on £1. and upwards in the shape of shares, and giving a voice in the management of the concern, they stimulate to prudential investments, and they educate in self-government the most important as well as most numerous class of society . . .

Part Three

Class and conflict–conciliation

1 Philanthropy

Those with a social conscience saw, as the Chartists saw, a country where many were desperately poor and where many felt severely oppressed. Such philanthropists were as worried by the hostility of the poor as they were saddened by their acute poverty. Some, like Shaftesbury, blamed a *laisser faire* state for reneging on its paternalist responsibilities, and sought to construct legislative defences for the most vulnerable members of society, its children and its insane (1a).

But most philanthropists believed that extreme poverty was due to individual failing, and the sense of oppression as a breakdown in the natural bonds of dependence and deference which should bind a society together. Personal, yet 'scientific', philanthropy, it was held, could overcome both. And compared with the concern and financial investment of the state and local authorities, the private philanthropic effort was highly impressive—in the 1850s it was estimated that at least £5 million a year was spent in charity in London alone, a figure several times higher than the state's domestic revenue. But the premises of scientific philanthropy made it unacceptable to the radical poor, and, as the century progressed, to the radical rich.

Scientific philanthropy, unlike the casual almsgiving of earlier generations, attacked not poverty as such, for that was considered inevitable in society, but the state of pauperism (1b). The poor man became a pauper when he could or would no longer maintain himself but became a burden on the community; this was not a fact about or a failing of society, but a fault in the individual who lacked the moral fibre to retain his independence. So the task of the new Poor Law (see above, p. 207) was to make the state of pauperism so unpleasant that no one would willingly enter it; and the task of philanthropy to build up the character so that no one would want or need to enter it. Thus the Quaker William Allen (1770–1843), favoured letters of introduction to charities as this would encourage working men to expose themselves to the view of the benevolent (1c); in 1819, Dr Chalmers (1780–1847), a Glasgow clergyman, refused to distribute alms to the poor because it would impair their responsibility to themselves and to each other (1d); Dr Kay (1804–77), the Manchester doctor who became the secretary to the Committee on Education, suggested that if the law helped the poor, then the rich would not; and class gulfs would grow wider (1e). And Harriet Martineau argued, in a tough-minded blend of the new philanthropy and the new political economy, that philanthropy was a cruelty to the poor as it destroyed their character, increased their families and diminished the wage fund on which their employment and their well-being depended (1f).

Such philanthropists therefore favoured charities which built character rather than dispensed alms; and these tended to be religious in their assumptions and scientific in their scrutiny of the poor. *Figaro*, a radical paper that freely satirized church and state, complained (1g) that such philanthropic piety was pretentious and hypocritical.

Suggestions for further reading

For a comprehensive survey, see D. Owen, *English Philanthropy* (1965); and its review by B. H. Harrison in *Victorian Studies*, June 1966. The most recent modern study of Shaftesbury is Geoffrey Best, *Shaftesbury* (1964).

1a Restlessness and responsibility

Shaftesbury, 'Infant Labour', *Quarterly Review*, 1840, quoted in E. Hodder, *Life and Work of the Seventh Earl of Shaftesbury* (1892 edn), pp. 173–4.

The two great demons in morals and politics, Socialism and Chartism, are stalking through the land; yet they are but symptoms of an universal disease, spread throughout vast masses of the people, who, so far from concurring in the *status quo*, suppose that anything must be better than their present condition. It is useless to reply to us, as our antagonists often do, that many of the prime movers in these conspiracies against God and good order are men who have never suffered any of the evil to which we ascribe so mighty an influence. We know it well; but we know also that our system begets the vast and inflammable mass that lies waiting, day by day, for the spark to explode it into mischief. We cover the land with spectacles of misery; wealth is felt only by its oppressions; few, very few, remain in these trading districts to spend liberally the riches they have acquired; the successful leave the field to be ploughed afresh by new aspirants after gain, who, in turn, count their periodical profits and exact the maximum of toil for the minimum of wages. No wonder that thousands of hearts should be against a system which establishes the relations, without calling forth the mutual sympathies of master and servant, landlord and tenant, employer and employed . . .

But here comes the worst of all—those vast multitudes, ignorant and excitable in themselves, and rendered still more so by oppression or neglect, are surrendered, almost without a struggle, to the experimental philosophy of infidels and democrats . . . Let your laws, we say to the Parliament, assume the proper functions of law, protect those for whom neither wealth, nor station, nor age has raised a bulwark against tyranny; but, above all, open your treasury, erect churches, send forth the ministers of religion, reverse the conduct of the enemy of mankind, and sow wheat among the tares—all hopes are groundless, all legislation weak, all conservatism nonsense, without this alpha and omega of policy; it will give content instead of bitterness, engraft obedience on rebellion, raise purity from corruption, and 'life from the dead'.

1b Poverty and pauperism

Patrick Colquhoun, *A Treatise on the Wealth, Power and Resources of the British Empire* (1814), chapter 14.

Poverty is that state and condition in society, where the individual has no surplus labour in store, or, in other words, no property or means of subsistence but what is derived from the constant exercise of industry in the various occupations of life. Poverty is therefore a most necessary and indispensable ingredient in society without which nations and communities could not exist in a state of civilization. It is the lot of man. *It is the source of wealth*, since without poverty there could be no labour; there could be *no riches, no refinement, no comfort*, and no benefit to those who may be possessed of wealth; inasmuch as without a large proportion of poverty, surplus labour could never be rendered productive in procuring either the conveniences or luxuries of life . . .

It is indigence, therefore, and not poverty, which constitutes the chief burthen to which civil society is exposed. It is the state of any one who is destitute of the means of subsistence, and is unable to procure it by labour to the extent nature requires. The natural source of subsistence is the labour of the individual, while that remains with him he is denominated *poor*; when it fails, in whole or in part, he becomes *indigent*. But it may happen, and does indeed frequently happen in civil life, that a man may have ability to labour and cannot obtain it. He may have labour in his possession without being able to dispose of it. The great desideratum, therefore, is to prop up poverty by judicious arrangements at those critical periods, when it is in danger of descending into indigence. The barrier between these two conditions in society is often slender, and the public interest requires that it should be narrowly guarded; since every individual who retrogrades into indigence becomes a loss to the body politic, not only in the diminution of a certain portion of productive labour, but also in an additional pressure on the community by the necessary support of the individual and his family who have thus descended into indigence.

1c The social utility of philanthropy

William Allen, Quaker philanthropist, 'A Review of Highmore's Pietas Londinensis', *Philanthropist*, iii, 1812, p. 4.

[Hospitals should not be free and open to allcomers but should require fees or letters of introduction from the poor.]

On the system of payment, it would but seldom happen that a truly deserving sufferer would be excluded, because it would very seldom happen that the circumstances of a truly deserving sufferer should not be known to some of the benevolent, who, if he was unable to pay for himself, would pay for him.

Nobody would be excluded upon this system, but he who could find no person, or set of persons, who would afford the expense to relieve him. Now, who is the sort of sufferer most likely to be in this unhappy situation? Undoubtedly he who is the least deserving. Now this is exactly the foundation on which wisdom and virtue would desire to see the matter placed. In this mode of application, charity operates as a real principle of virtue, as a motive to good conduct in the poor. It is the reward of merit. Throughout his whole life, the poor man, looking forward to the calamities to which his state is incident, must in this case be in the habit of asking himself, is my conduct such as to procure me friends in the house of need, to recommend me to the county of those who know me, in a period of sickness and want? Not only under the operation of these circumstances must the poor man be anxious to maintain a conduct which will recommend him to the kindness and friendship of those who may be able, if he should require it, to afford him relief; but he must be anxious to produce his conduct in the light. He must not withdraw into obscure and wretched corners, where he may indulge his vices unobserved;—a propensity so natural to the ill disposed, and so safe, when a provision independent of all knowledge of his conduct is legally provided for. He must endeavour to live under the eye of others, and study to make his conduct the object of their regard. It cannot but be visible, how strongly as a principle of virtue this must operate upon the poor; how powerful a motive to good conduct in all men it is to pass their lives under the full inspection of those whom they are bound to esteem, and whose kindness it is their interest to secure.

1d Pauperism relieved by the poor

Rev. W. Hanna, *Memoirs of the Life and Writings of Thomas Chalmers* (1850), ii, pp. 298–9, 301–11.

Dr. Chalmers . . . proposed . . . to provide for all his parish's indigence out of the fund raised by voluntary contributions at the church-doors . . . The new applications for relief were committed for investigation to the deacons . . . All depended on the watchful vigilance of those who, stationed at the out-posts, opened or closed the entry which led from poverty to pauperism . . .

To a deacon just entering upon office, Dr. Chalmers wrote . . . 'It may serve you as a sort of criterion of the adequacy of the means if you take along with you the fact that many are now working on the Green for 6*s*. a week, and are struggling with this as a temporary expedient for wearing through with their families—far from being a comfortable provision, we admit; but in times like the present, the burden is not all transferred from the poor to the rich, but is shared between them: it should be a compromise between the endurance of the one and the liberality of the other' . . .

A vast number of the primary applications melted into nothing under the pressure of a searching investigation . . .

In one district two young families were deserted by their parents. Had the children been at once taken upon the parochial funds, the unnatural purpose of the parents would have been promoted, and the parochial authorities would have become patrons of one of the worst of crimes. The families were left to lie helplessly on the hands of the neighbourhood, the deacon meanwhile making every endeavour to detect the fugitives. One of the parents was discovered and brought back, the other, finding his object frustrated, voluntarily returned.—An old and altogether helpless man sought parish aid. It was ascertained that he had very near relatives living in affluence, to whom his circumstances were presented, and into whose unwilling hands, compelled to do their proper task, he was summarily committed.—Typhus fever made its deadly inroads into a weaver's family who though he has sixpence a day as a pensioner, was reduced to obvious and extreme distress. The case was reported to Dr. Chalmers, but no movement towards any sessional relief was made; entire confidence was cherished in the kind offices of the immediate neighbourhood. A cry, however, of neglect was raised; an actual investigation of what the man had received during the period of his distress was undertaken, and it was found that ten times more than any legal fund would have allowed him had been supplied willingly and without any sacrifice whatever to the offerers.—A mother and daughter, sole occupiers of a single room, were both afflicted with cancer, for which the one had to undergo an operation; the other was incurable. Nothing would have been easier than to have brought the liberalities of the rich to bear upon such a case; but this was rendered unnecessary by the willing contributions of food and service and cordials of those living around this habitation of distress. 'Were it right', asks Dr. Chalmers, 'that any legal charity whatever should arrest a process so beautiful?' 'I never knew, during my whole experience in Glasgow, a single instance of distress which was not followed up by the most timely forthgoings of aid and of sympathy from the neighbours . . . though I have often distinctly observed, that whenever there was ostensible relief obtruded upon the eyes of the population, they did feel themselves discharged from a responsibility for each other's wants, and released from the duty of being one another's keepers . . .'

The result of these operations . . . was most striking and instructive . . . From one-tenth of the city, and that part composed of the poorest of its population, the whole flow of pauperism into the Town Hospital had been intercepted, and an expenditure which had amounted to £1400 per annum was reduced to £280 . . .

It was Dr. Chalmers' instinctive perception that much of the idleness and immorality of the lower classes was due to a legal security of support . . . 'At my first outset', says one of his agents, 'in surveying my proportion, I found so many families, and even clusters of families, without any visible means of support, that I could hardly sleep at night thinking of their starving condition, but after more matured observation I found out secret sources of supply, and became more easy in my mind'.

1e Charity, the chain of sympathy

Dr J. R. Kay, *Four Periods of Public Education* (1862), pp. 26–7.

Charity once extended an invisible chain of sympathy between the higher and lower ranks of society, which has been destroyed by the luckless pseudophilanthropy of the law. Few aged or decrepit pensioners now gratefully receive the visits of the higher classes—few of the poor seek the counsel, the admonitions, and assistance of the rich in the period of the inevitable accidents of life. The bar of the overseer is however crowded with the sturdy applicants for a legalised relief, who regard the distributor of this bounty as their stern and merciless oppressor, instructed by the compassionless rich to reduce to the lowest possible amount the alms which the law wrings from their reluctant hands. This disruption of the natural ties has created a wide gulf between the higher and lower orders of the community, across which the scowl of hatred banishes the smile of charity and love.

1f The folly of philanthropy

Harriet Martineau, *Illustrations of the Poor Laws* (1832 edn), pp. 38–43.

[*Cousin Marshall:* a discussion between Mr Burke and his sister on the evils of charity.]

'It would make your heart ache if I were to tell you how large a proportion of my Dispensary patients are children born puny from the destitution of their parents, or weakly boys and girls, stunted by bad nursing, or women who want rest and warmth more than medicine, or men whom I can never cure until they are provided with better food'.

'How you must sometimes wish that your surgery was stocked with coals and butcher's meat!'

'If it were, Louisa, the evil would only be increased, provided this sort of medicine were given gratis, like my drugs. There is harm enough done by the poor taking for granted that they are to be supplied with medicine and advice gratis all their lives: the evil is increasing every day by their looking on assistance in child birth as their due; and if they learn to expect food and warmth in like manner, their misery will be complete.'

'But what can we do brother? Distress exists: no immediate remedy is in the hands of the poor themselves. What can be done?'

'These are difficulties, Louisa, which dog the heels of all bad institutions. . . . The grand question seems to me to be this—*How to reduce the number of the indigent?* which includes, of course, the question, How to prevent the poor becoming indigent? . . . I would aim at two objects: increasing the fund on which the labourers subsist, and proportionating their numbers to this fund . . .'

'You would gradually abolish all charitable institutions then—O no! not all. There are some that neither lessen capital nor increase population. You would let such remain'.

'There are some which I would extend as vigorously and perseveringly as possible; viz. all which have the enlightenment of the people for their object. Schools should be multiplied and improved without any other limit than the number and capabilities of the people . . . The time will come, I trust, Louisa, when the poorer classes will provide wholly for themselves and their families; but at present we must be content with making them provide what is essential to existence. To enable them to do this, they must be educated; and as education is not essential to existence, we may fairly offer it gratis till they have learned to consider it indispensable. Even now, I would have all those pay something for the education of their children who can; but let all be educated, whether they pay or not.'

'The blind, and the deaf and dumb, I suppose, among others?'

'Yes; and in these cases I would allow of maintenance also, since the unproductive consumption of capital in these cases is so small as to be imperceptible, and such relief does not act as a premium upon population. A man will scarcely be in any degree induced to marry by the prospect of his blind or deaf children being taken off his hands, as the chances are ten thousand to one against any of his offspring being thus infirm. Such relief should be given till there are none to claim it.'

'I heard the other day, brother, of a marriage taking place between a blind man and woman in the asylum at X——'.

'Indeed! If anything could make me put these institutions on my proscribed list, it would be such a fact as that. The man could play the organ, and the woman knit, and make sash-line, I suppose?'

'Just so; and they could each do several other things, but, of course, not those common offices which are essential to the rearing of a family. It struck me immediately as a crime against society. Well—what other charities should stand?'

'Whatever else I resign, Louisa, I shall retain my office at the Casualty Hospital. I hope this kind of relief will be dispensed with in a future age; but the people are not yet in a condition to provide against the fractures, wounds and bruises which befall them in following their occupations. This institution may rank with Blind Asylums'.

'And what do you think of alms-houses for the aged?'

'That they are very bad things. Only consider the numbers of young people that marry under the expectation of getting their helpless parents maintained by the public! There are cases of peculiar hardship, through deprivation of natural protection, where the aged should be taken care of by the public. But the instances are very rare where old people have no relations; and it should be as universal a rule that working men should support their parents, as that they should support their children. If this rule were allowed, we might see some revival of that genial spirit of charity and social duty among the poor, whose extinction we mourn, without reflecting that we ourselves have caused it by the injudicious direction of our own benevolence.'

1g The other view of charity

Figaro in London, 8 September 1832.

British Benevolence

The income of the principal religious societies supported by voluntary contributions, for the year ending May, 1832, has been as follows:—

British and Foreign Bible Society	£81,700
Wesleyan Methodist Missionary Society	48,200
Church Missionary Society	48,700
London Missionary Society	34,500
London Hibernian Society	9,800

Society for Promoting Christianity among the Jews	11,000
British and Foreign Seamen and Soldiers Friend Society	5,000
Religious Tract Society	3,300
Irish Evangelical Society	3,000
Home Missionary Society	4,000
Naval and Military Bible Society	2,700
Prayer Book and Homily Society	2,700
British and Foreign School Society	2,500
Continental Society	1,900
Port of London Society	700
Christian Instruction Society	600
Ecclesiastical Knowledge Society	440
Sunday School Society	340
London Itinerant Society	390
Society for the Observance of the Lord's Day	240

The above is a lengthy and rather curious document, showing how liberal the rich people of England can be in their contributions for the *spiritual* good of the poor, while they leave their bodily care so entirely to other hands, that want and starvation are almost as abundant as bibles; unfortunately what is *meat* for the soul is anything but *meat* for the body, and consequently it is very questionable how far those persons positively do good, who open their purses with prodigality for the religious instruction of the poor, and leave them to shift for themselves in the matter of their worldly necessities. Holiness no doubt is a most comfortable thing, but so is a good dinner, and a clear conscience is a fine thing, but an empty stomach is not indispensable to its full appreciation. We should be the last to find fault with the system of giving religious instruction to the poor, but when twenty times as much money is devoted to the purpose as would clothe and feed some thousands of starving families, it becomes a matter for consideration what can be the source of so much exclusive liberality in the cause of piety. The fact is, that too many of the contributors to the Bible funds are actuated by the most interested motives; and taking in the literal sense the words 'He that *giveth* to the poor *lendeth* to the Lord', there are thousands who put down so much per annum in this manner, and look to their heavenly Father as they would to the bank for interest. They are charitable merely that they may be (as they imagine) sure of salvation, and consider a subscription to a bible fund as a sure means of booking their place to heaven, as a deposit of half a sovereign, paid at a coach office, would have the means of securing them a place to Birmingham. Charity is in many cases a mere matter of merchandize, and whoever sports most, often does so with a view of turning it to good account hereafter. If the charity be of a religious cast, it is considered to be killing two birds with one stone, and hence the prosperity of the Bible and Missionary Societies. It is disgusting to see religion thus degraded to a mere traffic,—as it is by some, who consider that, with their pew at church paid for a quarter in advance, and their name figuring in the lists of subscribers to at least a couple of pious societies, they are at least safe until the next call upon their pockets shall become due, and conceive their souls as safe, should they be cut off by death in the interim.

2 Education

The crucial issue that ran throughout the debates on education was whether educating the poor would aid or undermine a stable society, and whether in individual terms it would make men reconciled to or restive with their lot. Whigs and middle-class reformers expected that education would make for a stable society and a steady individual; Tories feared and working-class radicals very much hoped it would do the opposite.

In the early years of the century, it was argued that a properly religious education would build up the character of the poor and enable them to withstand sin and sedition. Giddies's pessimism was possibly a more acute judgment on this than Colquhoun's qualified approval of such schemes (2a). Similarly, in the great debates of the 1830s and 1840s on cheap newspapers, national schools and public libraries, middle-class reformers argued that no society could afford an ignorant and illiterate population. The need for useful knowledge could be measured quite precisely by a society's rate of crime, intemperance and turbulence (2b). Charles Knight of the SDUK added that it was no part of useful knowledge to make men dissatisfied with their lot in life. Tories insisted that useful knowledge was useless at best and dangerous at worst unless it was also moral knowledge (2c). Working-class radicals scoffed at it all—popular education was just one more way to obtain social and intellectual control over the populace (2d). One school inspector, the Rev. Noel, showed how education could bring contentment into the humblest home (2e); another, J. D. Morell, hoped that education would make such humble homes intolerable, for reasons and in language that would have pleased O'Brien (2f). In the same year, a rural clergyman could still defend an education for the agricultural poor which should be strictly limited in the interests of a properly stratified society.

Suggestions for further reading

See G. Best, 'The religious problem in English Education', *Cambridge Historical Journal*, 1956; R. K. Webb, *The British Working Class Reader* (1955); T. Kelly, *George Birkbeck* (1957), and M. Tylecote, *The Mechanics Institutes of Yorkshire and Lancashire* (1957), for Mechanics' Institutes; and J. F. Harrison, *Learning and Living, 1790–1960* (1961), for the working-class response. See also R. Johnson, 'Educational policy and social control', *Past and Present* No. 49, 1970.

2a The consequences of education

David Giddies, MP, *Hansard*, 13 July 1807.

[*Whitbread's bill to establish parish schools* was] more pregnant with mischief than advantage to those for whose advantage it was intended, and for the country in general. For, however specious in theory the project might be, of giving education to the labouring classes of the poor, it would, in effect, be found to be prejudicial to their morals and happiness; it would teach them to despise their lot in life, instead of making them good servants in agriculture, and other laborious employments, to which their rank in society had destined them; instead of teaching them subordination, it would render them factious and refractory, as was evident in the manufacturing counties; it would enable them to read seditious pamphlets, vicious books, and publications against Christianity; it would render them insolent to their superiors; and, in a few years, the result would be, that the legislature would find it necessary to direct the strong arm of power towards them, and to furnish the executive magistrates with much more vigorous laws than were now in force . . .

Patrick Colquhoun, *Treatise on Indigence* (1806).

These advantages are only to be attained by an attention to the education of the poor; not that species of instruction which is to elevate them above the rank they are destined to hold in society, but merely a sufficient portion to give their minds a right bias, a strong sense of religion and moral honesty; a horror of vice, and a love of virtue, sobriety and industry; a disposition to be satisfied with their lot; and a proper sense of loyalty and subordination, as the strongest barrier that can be raised against vice and idleness, the never-failing precursors of indigence and criminal offences—a barrier which cannot be too jealously guarded, since it is the state of society which not only increases the parochial rates, but also reduces the mass of productive labour upon which the strength and resources of the country depend.

. . . Let it not be conceived for a moment, that it is the object of the author to recommend a system of education for the poor that shall pass the bounds of their condition in society. Nothing is aimed at beyond what is necessary to constitute a channel to *religious* and *moral instruction*. To exceed that point would be utopian, impolitic and dangerous, since it would confound the ranks of society, upon which the general happiness of the lower orders, no less than that of those in more elevated stations, depends . . .

2b The economy of education

E. Bulwer Lytton, MP, *Hansard*, 15 June 1832.

The utility of knowledge

From an analysis, carefully made, of the cases of those persons who were committed for acts of incendiarism, etc. etc. in 1830, and the beginning of 1831, it appears that in Berkshire, of 138 prisoners, only 25 could write, and only 37 could read; at Abingdon, of 30 prisoners, 6 only could read and write; at Aylesbury of 79 prisoners, only 30 could read and write; of 50 prisoners tried at Lewes, one individual only could read well! . . .

If, then, it was true, as the facts he had stated seemed to him sufficient to prove, that there was an inseparable connection between crime and ignorance, it followed as a necessary consequence that it was their duty to remove all the shackles on the diffusion of knowledge—that poverty and toil were sufficient checks in themselves—that the results of any checks which they, as legislators voluntarily imposed, were to be traced, not in every violent and dangerous theory instilled into the popular mind, but in every outrage the people ignorantly committed, and every sentence of punishment, transportation, and death, which those outrages obliged them to impose!

Rev. John Dufton, *National Education, what it is and what it should be* (1847).

Our prisons have the extent of palaces, because our schools have been limited to sheds. The sums spent on cruel punishments would have paid thrice over for a system of salutary prevention.

Charles Knight, *The Old Printer and the Modern Press* (1854 edn), p. 307.

The object of the general diffusion of knowledge is not to make men discontented with their lot—to make the peasant yearn to become an artisan, or the artisan dream of the honours and riches of a profession—but to give the means of content to those who, for the most part, must necessarily remain in that station which requires great self-denial and great endurance; but which is capable of becoming not only a condition of comfort, but of enjoyment, through the exercise of those very virtues, in connection with a desire for that improvement of the understanding which to a large extent is independent of rank and riches.

2c The myth of useful knowledge

'The Progress of Social Disorganization, the Schoolmaster', *Blackwood's Edinburgh Magazine*, February 1834.

The whole system of the Educationists has been built upon a wrong foundation . . . They supposed that what they took pleasure in themselves, everyone would take pleasure in; and that Bacon, Newton and Locke would prove as effectual a counterpoise to sensual allurements or guilty excitation in the whole labouring population, as it did in

Herschel, or Brewster, or Babbage . . . But, disregarding such dry and uninteresting topics, the great bulk of mankind will fly to the journalist or the romance-writer, to abuse of their superiors, raillery at the Church, or invectives at the Government, which never fail to console them for the inequality of fortune; or stimulants to the passions, which the weakest intellect can understand.

The *Penny Magazines*, *Penny Cyclopaedias* etc. which have recently been issued under the direction of the great Central Societies in London for the Diffusion of Useful Knowledge, are certainly a great acquisition to the amusement of such of the poor as will read them, and they may have diffused much useful practical knowledge amongst them; but in a moral point of view, they have been and are nearly totally useless. It is not by being told about the caves at Elephanta, and the size of the Pyramids; the Upas Tree, and the Falls of Niagara; the diameter of the Earth, and the satellites of Jupiter; the architecture of Athens, and the Cathedral of York; the battle of Hastings, and the height of the Andes, that the labouring poor are to be taught the regulation of their passions, the subjugation of their wicked propensities, or the means of withstanding the innumerable sensual temptations by which they are surrounded. They may amuse an hour, but they will not improve a life; they may interest the imagination, they will not correct the heart . . . No, it is religion which must form the basis of every system of education which is to be really beneficial, and if that one ingredient is wanting, all that is mingled in the cup will speedily turned to poison.

This is an element in the case which the philosophic educationists appear to have never for one moment contemplated, but which, nevertheless, lies at the foundation of the whole question. They seem to have taken it for granted that they were for ever to have the entire moulding of the public mind, the exclusive direction of their studies, and that the labouring classes would never read anything but what issued from the presses of the Society for the Diffusion of Useful Knowledge. They never imagined, what has turned out to be the fact, that no sooner were the portals opened without any precautions against the admission of evil, than vice and corruption would rush in; that the inherent depravity of the human soul would give them a hearty welcome; and that at the gates formed by philosophic benevolence, sensual corruption or political extravagance would find a ready entrance. They never recollected, that while they were printing the *Penny Cyclopaedia*, another press might be throwing off Harriet Wilson; while they were circulating the Labourers' Institutes, another set might be disseminating the *Black Dwarf*; while they were dreaming of Bacon, a more numerous body might be thinking of Paine; while they were composing the *Penny Magazine*, a more popular publication might be got up in the shape of 'The Woman of Pleasure'.

2d Education as manipulation

Thomas Hodgskin, *Mechanics' Magazine*, 11 October 1823.

When government interferes, it directs its efforts more to make people obedient and docile, than wise and happy. It desires to control the thoughts, and fashion even the minds of its subjects; and to give into its hands the power of educating the people, is the widest possible extension of that most pernicious practise which has so long desolated society, of allowing one or a few men to direct the actions and control the conduct of millions. Men had better be without education, than be educated by their rulers; for their education is but the mere breaking in of the steer to the yoke; the mere discipline of the hunting dog, which, by dint of severity, is made to forego the strongest impulse of his nature, and instead of devouring his prey, to hasten with it to the feet of his master.

Bronterre O'Brien, *Destructive*, 7 June 1834.

Some simpletons talk of knowledge making the working classes more obedient, more dutiful—better servants, better subjects and so on, which means making them more subservient slaves and more conducive to the wealth and gratification of idlers of all descriptions. But such knowledge is trash; the only knowledge which is of service to the working people is that which makes them more dissatisfied, and makes them worse slaves. This is the knowledge which we shall give them.

A. Miall, *Life of Edward Miall* (1884), p. 67.

The main end of the system of education worked by the clergy seems to be to hinder the free development of the youthful mind and to produce a race of intellectual dwarfs . . . To do what they are bid, to think as they are taught, to believe what they are taught by clerical authority, to go to church without knowing why, to submit to government as it is without asking wherefore, to be reading and writing machines to subserve the purposes of the powerful and rich, mere living copies of primer and a prayer-book—this is what our rising generation are to gain by the generous aid of the Establishment.

E. Jones, *People's Paper*, 3 July 1852.

A People's Education is safe only in a People's own hands.

2e An inspector's report, 1841

Baptist Noel, school inspector, *Parliamentary Papers* (1841), xx, f. 171.

We have, then, to teach children, not that they should seek to raise themselves above the necessity of labour, but that labour which is the appointment of God, and while it secures the health also strengthens the understanding, is consistent with the greatest enjoyment of life; that, supplying a nation with all its comforts, and being a source of its opulence and strength, it must be creditable to individuals; and that a man of intelligence, wisdom and moral worth in a cottage has more true dignity than a sensual, selfish, ignorant and irreligious man, though he should be the owner of a palace. But, while education is not meant to raise the working classes above their condition, it may greatly multiply the comforts which they enjoy in it. It may preserve them from exchanging light, clean and cheerful cottages for comfortless cellars; it may give them better clothes, better food, and better health; it may deck their windows with fairer flowers; spread cleaner linen on their tables, and adorn their dwellings with more convenient furniture . . . By its aid they may learn to think so soundly, and to weigh evidence with so much acuteness, that the vile doctrines of a licentious infidelity may shock their understandings as well as revolt their hearts. And thus placed beyond the reach both of superstition and profanity, they may be led to seek and enjoy, through faith in Christ, the favour and the blessing of God. Education may thus raise the character of their enjoyments through life, and teach them, in the well founded hope of happiness beyond the grave, to meet death with tranquillity . . . It may further inspire them with loyalty to the Queen, and with love to their country; raise them above the temptation of a bribe in the exercise of any political rights which they may possess, and separate them from those who would seek any supposed amelioration of the laws by the methods of violence and injustice.

2f Education and social structure

J. D. Morell, school inspector, *The Progress of Society in England, as affected by the advancement of National Education* (1859).

[For those who believe in a] natural, and inevitable, nay, a providential separation between different classes in the community, and that no class can step out of its proper place without deranging and spoiling the social fabric . . . [and] that it is essential to our *existence* as a nation, that we should have distinct classes, occupying distinct positions, and severed to the core by a difference of privilege and culture, then undoubtedly those are correct who decry the further progress of popular education. For as sure as ever education becomes generally diffused in a country like our own, there must inevitably follow an ever-increasing tendency to level social distinctions, and to allow every man to occupy that place to which he may raise himself by his mental power, his personal industry, and his trustworthy character, independently of any consideration of rank, birth, or privilege. Those who would maintain the feudal type of society *at all cost* have an instinctive aversion to popular education, and their instinct, I consider, on their principles is perfectly correct. On the other hand, popular education is strictly speaking, the offspring and natural result of the modern and philosophic view of society; a theory which takes its start from the natural equality of all men, and which *must* regard it therefore as a crime and a wrong, that society should provide all the means of mental cultivation for one class, and none for another.

Now I am perfectly free to confess that I for one adopt *fundamentally* this last view of society; that I hold all men, socially speaking, to possess *equal rights* . . .

I maintain the doctrines of popular education, therefore, without *stint* or measure. I hold that we ought not only to educate all classes of the community, but that we ought to educate them *as highly as possible*; that there is no danger in teaching them too much; that our only drawback is, that we are sure to teach them too little . . .

It is sometimes said that to educate the poorer classes is likely to make them *discontented with their lot.*

I reply, so much the better if it does. No state of mind can possibly be more abject or incapable of improvement than that which sits down contentedly under the burden of ignorance and want. Here is a labouring man in Buckingham or Dorset, with a wife and half a dozen children; he earns seven or eight shillings a week—lives in a wretched hovel—feeds on the hardest fare—toils through the livelong day for a mere pittance—sees his wife in rags, his children in tatters, and ekes out a wretched subsistence for them by cringing at the great house to receive *in charity* what he ought to be receiving IN JUSTICE, as the proper and hard-earned wages of an honest man. Oh, says the squire, but you must not educate those children too well, or they will be discontented with their lot! Good heavens, then, would you *wish* them to be contented with it? Do we want to perpetuate this state of serfdom without its privileges, for ever? Would it not be as well, think you, to teach those children *that* which will make them aspire to something better than the wretched prospect of life that lies before them? . . .

The whole of the popular objections to education are, in fact, based upon the *presupposition*, and perhaps the *wish* that society may always remain *as it is*, and that the lower classes may never rise to a higher position than that which they at present occupy. With this supposition (still more with this *wish*), I cannot possibly bring my mind to coincide.

Rev. J. Fitzygram, *Hints for the Improvement of village Schools* (1859).

I am no advocate of any 'high pressure' system of education. It seems to me to be of the utmost importance to keep each class of society in its proper place; and with this view, to give to each child such a measure of instruction as its station in life is likely to require, and *no more*. For *is* it not *right* that the farmer should be better educated than the labourer, and the gentleman better than the farmer? *Are* we not in danger of doing much mischief, if we educate highly the class of *labourers*, while we neglect the classes immediately above them?

3 Religion

Built into the premises of Victorian society was Victorian religion. It offered that common set of standards, beliefs, principles and assumptions which held a society together and without which a society would disintegrate. Secularism, on this account, presented as much a threat to civilized society as socialism. Indeed not all Victorians clearly distinguished between them, for both were anarchic in their consequences.

Religion was perhaps the most obvious way in which the poor became reconciled to their lot. This could come from an authentic otherworldliness which encouraged men to ignore the woes of this world; less attractively, religion could be used quite deliberately to sanctify a civil order and place it above criticism. Religion for the poor inculcated two character traits in particular, resignation (3a), and moral self-discipline (3b). So working-class radicals not surprisingly insisted that official religion was made the opium of the people (3c) and church extension was extending employment for unplaced clergy. (See also above, p. 15.)

However, from the 1830s on, even working-class radicals were willing to admit that the clergy had found their social conscience. They were adding charities to their churches, building schools and libraries, working in the fields of public health and housing (3d). The most significant development was Christian Socialism (3e). Charles Kingsley (1819–75), and F. D. Maurice (1805–72) headed a group of laymen and clergy who, in the face of 1848, sought to reforge class bonds and infuse working-class movements with practical Christianity, so that Chartists would seek moral and personal improvement as assiduously as they sought political reform. The Christian Socialists wrote novels, pamphlets and papers; and went on to form working-class co-operatives in London in tailoring and shoemaking. Though their practical success was limited, the Christian Socialists had a profound impact on Victorian social philosophy, with their emphasis on the organic nature of society, their hatred of the iron laws of political economy, and their sympathy for working-class aspirations.

Suggestions for further reading

See R. Soloway, *Prelates and people 1783–1852* (1969); J. Welsh, 'Bishop Blomfield and Church Extension in London', *Journal of Ecclesiastical History*, 1953, for the Church's social policy; O. Chadwick, *The Victorian Church* (1966), for a comprehensive study; and T. Backstrom, 'The practical side of Christian Socialism', *Victorian Studies* 1963, J. Saville; 'The Christian Socialists of 1848', in *Democracy and the Labour Movement*, and T. Christennsen, *Origin and history of Christian Socialism* (1962).

3a Faith and tranquillity

Archdeacon Lyall of Colchester, 1833, quoted in G. Best, *Temporal Pillars* (1964).

Take away the restraints of religion from their minds, and immediately all the arrangements of society become changed in their eyes, as if seen through a distorting medium . . . It makes all the difference in the view of a man who can with difficulty earn his daily bread, whether the subordination of ranks, and the inequalities of condition in society, be considered by him as founded upon God's will, or merely upon the will of his fellow men. Bid him understand that these things are of human contrivance—and rulers and superiors become in his eyes only so many taskmasters, whom he is compelled to serve—the laws under which he lives, merely the instruments of that oppression, by which his labour is exacted. The belief in God is, in the moral world, what the principle of gravitation is in the physical—that which binds all the discordant elements in one harmonious system.

W. Cooke Taylor, *Notes of a Tour* (1842), pp. 301–2 in the 1968 edn.

The progress of Socialism and infidelity has been effectually checked in the manufacturing districts. The pressure of affliction has induced many who were previously negligent of religion to 'turn unto the Lord their God' . . . In the houses of the needy and afflicted I have often found the

Bible the last piece of furniture remaining; I have heard the miserable proclaim the patience they had learned from its precepts and the consolation they had derived from its promises. If any man doubted the benefits which Christianity has conferred upon mankind, he would be cured of his scepticism by witnessing its soothing influence on the distress and suffering of Lancashire.

F. Oakeley, *The Dignity and Claims of the Christian Poor* (1840).

The sufferings of poverty are probably less, and its alleviations greater, than its formidable appearance suggests . . . To the poor, then, I say, bless God, who has chosen you out of this miserable world to the enduring riches of His grace. If you want comfort in the midst of your privations, which are indeed many and grievous, come to Church.

The Rev. Sinclair's Charge to the clergy of the archdeaconry of Middlesborough, 1849.

As to the late disturbances, they would not have occurred, had the spiritual wants of the population been previously attended to . . . I am quite sure that nothing will ever improve the character of the lower orders, or give the upper security and peace, but a multiplication of schools and churches.

A. Ure, *Philosophy of Manufactures* (1835), pp. 423–5.

The first and great lesson—one inculcated equally by philosophy and religion—is that man must expect his chief happiness, not in the present, but in a future state of existence. . . . How speedily would the tumults which now agitate almost every class of society, in the several states of Christendom, subside, were that sublime doctrine embraced as it ought to be! . . . Where then shall mankind find this transforming power?—in the cross of Christ . . . It atones for disobedience; it excites to obedience; it purchases strength for obedience; it makes obedience practicable; it makes it acceptable; it makes it in a manner unavoidable, for it constrains to it; it is, finally, not only the motive to obedience, but the pattern of it.

3b Faith and self-discipline

J. A. James, 'The Poor', *Church Members' Guide* (1822).

Contentment with such things as they have, and an unmurmuring submission to the appointment of Providence, are most obviously their duty, and should be conspicuously manifested in their deportment. It should not appear as if they thought it hard, that their lot was cast in the humble vale of poverty. A cheerful resignation to the irremediable ills of their station, a frame of mind that looks as if they were so grateful for the blessings of grace, as to be almost insensible to the privations of poverty, is one of the many ways in which poor Christians may signally glorify God.

The poor should watch against an envious spirit . . . They should be conspicuous for their industry, nor wish to eat the bread of idleness . . . The poor have no right, therefore, to expect, that in consequence of their association with a Christian church, they are in any measure released from the obligation of the most unwearied industry. They are not to be supported by society in idleness, nor ought they to look for any pecuniary allowance while able to provide for themselves and their family. The religion of Jesus Christ was never intended to establish a system of religious pauperism . . .

The factory owner's version of the new moral world

A. Ure, *The Philosophy of Manufactures* (1835), pp. 417–18.

It is, therefore, excessively the interest of every mill-owner, to organize his moral machinery on equally sound principles with his mechanical, for otherwise he will never command the steady hands, watchful eyes, and prompt co-operation, essential to excellence of produce. Improvident work-people are apt to be reckless, and dissolute ones to be diseased: thus both are ill-qualified to discharge the delicate labours of automatic industry, which is susceptible of many grades of imperfection without becoming so obviously defective as to render the work liable to a fine. There is, in fact, no case to which the Gospel truth, 'Godliness is great gain,' is more applicable than to the administration of an extensive factory.

The neglect of moral discipline may be readily detected in any establishment by a practised eye, in the disorder of the general system, the irregularities of the individual machines, the waste of time and material from the broken and pieced yarns . . . It is, therefore, as much for the advantage as it is the duty, of every factory proprietor, to observe, in reference to his operatives, the divine injunction of loving his neighbours as himself; for in so doing he will cause a new life to circulate through every vein of industry.

R. Lowery, 'Passages in the life of a Temperance Lecturer', *Weekly Record*, 14 June 1856.

The colliers of Northumberland and Durham are a century in advance of their class in any other mining district in England, Scotland or Wales . . .

The owners had early seen the capability of the organization and labours of the Methodists being especially adapted to improve the population; for the colliery people were collected in places mostly lying apart from the established parish churches, which then had no curates or scripture readers going forth to reach such people. The owners wisely facilitated the operations of the Wesleyans in opening Sunday schools and chapels. Many of the colliers became local preachers, and promoted the mental culture of their own class.

3c Anti-clericalism

Chartist Circular, 30 November 1839.

The religious education of the people

In the school and the church, the people are taught that passive obedience is a virtue,—that *faith* is paramount to knowledge, and that the fear of hell is more salutary for the poor man's soul, than to confide in the mercy of God . . . They are taught to believe that they are mercifully created to endure poverty, and that the rich are very unfortunate in being born to the care and trouble of ruling over the poor. They are also taught, that God has created them poor, for the salvation of their immortal souls; and that through tribulation they must enter Heaven. They are taught that to fret at their earthly privations, is to rebel against the goodness of God, and for which, they must incur his everlasting displeasure . . .

The poor are also religiously instructed to be thankful for the present condition which God has so mercifully assigned them. They are not to consider that 'man's inhumanity to man, makes countless thousands mourn'; but that it is the *doing* of the Lord, for the salvation of their souls. They are to be thankful; but for what are they to be thankful? Thankful for permission to toil for a selfish master, who cares more for his dogs than for them! for permission to exist in artificial society, moved, and moving, like the wheels of a 'machine'. Permission to pay grievous taxes over which they have no control? Permission to obey laws which they have never made and which they feel to be oppressive and unjust? Permission to be 'hewers of wood, and drawers of water' for the rich? Permission to reside in hovels, often with a log of wood for a chair, and a bundle of straw, with a ragged sack, for a bed, with the wind and rain and sleet beating on the patched casements, and broken roofs, and rendering their habitations comfortless and damp; and when on their pallets of straw, they huddle together at night with hungry appetites, and aching heads, exposed to rheumatism and fever? is it for permission to pine and starve at the loom? or to toil and groan unheard in the bowels of the earth, in danger every moment of being crushed beneath the pendant rocks? Permission to creep along the streets covered with soot, and to carry it in bags from a rich man's chimney? These are the enjoyments of the poor, for the rich are never employed in these heart-sickening occupations; and is it for those blessings that the poor are to be thankful? and to which if they refuse to submit with passive obedience, they are in danger of hell . . .

I lately entered a church and heard a preacher describing the torments of the damned, and consigning to these torments the ungrateful poor, who rebel against God, by daring to repine at their poverty . . . The rich are leagued together to oppress them, and the priests describe the penalty of discontentment to frighten them into passive obedience, which they politically misname *Christian humility*.

Church extension

Northern Star, 11 July 1840.

The *Clique* . . . have dared to propose a grant of a large sum of money for the building of a greater number of churches! . . . Did the religion of these men urge them to propose relief to the poor and suffering? Did it impel their energies in favour of the oppressed and unfortunate—the enslaved and the groaning? Did it even make them offer to increase . . . a number of free seats, so that the poverty stricken may at least pray, without having the pride and pomp of distinction and rank flung into his teeth! Oh no; far from this. They wish to raise more churches . . . so that their younger brothers and their younger sons may be provided with snug berths, receive much for doing nothing . . . and even have a chance of a bishopric . . . The churches that we have . . . are generally not more than *half filled*!

3d Religion and social responsibility

R. Lowery, 'Passages in the life of a Temperance Lecturer', *Weekly Record*, 2 August 1856.

Every denomination of religion is more active in its operations to do good since then, and especially the Church of England clergy. The mere fox-hunting, sporting, and jolly-living parson who entered the church for the living has almost died out, and a new race of earnest men devoted to the duties of their office have sprung up. Twenty years ago when moving about I found a general disrespect for the parsons, as they were called. The word was used to express contempt and condemnation, as of one who drew the salary and did not fulfill the duties of an office . . . Now the churches are extended, the clergy and the curates generally respected, and active in instructing the poor.

3e Christian socialism

A Working Parson [Charles Kingsley], April 1848, to working men.

You say that you are wronged. Many of you are wronged; and many besides yourselves know it. Almost all men who have heads and hearts know it—above all, the working clergy know it. They go into your houses, they see the shameful filth and darkness in which you are forced to live crowded together; they see your children growing up in ignorance and temptation, for want of fit education; they see intelligent and well-read men among you, shut out from a Freeman's just right of voting; and they see too the noble patience and self-control with which you have as yet borne these evils. They see it, and God sees it.

Workmen of England! You have more friends than you think for. Friends who expect nothing from you, but who love you because you are their brothers, and who fear God, and therefore dare not neglect you, His children; men who are drudging and sacrificing themselves to get you your rights; men who know what your rights are, better than you know yourselves, who are trying to get for you something nobler than charters and dozens of Acts of Parliaments . . . You may disbelieve them, insult them—you cannot stop their working for you, beseeching you as you love yourselves, to turn back from the precipice of riot, which ends in the gulf of universal distrust, stagnation, starvation. You think the Charter would make you free—would to God it would! The Charter is not bad; *if the men who use* it are not bad! But will the Charter make you free? . . .

Parson Lot's Letters to Chartists

Charles Kingsley, 6 May 1848, printed in *Charles Kingsley, His Letters and Memories of his Life* (1888), p. 65.

MY FRIENDS,

. . . My only quarrel with the Charter is, that it does not go far enough *in reform*. I want to see you *free*; but I do not see how what you ask for will give you what you want. I think you have fallen into just the same mistake as the rich of whom you complain:—I mean, the mistake of fancying that legislative reform is social reform, or that men's hearts can be changed by Act of Parliament. If anyone can tell me of a country where a charter made the rogues honest, or the idle industrious, I shall alter my opinion of the Charter, but not till then. It disappointed me bitterly when I read it. It seems a harmless cry enough, but as poor, bald, constitution-mongering cry as I ever heard.

Charles Kingsley to Thomas Cooper, 19 June 1848, printed in *Charles Kingsley, His Letters and Memories of his Life* (1888), p. 73.

It seemed to me to be intolerable to be so misunderstood . . . My ancestory fought in Cromwell's army, and left all for the sake of God and liberty, among the pilgrim fathers; and here were men accusing me of 'medieval tyranny'. I would shed the last drop of my life blood for the social and political emancipation of the people of England, as God is my witness; and here are the very men for whom I would die, fancying me an 'aristocrat'. It is not enough for me that they are mistaken in me. I want to work with them. I want to realize my brotherhood with them. I want some one like yourself, intimately acquainted with the mind of the working classes, to give me such an insight into their life and thoughts, as may enable me to consecrate my powers effectually to their service. For them I have lived for several years. I come to you to ask you if you can tell me how to live more completely for them . . . I send you my poem as something of a 'sample'. At first sight it may seem to hanker after feudalism and the middle age. I trust to you to see a deeper and somewhat more democratic moral in it . . .

F. D. Maurice, *On the Reformation of Society and how All Classes May contribute to it* (1851).

There is one class of our countrymen, and that the mightiest of all, the one which makes up the great mass of our population, the one which we sometimes describe by the rude and coarse phrase 'the masses'. This class . . . is suffering more than any other from that principle of mutual strife and rivalry, which has been degrading all. Our phrase 'the masses' indicates the feeling which we have, that they form a rude chaos, scarcely a part of organized society. There are some who would wish them to remain in this state, who think they are safer in it, who dread the thought of their uniting lest they should become formidable. I cannot conceive a notion more selfish and wicked, and at the same time more utterly foolish than this. A wild floating mass of atoms is the most perilous of all things to exist near a society which has any order. They must combine in some way. Be sure if they do combine without having any principle to hold them together, it must be for purposes of destruction. I would say to the upper and middle classes, for their own sake, for yours, encourage them to unite, to organize themselves. Tell them that they are meant to work together, and that they can work together. Tell them that they are not a set of separate creatures striving one against another. Claim them as living portions of a living and united society. I say, do this for your own sake. All hope for the reformation of the other portions of English Society lies now in the reformation of this one. If the members of it can overcome the impulses to division and disorganization which have worked, and are working in them so strongly, and which we have encouraged, if they can feel that they have a common life and a common object, and that all the powers they have may contribute to it, then there is hope that in their rise all other portions of society will rise; that when they begin to think, speak, and act as men, we shall recover our manliness also. And therefore any effort, proceeding from themselves for such an object as this, I think, should be hailed as one of the most blessed symptoms of returning life to the whole community. Such efforts are beginning to be made by working-men in all parts of England.

4 Politics or paternalism?

After the repeal of the Corn Laws in 1846, supporters of the League formed and joined radical pressure movements, the Parliamentary and Financial Reform Association, the Freehold Land Society for land reform, the temperance movement, the Anti-State Church Society which became in 1853 the Liberation Society to obtain church reform, and the Public School Association, which worked for non-sectarian and rate-financed schools. All of these sought to bring pressure on government in the name of both the middle and working classes; and they remained the main planks of rank and file liberalism into the next century.

Hume's Little Charter was a precursor of the Parliamentary and Financial Reform Association; and it advocated household suffrage to ensure that Parliament represented all classes and heard all grievances (4a). Russell rejected this because it paid too much attention to the mere quantity of electors and not enough to the quality of the elected and the fabric of Parliament. Cobden thought such a distinction unacceptable. Parliament was responsible to public opinion, and usually showed itself to be responsive to public opinion; and if Parliament refused to extend the vote, it must expect agitation and unrest from those excluded. Cobden then went on to form the Freehold Land Society which bought up large estates and sold them off in small lots to provide forty-shilling freehold votes (4b). He hoped this would simultaneously enfranchise the thrifty and undermine the aristocracy's grip on the land.

The Tories' position was clear: the working classes were not fit judges of their own best interests. If their economic wrongs were alleviated, the lower orders would no longer clamour for the political independence for which they were so ill-qualified (4c). Such alleviation, even working-class commentators agreed, did occur and did much to heal class relations in the 1850s (4d). But the *Edinburgh Review* (4e) pointed out the unwelcome paternalism that lay behind this flowering of benevolence. And J. S. Mill (1806–73) (4f), summed it up; on Tory theory, the poor were children. This was as unhealthy as it was unacceptable. The poor were now determined to control their own economic and political destiny.

Suggestions for further reading

For a general account, see F. Gillespie, *Labour and politics in England, 1850–1867* (1927); for Cobden and Bright, there are studies by H. Ausubel (*John Bright, Victorian Reformer*, 1966), D. Read (*Cobden and Bright*, 1967), N. McCord (in R. Robson (ed.), *Ideas and Institutions of Victorian England* 1967) and some comments in J. Vincent, *The Formation of the Liberal Party* (1966). For the wider issues of class co-operation and pressure groups, see P. Hollis (ed.), *Pressure from without* (forthcoming).

4a The Little Charter

Hansard, 20 June 1848.

Mr. Hume rose to move:

'That this House, as at present constituted, does not fairly represent the population, the property, or the industry of the Country, whence has arisen great and increasing discontent in the minds of a large portion of the People; and it is therefore expedient, with a view to amend the National Representation, that the Elective Franchise shall be so extended as to include all Householders—that all votes shall be taken by Ballot—that the duration of Parliaments shall not exceed three years—and that the apportionment of Members to Population shall be made more equal.'

. . . Parliament was a mere engine by which a constitutional country was to be governed, and which, according to our constitution, purported to attend to the interests of all classes upon all occasions . . . If the House did not represent all classes alike, some classes must be injured, and they were now discontented because they were excluded from the pale of the constitution, and placed in a situation where they were obliged to suffer and undergo whatever laws might be passed affecting them, without as freemen having any voice in the election of those who made such laws. If, then, Parliament did not represent all classes, it became a bad engine—an engine in the hands of the few, who had power as against the many; and it might be better, if we were not to have a good Parliament, to have no Parliament at all.

Hansard, 20 June 1848.

Lord John Russell:

In my opinion, that which not only every man of full age, but the whole population of the kingdom, have a right to, is the best government and the best kind of representation which it is possible for the Legislature to give them. The main object of our institutions is good government and the welfare of the people; and we ought not, for the sake of some abstract principles, to lose sight of that great object . . . Let us see, then, whether a Parliament elected by the householders and lodgers would be a better Parliament—would afford a better representation of the people than the present Parliament. It appears to me that if you establish a really household suffrage, the objection . . . that you get a representation of brick and mortar, applies . . . But then, if you are to make it more general—if you are to make the suffrage universal . . . you could hardly avoid that division into equal districts, of equal population, which it is the proposal of the advocates of the Charter to introduce. Now, if I am asked whether such a division into districts and universal suffrage—the suffrage in every male person of full age—would give a better representation of the people at large than the present, and more conducing to the people's interest—I must deny that it would do so. You would have a great number of representatives of the large towns, some fifty representatives for this metropolis, some ten or twenty for other large towns, all of them imbued with the spirit of those towns, and the excited feelings of the population of those towns, but, on the other hand, destroying the smaller boroughs and the middle sized towns in the country: you would have representatives of the agricultural class, of a totally different character, firmly attached perhaps to the present institutions, but unwilling to adopt reforms which this House, and other Houses of Parliament framed under the Reform Act, have been willing to adopt. I should fear, with a representation so composed, of men totally differing in their political views—one too much inflamed with ideas of extensive amelioration, the other adverse to progress and improvement—you would have a collision and a contest which would be dangerous to its operation, and, above all, would not fairly represent the country which it would affect to represent . . . Considering that this is a country which has not only commerce and agriculture; . . . that there are many in active and many who are not in active life, whose intelligence fits them to be representatives in Parliament, but whose habits do not induce them to seek or qualify themselves for either county representation or the representation of such places as Manchester or Birmingham—the country would not be fitly represented if we merely had representation attached to a certain amount of population . . . If I am right in saying that mere numbers ought not to constitute the basis of your representation—that you should endeavour rather to have your House of Commons, like the country itself, composed of various classes and men of various occupations, then the whole argument founded upon the disparity of numbers falls at once to the ground . . .

Hansard, 6 July 1848.

Richard Cobden:

I ask, what danger is there in giving the franchise to householders? They are the fathers of families; they constitute the laborious and industrious population. What would be endangered by giving this class the franchise? . . . The people would continue, as at present, to choose their representatives from the easy class—among the men of fortune; but I believe this extension of the suffrage would tend to bring not only the legislation of this House, but the proceedings of the Executive Government, more in harmony with the wants, wishes, and interests of the people . . .

What are the two things most wanted? . . . What but greater economy, and a more equitable apportionment of the taxation of the country? I mean, that you should have taxation largely removed from the indirect sources from which it is at present levied, and more largely imposed on realised property. . . . and this the people . . . would . . . enable you to accomplish . . .

You glorify yourselves that you have abolished the slave-trade and slavery . . . Whatever you have done to break down any abomination or barbarism in this country has been done by associations and leagues out of this House; and why? Because, since Manchester cannot have its fair representation in this House, it was obliged to organize a League, that it might raise an agitation through the length and breadth of the land, and in this indirect matter might make itself felt in this House. Well, do you want to get rid of this system of agitation? Do you want to prevent those leagues and associations out of doors? Then you must bring this House into harmony with the opinions of the people. Give the means to the people of making themselves felt in this House. . . . [For] is this not a most cumbrous machine?—a House of Commons, by a fiction said to be the representatives of the people, meeting here and professing to do the people's work, while the people out of doors are obliged to work? . . .

It is not with a view of overturning our institutions that I advocate these reforms in our representative system. It is because I believe that we may carry out those reforms from time to time, by discussions in this House, that I take my part in advocating them in this legitimate manner. They must be effected in this mode, or they must be effected, as has been the case on the Continent, by bayonets, by muskets, and in the streets . . . You have had your government of aristocracy and tradition; and the worst thing that ever befell this country has been its government for the last century-and-a-half. All that has been done to elevate the country has been the work of the middle and industrious classes; and it is because I wish to bring such virtue, such intelligence, such industry, such frugality, such economy, into this House, that I support the Motion of the Hon. Member for Montrose. [J. Hume.]

4b The Parliamentary Reform Association

T. Frost, *Forty Years' Recollections* (1880), pp. 203–9.

In Croydon, as elsewhere, there were many of the middle classes who desired Parliamentary reform quite as much as the working men, though with a different aim; but they wished for what they called a moderate measure, by which they meant one that would enfranchise the shopkeepers of the large unrepresented towns which had been growing into importance during the preceding twenty years, and still exclude the majority of the working men. As the Chartist agitation quietly died out after the excitement of 1848, a new movement was commenced, therefore, and a branch of the Parliamentary Reform Association, which had just been launched into existence under the auspices of Sir Joshua Walmsley and Joseph Hume, was formed among the shopkeepers of the town and neighbourhood, with a sprinkling of other grades of the middle class, such as yeomen, farmers, brewers &c.

Finding the Chartist organization broken up, and discerning in the new movement a power that might be used with good effect against any Government that took its stand on the finality of the legislation of 1832, I proposed to the Chartists of the locality that we should join it, and endeavour to use its machinery for the furtherance of our own aims. They were at first reluctant to move in that direction, but when the example had been set by Hodges and myself, most of them followed. Their adherence added so considerably to the numerical strength of the new association, that I deemed it only fair, as they were nearly all working men, while the majority of the original members were shopkeepers, that they should be represented in the committee... The result of the election was the re-election of three tradesmen and two mechanics, and the substitution of three artisans and myself for two yeomen, a farmer, and a brewer . . . It was always clear to my own mind that every movement for the extension of the franchise must lead eventually to manhood suffrage, with new electoral divisions, so arranged as to give every voter the same amount of political power . . .

What the middle classes most wanted was a diminuation of the pressure of taxation, then much greater than at the present day; and if that object could have been gained without Parliamentary reform, they would gladly have refrained from touching that question. But they could not see their way to its accomplishment without an increase of the voting power of the shopkeeping classes; and that involved the difficulty that always stood in the way of their success. They could not bring pressure from without to bear upon Parliament with sufficient force for the purpose without union with the working classes, and the support of the latter could be obtained on no other terms than the adoption of the principle of manhood suffrage.

When the Council of the Association convened a conference on the question, the members of the Croydon branch elected me as one of their delegates, giving me for a colleague a clothier, named Talbot, a representative of the moderate party. Among the ultra Liberals whom we met in St. Martin's Hall on that occasion were Macgrath and Clark—who had been members of the Chartist executive in 1847—Ernest Jones, George W. Reynolds, and Mr. Holyoake; but the representatives of the moderate section constituted the majority. Joseph Hume was voted to the presidential chair, and a debate commenced which extended over two days, and did not terminate without provoking considerable exasperation on the part of the ultras.

It was made evident, at an early stage of the proceedings that the representatives of the trading or moderate section were much more earnestly intent upon increasing their own power in the House of Commons, for their own purposes, than upon achieving the enfranchisement of the majority. They could not be urged beyond a rate-paying qualification for the franchise, though they knew that the majority of the working classes would be excluded by the operation of the Small Tenements Rating Act, and that in London the majority of the unenfranchised of all classes were lodgers. Hence, the dissensions that arose in the Conference on the second day, and which culminated in Ernest Jones's vehement denunciation of Joseph Hume as a reactionist.

The agitation collapsed shortly afterwards, nor was there any earnest renewal of the struggle for more than a dozen years afterwards, though the question was brought before Parliament on two or three occasions by Mr. Bright and the late Earl Russell.

4c Freehold land society

R. Cobden, *Speeches*, 26 November 1849.

It is an association framed for the purpose of enabling individuals, by means of small monthly contributions, to create a fund by which they may be enabled in the best and cheapest way, to possess themselves of the county franchise. You will see then that this society has a double object in view: it is a deposit for savings, and a means of obtaining the vote . . . The plan of that society is, to purchase large estates . . . and to divide them amongst the members of the association at cost price . . .

Can you by this means effect a great change in the depository of political power? Because I avow to you that I want, by constitutional and legal means, to place, as far as I can, political power in this country in the hands of the middle and industrious classes; in other words, the people. When I speak of the middle and industrious classes, I regard them, as I ever did, as inseparable in interest. You cannot separate them. I defy any person to draw the line where the one ends and the other begins . . . Nothing of importance is ever done by Parliament until after a seven-years' stand-up fight between the people on one side, and those who call themselves the people's representatives on the other . . .

As everybody admits that we must not go into the streets to fight, let me ask my friends what other step they intend to take? Petition Parliament! Petition Parliament to reform itself! Why no; the clubs would not like that; it would not suit their cards. Nobody thinks of getting a reform of Parliament by petitioning. Well, then, how are you to get it? . . . We must fight the enemy by means of the 40*s*. freehold.

Now what chance have we of succeeding? . . . We have as near as possible a million of registered electors for the whole kingdom . . . What proportion of them do you suppose are the votes of occupying tenants? 108,790. . . . Why, half the money spent in gin in one year would buy as many county freeholds as would counterpoise these 108,790 tenant-farmers . . . Why, if one in ten of the men who are not qualified to vote in London and Southwark, would purchase votes in the neighbouring counties, it would almost suffice to carry every good measure that you and I desire . . . When I speak of the mechanics and artisans of our great towns, I will say, there is not one of them that, if he resolutely set to the work, may not possess the county franchise, in a few years . . .

In proportion as you exert yourselves for this great movement, you will become powerful. Every class of men that sets itself vigorously to work, by means of the 40*s*. qualification, to place as many as possible of that class on the register, will find itself elevated, politically and socially, by the position it has given itself . . . I say to no class, come and gain exclusive power or influence in the country; I am against class legislation, whether from below or above; but, I say, if you wish to have your interests consulted—your legitimate rights respected; if you wish no longer to have your very existence ignored in the counties; then come forward, and join such a movement as this, and by every possible means promote the extension of the 40*s*. freehold qualification.

R. Cobden to John Bright, 1 October 1849, quoted in J. Morley (ed.), *Life of Cobden*, ii, p. 53.

. . . The citadel of privilege in this country is so terribly strong, owing to the concentrated masses of property in the hands of the comparatively few, that we cannot hope to assail it with success unless with the help of the propertied classes in the middle ranks of society, and by raising up a portion of the working-class to become members of a propertied order; and I know no other mode of enlisting such cooperation but that [the 40*s*. freehold scheme] which I have suggested . . .

4d In loco parentis

John Fullerton, 'The Condition of the Labouring Classes', *Quarterly Review*, January 1832.

We will not give place to any in sincere anxiety for the general spread of education, moral, religious and intellectual . . . [but] . . . We are not such zealots in the cause as to believe or assert that it is to do everything for the poor, or enable them to do everything for themselves. We do not believe that any education which it is possible to give them will ever render the working classes capable of thoroughly understanding, and consequently, of being trusted with the regulation of their own interests, so as to relieve their superiors from the duty of guiding and protecting them.

How to disarm the Chartists

Blackwood's Edinburgh Magazine, June 1848.

A uniform system of voting, such as a £5 or household suffrage, which is now proposed as a remedy for all the evils of society, is of necessity a *class representation*, and the class to which it gives the ascendency is the *lowest* in whom the suffrage is vested . . . But if the suffrage is reduced so low as to admit the representatives of the operatives and 'proletaires', or those whom they influence, (which household or a £5 suffrage would undoubtedly do), what measures in the present state of society in this country, and feeling throughout the world, would they immediately adopt? We have only to look at the newly formed republic of France, where such a system is established, to receive the answer. Repudiation of state engagements (as in the case of the railways); confiscation of property under the name of a graduated income tax; the abolition of primogeniture, in order to ruin the landed interest;

the issue of assignats, in order to sustain the state under the shock to credit which such measures would necessarily occasion, might with confidence be looked for. And the question to be considered is, would these measures in the end benefit *any class of society*, or, least of all, the operative, in a country such as Great Britain, containing, in proportion to its population, a greater number of persons dependent on daily wages for their existence than any other that ever existed?

What is to be expected from such ruin to credit and capital but the immediate stoppage of employment, and throwing of millions out of bread? Even if the whole land in the country were seized and divided, it would afford no general relief—it would only shift the suffering from one class to another . . .

But what is required is not to augment the political power of the working classes, but to remove their grievances;—not to give them the government of the state, which they can only exercise to their own and the nation's ruin, but to place them in such a condition that they may no longer desire to govern it. This can be done only by abandoning the system of class government for the interest chiefly of the moneyed interests, and returning to the old system of general protective and national administration . . .

There is no way of really improving the condition of the working classes, but by augmenting the demand for labour. This is what they want; we never hear of them petitioning for wash-houses and cold baths, or a health-of-towns bill; it is a 'fair day's wage for a fair day's work' which they always desire. Rely upon it, they are right. By all means give them wash-houses and cold baths; broad streets and common sewers; airy rooms and moderately sized houses; but recollect, if you do not give them work at the same time, it will all prove nugatory . . . Restore protection to colonial industry; relieve the great works in progress throughout the empire; engage in a great system of government emigration; give the country a currency adequate to its necessities, and commensurate to its transactions; and you may bid defiance to Chartist agitation . . .

4e The assumption of responsibility

Weekly Record, 12 April 1856; 2 August 1856.

The best of the working men are often placed in antagonism to the upper classes, and much of the truth uttered by the press is neutralized in their minds. Until lately, and to a great extent even yet, there was but little communion or sympathy on either side between the working people and the wealthy orders; labouring men only met with their employers in the workshop, or counting-houses, receiving orders, or disputing wages or time; neither knew much of the home life, inner thoughts, or virtues, of the other . . .

It is pretty generally admitted that at present there is a much higher sense of class and individual responsibility . . . There is less class antagonism; people of wealth and station are more alive to their responsibilities, and take more interest in aiding improvement, especially in the higher or more wealthy commercial class; then they thought little of those whom they employed, except as mere workers in their establishments. Now they take interest in all their concerns; they look to their dwellings, their pursuits and recreations, to their means of mental, moral and religious culture; they mix more frequently with them, they feel gratified in having good men in their establishment as well as good workmen. Formerly there was rather a race after gold than after happiness within . . . Experience convinced them, that in widening the sphere of their activities, in using their wealth and position to promote mental and moral improvement, they would find their highest profit and pleasure; better workshops, dwellings, schools, public parks, libraries, peoples' colleges, social jaunts and festivals for the work-people, were promoted by them. By these means the characters and enjoyments of both classes are improved, while mutual confidence and respect are increased . . .

4f The new philanthropists

'The claims of Labour', *Edinburgh Review*, April 1845.

The democratic movement among the operative classes, commonly known as Chartism, was the first open separation of interest, feeling, and opinion, between the labouring portion of the commonwealth and all above them. It was the revolt of nearly all the active talent, and a great part of the physical force of the working classes, against their whole relation to society. Conscientious and sympathizing minds among the ruling classes, could not but be strongly impressed by such a protest . . . If the poor had reason for their complaints, the higher classes had not fulfilled their duties as governors; if they had no reason, neither had those classes fulfilled their duties in allowing them to grow up so ignorant and uncultivated as to be open to these mischievous delusions . . . It was no longer disputable that something must be done to render the multitude more content with the existing state of things . . .

> [The author attributes the spread of such ideas to the writings of Carlyle, the speeches of Young England, and the distress revealed by the Poor Law and Corn Law agitations. The result has been a mushrooming of reforms, from baths to factory legislation, and allotment schemes.]

The new schemes of benevolence . . . are propounded as instalments of a great social reform. They are celebrated as the beginning of a new moral order, or an old order revived, in which the possessors of property are to resume their places as the paternal guardians of those less fortunate; and which, when established, is to cause peace and union throughout society, and to extinguish, not indeed poverty—that hardly seems to be thought desirable—but the more abject forms of vice, destitution, and physical wretchedness . . .

Their theory appears to be in a few words this—That it is the proper function of the possessors of wealth, and especially of the employers of labour and the owners of land, to take care that the labouring people are well off;—that they ought always to pay good wages; . . . that, at these good wages, they ought to give employment to as great a number of persons as they can afford; and to make them work for no greater number of hours in the twenty-four than is compatible with comfort, and with leisure for recreation or improvement . . .

It is quite possible to impose, as a moral or legal obligation, upon the higher classes, that they shall be answerable for the well-doing and well-being of the lower. There have been times and places in which this has in some measure been done. States of society exist, in which it is the recognized duty of every owner of land, not only to see that all who dwell and work thereon are fed, clothed, and housed, in a sufficient manner; but to be, in so full a sense, responsible for their good conduct, as to indemnify all other persons for any damage they do, or offence they may commit. This must surely be the ideal state of society which the new philanthropists are contending for. Who are the happy labourering classes who enjoy the blessings of these wise ordinances?—The Russian boors. There are other labourers, not merely tillers of the soil, but workers in great establishments partaking of the nature of Factories, for whom the laws of our own country, even in our own time, compelled their employers to find wholesome food, and sufficient lodging and clothing. Who were these?—The slaves on a West India estate . . . But this obligation never has existed, and never will nor can exist, without, as a countervailing element, absolute power, or something approaching it, in those who are bound to afford this support, over those entitled to receive it. Such a relation has never existed between human beings, without ultimate degradation to the character of the dependent class . . .

They cannot mean that the working classes should combine the liberty of action of independent citizens, with the immunities of slaves. There are but two modes of social existence for human beings;—they must be left to the natural consequences of their mistakes in life; or society must guard against the mistakes, by prevention or punishment. Which will the new philanthropists have?

4g The poor and their position: two conflicting accounts

J. S. Mill, *Principles of Political Economy* (1848), iv, chapter 7.

The one may be called the theory of dependence and protection, the other that of self-dependence.

According to the former theory, the lot of the poor, in all things which affect them collectively, should be regulated *for* them, not *by* them. They should not be required or encouraged to think for themselves, or give to their own reflection or forecast an influential voice in the determination of their destiny. It is the duty of the higher classes to think for them, and to take the responsibility of their lot, as the commander and officers of an army take that of the soldiers composing it. This function the higher classes should prepare themselves to perform conscientiously, and their whole demeanour should impress the poor with a reliance on it, in order that, while yielding passive and active obedience to the rules prescribed to them, they may resign themselves in all other respects to a trustful *insouciance*, and repose under the shadow of their protectors. The relation between rich and poor should be only partially authoritative; it should be amiable, moral, and sentimental: affectionate tutelage on the one side, respectful and grateful deference on the other. The rich should be in *loco parentis* to the poor, guiding and restraining them like children. Of spontaneous action on their part there should be no need. They should be called on for nothing but to do their day's work, and to be moral and religious. Their morality and religion should be provided for them by their superiors, who should see them properly taught it, and should do all that is necessary to ensure their being, in return for labour and attachment, properly fed, clothed, housed, spiritually edified and innocently amused . . .

As the idea is essentially repulsive of a society only held together by bought services, and by the relations and feelings arising out of pecuniary interests, so there is something naturally attractive in a form of society abounding in strong personal attachments and disinterested self-devotion. Of such feelings it must be admitted that the relation of protector and protected has hitherto been the richest source. The strongest attachments of human beings in general are, towards the things or the persons that stand between them and some dreaded evil . . . The error in the present case lies in not perceiving, that these errors and sentiments, like the clanship and hospitality of the wandering Arab, belong emphatically to a rude and imperfect state of the social union, and that the feelings between protector and protected can no longer have this beautiful and endearing character where there are no longer any serious dangers from which to protect. What is there in the present state of society to make it natural that human beings, of ordinary strength and courage, should glow with the warmest gratitude and devotion in return for protection? The laws protect them: where the laws do not reach, manners and opinions shield them . . .

Of the working classes of Europe at least it may be pronounced certain, that the patriarchal or paternal system of government is one to which they will not again be subject. That question has been several times decided. It was decided when they were taught to read, and allowed access to newspapers and political tracts. It was decided when dissenting preachers were suffered to go among them, and appeal to their faculties and feelings in opposition to the creeds professed and countenanced by their superiors.

It was decided when they were brought together in numbers, to work socially under the same roof. It was decided when railways enabled them to shift from place to place, and change their patrons and employers as easily as their coats. The working classes have taken their interests into their own hands, and are perpetually showing that they think the interests of their employers not identical with their own but opposite to them. Some among the higher classes flatter themselves that these tendencies may be counteracted by moral and religious education; but they have let the time go by for giving an education which can serve their purpose. The principles of the Reformation have reached as low down in society as reading and writing, and the poor will no longer accept morals and religion of other people's prescribing . . .

It is on a far other basis that the well-being and well-doing of the labouring people must henceforth rest. The poor have come out of leading strings, and cannot any longer be governed or treated like children. To their own qualities must now be commended the care of their destiny. Modern nations will have to learn the lesson, that the well-being of a people must exist by means of the justice and self-government, the *dikaiosune* and *sophrosune* [justice and temperance] of the individual citizens . . . The prospect of the future depends on the degree in which they can be made rational beings.

There is no reason to believe that prospect other than hopeful. The progress indeed must always be slow. But there is a spontaneous education going on in the minds of the multitude, which may be greatly accelerated and improved by artificial aids. The instruction obtained from newspapers and political tracts is not the best sort of instruction, but it is vastly superior to none at all. The institutions for lectures and discussion, the collective deliberations on questions of common interest, the trades unions, the political agitation, all serve to awaken public spirit, to diffuse variety of ideas among the mass, and to excite thought and reflection among the more intelligent. Although the too early attainment of political franchises by the least educated class might retard, instead of promoting, their improvement, there can be little doubt that it is greatly stimulated by the attempt to acquire those franchises. In the meantime, the working classes are now part of the public; in all discussions on matters of general interest they, or a portion of them, are now partakers; all who use the press as an instrument may, if it so chances, have them for an audience; the avenues of instruction through which the middle classes acquire most of the ideas which they have, are accessible to, at least, the operatives in the towns . . .

From this increase of intelligence, several effects may be confidently anticipated . . . They will become even less willing than at present to be led and governed, and directed into the way they should go, by the mere authority and *prestige* of superiors . . . The theory of dependence and protection will be more and more intolerable to them, and they will require that their conduct and condition shall be essentially self-governed . . .

. . . To work at the bidding and for the profit of another, without any interest in the work—the price of their labour being adjusted by hostile competition, one side demanding as much and the other paying as little as possible—is not, even when wages are high, a satisfactory state to human beings of educated intelligence, who have ceased to think themselves naturally inferior to those whom they serve . . . The problem is, to obtain the efficiency and economy of production on a large scale, without dividing the producers into two parties with hostile interests, employers and employed, the many who do the work being mere servants under the command of the one who supplies the funds, and having no interest of their own in the enterprise, except to fulfill their contract and earn their wages.

It is this feeling, almost as much as despair of the improvement of the condition of the labouring masses by other means, which has caused so great a multiplication of projects for 'the organization of industry' by the extension and development of the co-operative or joint-stock principle . . . The French revolution of February, 1848, at first seemed to have opened a fair field for the trial of such experiments, on a perfectly safe scale, and with every advantage that could be derived from the countenance of a government which sincerely desired their success. It is much to be regretted that these prospects have been frustrated, and that the reaction of the middle class against anti-property doctrines has engineered for the present an unreasoning and undiscriminating antipathy to all ideas, however harmless or however just, which have the smallest savour of Socialism . . . Socialism has now become irrevocably one of the leading elements in European politics. The questions raised by it will not be set at rest by merely refusing to listen to it; but only by a more and more complete realization of the ends which Socialism aims at, not neglecting its means so far as they can be employed with advantage.

Index